MARY FISHER

My

NAME IS MARY

A MEMOIR

SCRIBNER

NEW YORK   LONDON   TORONTO   SYDNEY   TOKYO   SINGAPORE

SCRIBNER
1230 Avenue of the Americas
New York, NY 10020

SCRIBNER and design are trademarks of Simon & Schuster Inc.

Set in Bauer Bodoni
Designed by Jennifer Dossin

Manufactured in the United States of America

1 3 5 7 9 10 8 6 4 2

Library of Congress Cataloging-in-Publication Data is available.

ISBN 0-684-81305-X

FOR MY MOTHER, MY FIRST FRIEND

ACKNOWLEDGMENTS

This book has been just an idea for some time. It was Bruce Buursma and his colleagues at Copywriters Incorporated who pored through months of research, did the hard interviews, and then guided the writing process—enabling me to translate a jumble of memories into a coherent story.

My cousins Michael Saag, an eminent physician and AIDS researcher at the University of Alabama at Birmingham, and Barby Dale, creator of the greeting cards ("Dale Cards") that amuse America, spent hours recalling family stories and improving my faulty recollection. My father and my brother, Phillip, read earlier manuscripts, spotting errors and supplying missing pieces. I'm grateful to all of them for their affection and their help.

Some friends named in the book also helped with particular portions of it, notably: David Carpenter, Sally Fisher, Betty Ford, Ron Konecky, Renee Monell, Patty Presock, Joy Prouty, Judy Sherman, and Stu White.

The staff at Scribner has also made enormous contributions to this work.

Three people took special pains to keep me joyful, or sane, while producing this memoir: My sister-in-law Tina Campbell was the other adult in the house when one was desperately needed; David Landers kept urging me to tell the truth lovingly, no matter how difficult I found it; and Rosie O'Donnell made me a godmother while I was midway through this project, reminding me that children are more important than books.

My own children, Max and Zachary, have tolerated sharing their mother with another project—this book—in recent months. They are my joy.

A. James Heynen, whom you will meet here, is more than the friend and colleague who helped create this memoir. He's also the person who has enabled me not merely to live my life in recent years but to live it with purpose.

I dedicated this book to my mother. Parts of the book are our shared story, and neither of us has enjoyed examining every memory. In the final days of working on the manuscript, Mother wondered, quite pointedly, if we really needed to tell all these stories in public. But when we'd had nearly our last word on the subject, she said, "Well, whatever, Mary—I love you."

If my children grow to love and respect me as deeply as I love and respect my mother, I'll be a very satisfied woman. Mother was my first friend, and she has grown into my finest mentor. Beyond all the other courageous people I've known and loved, it's Mother who most of all has taught me that one person can truly make a difference.

Mary Fisher
Thanksgiving Day, 1995

Contents

PROLOGUE

It's true that I have a virus, and that my virus is deadly. But I am not a "patient" or a "case" for anyone. I do not focus on dying with this virus; I concentrate on living with it. I am, like you, a pilgrim stumbling along the way, a common pilgrim with a common name: Mary.

If I could, tonight, I would offer healing and a cure. I would promise health. I would laugh at the virus and invite you to join in the laughter. But the only healing I have to offer is prayer. The only cure I know is to be surrounded by a family of people full of compassion, ready to love you sick or not, cured or not.

And for all, I share this comfort: God knows us by our names. Once, long ago, early on a Sunday morning, a grieving woman was moving toward a loved one's borrowed tomb. In the scant light of sunrise, she heard a voice. And then she heard him say, "Mary." He called her by her name—my name.

Those whom we have lost have not been lost to God. As surely as my children hear me calling them to come to me—"Max! Zack!"— those who've gone ahead have heard their Father issue a call to them by name. Those who fear death, who dread illness, who suffer terror in the night: Listen closely, and you will hear Him calling you—by your name.

For all who hear the call of their names, there is the promise of grace and peace. I know this promise, as surely as I know that my name is Mary.

—Adapted from Mary Fisher's address at an Ecumenical Memorial Service for those lost to AIDS, St. James Catholic Church, Grand Rapids, Michigan, April 22, 1993.

CHAPTER I

"On a Clear Day"

All my life I've wanted to be good. As far back as I can remember, it was not punishment I feared. What I dreaded was simply, purely, not being good. Any act that smacked of naughtiness, any violation of household expectations, mystified and even frightened me.

Children from our Louisville neighborhood once hid behind our backyard wall, hurling insults at us for our Jewishness. An offended cousin responded from our side with a volley of stones lobbed in the direction of the taunting voices. I didn't like being insulted. But even more, I didn't like the idea that we weren't being good. Despite our youth, despite the name-calling, despite any excuse, we absolutely, positively, *had* to be good.

I tried explaining this concept to my little brother, Phillip, when I was six and he was three. He had attacked my dolls, and I'd gone to their rescue. I sat him down as a six-year-old sits down a three-year-old, and I explained that his behavior—setting aside the question of whether or not it was evil—was simply not possible. He *had* to be good. It wasn't an order; it was an explanation. We had to be good, just like we had to keep our noses above water when we swam. It was not about rules and obedience, but about how things are in life. To live, we must breathe; therefore, we keep our noses above water. To live, we must be good; therefore, we keep our hands off other people's dolls.

The lesson did not take. Phillip answered my earnestly delivered wisdom with a well-aimed kick to my shin.

Neither that kick nor any other delivered in the course of the past four decades has knocked out of me the abiding desire to be good. From earliest adolescence to the dim haze that covered my twenty-year romance with alcohol; from innocent mornings at grade-school bus stops to the stunning discovery, one morning forty years later, that I had acquired the AIDS virus—I cannot remember a time or condition, no matter how public or private, how saintly or sleazy, when I did not long to be good.

The problem, of course, is that I was not always good. As a result, self-loathing came frequently and easily. Since I believed that being good—being perfect, really—was the natural state of things, each time my actions contradicted my belief, I wondered what shame I had brought to my family now. What kind of ungrateful wretch was I, if I could fail my mother and others so? Why couldn't I just be normal—that is, why couldn't I just be perfect?

I've spent most of my life uncertain about who I am. But always I knew this about myself: I wanted to be good. For my mother, for my fathers, for my teachers, for our family's dog, Octane—for all of them—I wanted desperately to be the one thing I was sure I was not: a good girl.

My last drink was a margarita. No particular drama was attached to the occasion. My father, my sisters and brother (plus their respective spouses), and I had all gathered near the Betty Ford Center where Mother was riding the fresh wave of recovery in her battle with alcohol. All of us, except Mother, were having dinner together in one of my favorite restaurants, Las Casuelas in Rancho Mirage, California. It was December 10, 1984.

At the bottom of the margarita glass a limp slice of lime slumped over the melting ice cubes. I remember staring into the glass where the drink had been. If my life had been a movie script, this would have been the moment when I'd have taken an emotion-laden vow of abstinence and sealed it by shattering the glass against the wall behind the bar. But I wasn't on a movie set, and I certainly had no script.

I was dreading the week ahead, the so-called family week in which the Betty Ford Center staff explored the dynamics of a family racked by alcoholism. I imagined our family awkwardly discussing, in front of strangers, things we'd never discussed with one another, even in private. Perhaps I feared what others would say of me. Maybe I wanted to protect Mother from scars left as evidence of wounds inflicted during forgotten moments.

What seemed clear, that night, was that the coming week would be all about Mother. She was "it." This was her problem, her treatment, her recovery. I was here—we all were here—for her, to help her stop drinking and stop crying. She should have been responsible for herself, but since she hadn't been, we all needed to pitch in and help.

By contrast, I was also indulging the belief that night that whatever problems I suffered in life were also my mother's fault or, on a long day, my mother's and either or both of my fathers'. What I really wanted was my mother, or my parents, to accept responsibility for their own problems, and then also to shoulder the burden of mine. Other children in the family may have enjoyed the same delusion, the liberating and mistaken notion that we were not responsible for ourselves. But before the week had passed, and before I was able to work up a hundred compelling reasons to deny what was becoming obvious even to me, I'd been encouraged to stay on when the family's week ended. I had become "it," too.

Some miracles occur so gently that you later wonder how such impressive change could have passed unnoticed. In the months that prefaced the Betty Ford Center, the volume of my own discontent had escalated. I needed a new life; I had begun, almost against my own will, to explore the part of me that had grown up shrunken and shriveled, the malformed child of a gifted but frustrated woman. In the days at Betty Ford, my exploration evoked a shudder that dissolved into tears and finally degenerated into long, low moans. When the grief and self-pity lifted, in the quiet between the southern California mountains, I tried peeling away the layers of my life to find what was buried beneath years of well-developed roles, to locate and get to know *me.* But it was not in searching that I found Mary; it was in letting go. The act of surrender opened a door for me to the truth.

And the truth was breathtakingly simple. I discovered that I am Mary, and that being Mary is enough—not perfect, of course, but enough. And maybe even good.

I drank because, when I felt anxious or unsure, alcohol drained my tension and filled me with security. It made me acceptable, especially to myself. It was an old, old pattern in my life: looking for a way to be acceptable—and accepted.

I did not start out as Mary Fisher. I was born Lizabeth Davis Frehling. Weeks later my mother—who'd wanted to name me Elizabeth but had been overruled by my father George—organized a Sunday afternoon temple ceremony in which my name was formally changed to Mary. It was a more acceptable name, having previously belonged to a family matriarch who'd just died.

Four years later, my mother and father George divorced. Within a year, Mother had married Father, Max (Fisher). When their honeymoon ended, Phillip and I were moved from Louisville and its circus of crazy, cavorting relatives to Detroit and a life of more subdued financial security. In Louisville, our family had been in vaudeville and theater; in Detroit, our family was in gas and oil. The only neighborhood I'd known, which had "aunts" in every house lining the street, was gone; in its place were business dinners and country clubs. I went from being my mother's oldest child, and Phillip's big sister, to being younger by ten years than my stepsister, Jane, who was then fourteen.

Jane Fisher, Max's only child from his first marriage, had lost her mother to a slow-paced, degenerative illness. Jane was, naturally, doubly attached to her father. Into, or between, their relationship came my mother, a beautiful and youthful twenty-nine-year-old. It was no wonder that, as a motherless teenager, Jane reacted to our arrival with a mixture of horror and disdain. Nor was it any wonder that, as a transplanted five-year-old, I saw her only as an angry threat to our fragile existence. She reacted with violent adolescent outbursts; I responded by pulling Phillip closer and covering up for anything I imagined my mother had done wrong.

Julie, the first child born to my mother and Max Fisher, arrived in 1955. Two years later, Margie was born. I loved being the big sister and hardly noticed that the household staff grew larger with each addition. But I certainly noticed when we moved from the edge of Detroit to an expansive suburban home overlooking the immaculately groomed links of the Franklin Hills Country Club.

Mother had always been a creative woman with flashing wit and sometimes slashing humor. She was a natural entertainer, the ideal Southern hostess for a successful man's dinner parties. Dad—as I had come to call, and still think of, my stepfather—was becoming a potent force in national discussions of his one great love: the state of Israel. As Mideast tensions rose and fell, and as Washington's zeal for Israel waxed and waned, his trips became longer and more frequent. Perhaps it was his absence that Mother was filling with more and more drinks; perhaps it was an absence in herself. I never knew.

In the classroom, meanwhile, I could do no wrong. I pleased my teachers. When sports were available, I pleased my coaches. As socializing became important, I pleased my friends. In high school I was elected freshman class president. Then sophomore class president. Then junior, then senior. I was a student the teachers would describe with smiles as "one of the really good kids," because I was good at pleasing.

But in the one place where most I wanted to please, at home, I couldn't. When she wasn't drinking, Mother was unhappy and generally unpleasable. If she took a drink or two, she would revert to her entertaining self: charming, funny, a joy to be with. But it was a brief transition, a happy but small oasis, between not-drinking and, increasingly, overdrinking. Several drinks later the joyfulness would be gone. As Mother would continue to sip, she'd grow silent. I soon learned I could not please her in this condition either and began experimenting with ways merely to protect her.

The family messages I read most clearly about myself—some given with a subtle look or silent glance, some rendered with clear analyses and prescriptions—had a steady theme: I was unsatisfactory. I was too short. The problem: thyroid. The solution: pills. I was too heavy. The problem: diet. The solution: pills. The pills made me hyperactive, so I couldn't sleep. The solution: sleeping pills. When these pills left me drowsy in the morning, a new prescription cured me almost back to hyperactivity. By the time I graduated from high school, I was a walking pharmacy. I cleared early hurdles in adulthood—trying a few colleges, a few relationships, and a few careers—filling prescriptions with a joyless sense of duty and a growing edge of self-loathing, wondering if everyone felt like I did and, if not, what were they taking? What made them so acceptable?

Years passed, and I grew busy. If this relationship failed, I'd grab for that one. If this pill didn't satisfy, they'd prescribe another. I'd throw myself into a school or a job; if it didn't work out, I'd throw myself somewhere else. I'd staff a public television auction to raise support; I'd produce a live morning show; I'd create a new business, decorate a new apartment, seize a new challenge. First in Detroit, then Ann Arbor, then Birmingham, then New York, then Washington, D.C., then Detroit again, and New York again, and even Paris—nothing lasted, except my capacity to cross the line from busy to frantic, and my conviction that I was not yet acceptable.

Then came December 10, 1984, when I swirled the lime and ice around the bottom of an undistinguished margarita glass and walked into a new future. My former life was over, even before I knew it.

Betty Ford is a person, not merely a name on a masthead, in my life. I knew who she was but did not know her well until I began to work for her husband in the White House. He has always been "the President" for me; she was then "Mrs. Ford." Friendship—deep friendship—came later. Today, it's the President and "Betty" who are godparents of my son Max.

The place named for her, the Betty Ford Center, is a tidy complex of buildings in Rancho Mirage, California, surrounded by lush private lawns and golf courses. The environment, within the center and outside, speaks softly of serenity. Beyond the watered green is the desert, where Santa Ana winds push away the encroaching smog from the Los Angeles basin, baking the desert floor hard and dry. Framing the desert are mountainsides, a tangle of greens and yellows and oranges and browns, sometimes snow crested and sometimes fog shrouded. Late afternoon, listening to winds move sand around cactus, wondering if a rattlesnake can muster the energy to chase down a passing pack rat, the desert is forlorn and abandoned. But life and color constantly flow off the mountains.

Fresh as I was from a world of synthetic busyness, I was slowed and quieted by the sheer majesty of this place. The "Mary" who'd always failed at being good began to fade here; in her place rose a new Mary—me. I had always needed to be in charge. But here I learned the confession that I was not in charge, that I could live only by the grace of (in the words of Alcoholics Anonymous) "a Higher Power." If I were not in charge, there would be room and work for God. And if God would kindly take charge, I could be free to be myself.

All this came clear during early-morning walks when the desert air was still crisp. Wrapped in a sweater, clutching it tightly, I would repeat to myself as a prayer and a plea: "God grant me the serenity . . . the courage . . . the wisdom . . ." I did not claim a particular religion or write an enduring dogma. But I did realize that something, Someone, was at work in my life. I sensed God holding me, cradling me, hugging me, enabling me to know, and to be, myself.

I remember the morning that, turning back toward the center, I caught sight of the rising sun as it filled the mountain basin with a warm apricot glow. It was a single moment in a longer process, but it was also the instant in which God said to me most clearly, "Mary, I'm in control." It came as a drenching comfort, an overwhelming release, like that of a lost child being swept up into a mother's arms and wrapped in serenity, free to sob at last because she has been found. I have never, since that morning, seriously doubted that life has purpose—or that I, even when I have not been good, have a place within that purpose.

I left the protective life of the Betty Ford Center in March 1985. I had only begun to know myself. Hard questions had been asked and not answered. Uncertain where to go next, on advice of the center's staff I agreed to spend a few months in an "aftercare" program at Parkside Lodge in Florence, Colorado.

The days spent at Betty Ford and Parkside were uneven. I lived a roller-coaster existence. One moment I'd celebrate a new insight, the next I'd pick at old wounds. My journal from that time spins and whirls between the brave new me, soaring to new promises, and the familiar old me, plummeting into a hole of self-hatred so deep and dark I feared I'd never climb out.

Monday, April 15: "Decided I'm making it big."

Tuesday, April 16: "Sad, crying, confused—don't know what the hell I'm doing here—feel lonely, feel overwhelmed. . . ."

Wednesday, April 17: "Felt so much better today . . . I'm willing to take liberties, be spontaneous, be nurturing of myself. I enjoyed today—didn't feel teary, felt closer to people."

Thursday, April 18: "Feeling my anger . . ."

It was a period of tremendous intensity and introspection that careened between self-doubt and self-discovery. After only a few days at Parkside, I sent a telegram to my family that was terse and exactly what my counselors wanted to hear: "I'm resigning the position of problem child." The term "problem child" was the language counselors wanted me to use, so I used it. In fact, the only sense in which I had been the "problem child" was that I'd always tried to fix everyone else's problems. My demon hadn't been naughtiness; it had been attempted goodness. And I was still at it, still trying to please the authority figures by being what I thought they wanted me to be.

After two months, preparing to leave Parkside, I wrote a much longer letter to my parents that included another declaration of resignation: "Most of my life has been spent living through you and others, . . . seeking the approval of others and especially you. I am resigning from that line of work." The search for approval had haunted me, but what I was not yet saying—perhaps not yet thinking—was that I wanted to feel loved. It was a long, one-step-at-a-time journey.

Reading again through my journal from Parkside, I see that a new theme began to emerge there: I was experimenting with the belief that we can be loved totally and unconditionally. There are pages of poetry laced with spiritual conversations. I wrote of an "endless emptiness" now "filled by God." I offered the prayer that

> If I could but Your Abby (my counselor) be
> And have You, Father, within me
> Reveal my mission
> Show Your truth
> Like a butterfly I'd be set free. . . .

When I left Parkside, I took with me not only a knowledge of who Mary is psychologically, but also a conviction about who Mary is spiritually. I am God's—never perfect, but always God's.

Perhaps it was seeing the Master Artist at work in the mountains; perhaps it was merely awakening what had too long been sedated first by pills and then by alcohol—whatever the explanation, on April 10, 1985, sitting on a porch at Parkside with a bit of charcoal and a drawing pad, I drew a crude sketch of a table set between

some trees in the fence-enclosed backyard and patio. Even in the painfully simple lines of a picnic table and a leafless aspen, there was symmetry and shading and texture. My art therapist had been saying, "Mary, you're an artist." And I'd been saying, "Not possible." Creative, maybe; some "art instincts." Although I'd been actively, daily offering the prayer "Reveal my mission," I could not, would not, accept the identity of artist. Until April 10, when for the first time I looked down and said, "Maybe I am an artist." And I recorded in my journal, "I am God's creation."

The next day—April 11, 1985—my brother Phillip wrote "to tell you that I love you and [to] give you the circumstances of your nephew's birth." My little brother, Phillip, had become a father. As early as I could remember, I'd wanted to be a mother. I'm sure I startled many of the men I dated by announcing my intention to produce a brood of children. In listening to Phillip describe the euphoria of parenthood, I wondered how long it would be before I would become a mother. And I recorded in my journal, "Thy will be done."

I've learned new lessons since those days, but none more fundamental. I knew then, in the spring of 1985, that Mary matters. I matter to me. I matter to God. The days we are given are always numbered, undeniably finite, but we can make them count for something. If I choose to, I can make a difference.

"The caretaking has to be done," Mary Catherine Bateson reminds us in *Composing a Life*. "Somebody's got to be the mommy." But I had begun caretaking too early for a little brother, then for an uncertain and depressed mother, and finally for two little half sisters. "Somebody's got to be the mommy." But not me. Not, that is, until recovery. When I left Betty Ford and Parkside—and the experience is anchored in both of them—I was ready for adulthood, even for motherhood.

For a while, I was "Miss AA" to all my friends. Some acquaintances fell away; what had bonded us, we soon realized, wasn't our intellects but our appetites. Once there were no drinks to pour, there was nothing to hold us. I headed back to New York. I reconnected with a man I'd met earlier, Brian Campbell, and we rekindled a friendship that eventually grew into love.

I hadn't known Brian during his fastest days of dangerous experimenting with drugs and alcohol, although he'd shared enough for
me to know how close he'd lived to the edge. When we caught up
with each other in New York, he wanted to "get clean and sober." In
his own good time (which is when Brian typically chose to act), he
took on his own recovery. But what bonded us most wasn't recovery; it was art.

Brian was a seasoned artist and designer. He knew techniques I
could only admire, and he was willing to teach me. During our early
months together, it was his role as mentor, not yet as lover, that
made me hold to him so tightly.

Later, at the bar of the Sherry-Netherland Hotel in New York
City one night, Brian pulled from his wallet a crumpled piece of
paper. He handed it to me so I could read what he had copied onto
the paper, words from the sculptor David Smith: "Art is made from
dreams and visions, and things not known, and least of all from
things that can be said. It comes from the inside of who you are,
when you face yourself." This was the Brian I loved: tender, sensitive, vulnerable, gentle.

Brian always knew why he was an artist. "It's who I am," he'd
say simply, when asked. For me, it was never that simple. But when
I read Anne Truitt's *Daybook: The Journal of an Artist*, I felt as if
someone had finally understood my soul:

> I do not understand why I seem able to make what people call
> art. For many long years I struggled to learn how to do it, and
> I don't even know why I struggled. Then, in 1961, at the age of
> forty, it became clear to me. . . .

Like Truitt, I'd discovered that I was an artist only because I saw
that I was making art. When Brian would show me a new technique, I'd insist that I couldn't possibly do what he was asking.
"I'm not an artist," I'd explain. I'd never done it before. He'd smile
and say, quietly, "Just try." I did, and it worked. And so I discovered, as Anne Truitt had before me, that "if I'm an artist, being an
artist isn't so fancy because it's just me."

By the summer of 1986 Brian and I were together in New York.
As our relationship grew, so did our plans. We were two artists in
love, both wanting children, neither imagining that a New York

City loft was the place to raise them. Mother and Dad were in Florida more months each year, and Mother helped persuade us that her Southern neighborhood was the right place to have her grandchildren. Brian was intent upon giving a child his name, Campbell, and used the word "marriage." I had chartered *The Magic Lady* for a winter sail in the Caribbean, which provided an occasion. And so we married at my parents' Florida home and took our honeymoon aboard *The Magic Lady*. A month after the honeymoon I received the news: I was pregnant with Max. In the opening page of Max's journal I note that we received the news on February 12, 1987, and "Dad was happy and I cried with happy, happy tears."

Someone has said that adult children of alcoholics do not know what "normal" is. I wept at the news of my pregnancy because I had, finally, uncovered normalcy. God had given me sobriety first, and then peace, and then purpose, and now a child. Later, I would weep and wonder again about normalcy when word came that I was HIV-positive.

But the day I received the confirming word that I was pregnant, I wept with gratitude because for once I had it all: a husband, my own family, normalcy, a future. It was—I was—acceptable. And for a deliciously long moment I knew that I had never been better, more full of joy, more conscious of the fact that I was Mary and that being Mary was very, very good.

CHAPTER 2

"The Life and Times of Lizabeth Davis Frehling"

My father died in Houston. His funeral was in Miami. He was buried in Louisville. Everything about George Frehling demanded an explanation. His life was never straightforward, his commitments always subject to revision. Things always became complicated when my father, George, became involved. Even his own dying.

At the end, I was with him. I held his hand. I told him I loved him. I raged at him for not coming back when he promised he would, for never being there when Phillip and I needed him. Dying, he still wasn't there. He lay in a Houston hospital bed, his heart damaged beyond repair, his body in a coma already leaning into death.

Although he was unable to speak and in all likelihood unable to hear, I tried to communicate love with a touch. Someone described this as "loving with wordless eloquence," but it did not feel eloquent to me. It felt grim and sorry. Even here, at his deathbed, I wanted to be his good, adoring little girl. I wanted him to be my powerful, loving, forever daddy. And in the middle of my childish wanting, he slipped away, again, for the last time. I can't recall now if it was before he went or after that I said, as much to myself as to him, "I forgive you, Daddy."

It was George Frehling's absence that made him a figure of great power and mystery and anguish in my life. If I did not idolize him, it was only because I could not. As I grew older, I realized that my mother's memories and the hard facts both showed a George Frehling who was a seriously flawed man. Since I couldn't, under such circumstances, idolize him, I did what I could to rehabilitate him. I thought of George as misunderstood. He was absent and so he couldn't defend himself. But he couldn't have been *that* bad, because he loved me. "Maybe," I thought, "when he comes back, he'll have done something wonderful. He'll be a hero. Then everyone will see. . . ."

Throughout my childhood I improved him. In my mind, George grew into a composite sketch of Ozzie Nelson, Ward Cleaver, and the wise and wonderful Mr. Anderson of "Father Knows Best." Out of the unreality of fictional TV fathers, a picture of George, my own largely fictional father, emerged. He was gentle, caring, smart, handsome, fair, strong—and gone. I missed him, wherever and whoever he was.

Now, long past my childhood, he was dead. He had gone to Houston because his third wife was undergoing therapy for cancer at the M.D. Anderson Clinic in that Texas city, half a continent away from their Miami home. While there, at age sixty-four, he was stricken with a massive heart attack. In a final irony, his ailing wife outlived him.

At his Miami funeral, George's family told me I should never doubt how much he loved me. It was reassuring to hear that my years of childish imagination had not been entirely mistaken. But it also fueled a lasting melancholy, a grief not for his dying but for the life we never had, for the daddy I'd always wanted. I felt overwhelming regret—and found it expressed in a blazing flash of anger—that I had been forced to imagine that he loved me, because I never knew. I just never knew.

His final resting place was Louisville, my birthplace and the hometown for both George and my mother. While traveling for the memorial and burial observances, I conjured, as best I could, my childhood memories of George. I remembered mostly the sweet times: vacations and restaurant meals, the small airplane he owned (at least I believed he owned) and called the *Merry Mary*, in my honor. I remembered how good the pungent aftershave lotion smelled on his skin, how good-looking he was. I remembered how very safe I felt when I was with him and how he made me believe that I was important to him.

Although George may never have been a gambler, he could have been; his ever-present smile had just a hint of riverboat in it. He'd once owned a German shepherd that he loved and Mother hated. One day she issued an ultimatum: either the dog went, or she would. The story became a family legend because, it's said, George grinned and thought a good while—like a poker master measuring his opponent but not yet showing his cards—before deciding which companion he preferred, his dog or his wife.

I remember the Easter Sunday he and I were to celebrate my fifth birthday with a daddy-daughter dinner at the Brown Hotel, a regal landmark in downtown Louisville. Riding with him to the hotel, I just knew I was the center of the universe. It was going to be a lovely and intimate afternoon. But it wasn't. It was a party; George had invited all his friends—and George was, whether he intended it or not, the star of the party. I was along as his birthday girl, his little bouncy prop, the token kid worthy to be seen but not heard.

At some point long after his and his mother's divorce, George stopped sending birthday cards and presents. Because such arrivals had been erratic in the best of times, it took years for me to admit that even his infrequent contact with Phillip and me had finally ground to a halt. By then we had a stepfather whom we loved and who had adopted us. Max Fisher was "Dad." But George remained the mythical daddy. No longer a seamless part of our life, he became a remnant piece of my heart.

In fact, George was off creating another family in another place. But as a child, I did not know. And so, not knowing, I imagined. When I felt unloved, I imagined that George would love me, if only he knew me, if only I could find him. When I felt abandoned, I imagined that George would come back and sweep me into his arms. When I felt alone, I remembered the smell of him hugging me. When I wept, it was often his name that I called out—not "George," but "Daddy."

When I found him at the end, he was comatose and I was an adult already past forty. Across three cities spanning nearly two thousand miles, I kept him company during memorials and eulogies and good-byes. I wanted to be there. Perhaps I needed to be there, both for him and for me.

Louisville is the gateway of the American South. The Ohio River snakes along the city's northern and western limits, rolling by luxu-

rious neighborhoods and decaying industry, dividing Kentucky from Indiana, the South from the North. Our family was always clear that we were in the South. And we meant for people to know it, with every word we drawled.

My mother can scarcely remember a time when she wasn't somehow linked to George Frehling. Their respective grandparents—my great-grandparents—had been friends in Louisville's tightly knit Jewish community and would often vacation together. The Switow family of my mother's side and the Matz family of my father's maternal side had joint dealings in the theater business. Even after their divorce, the links never fell away entirely. Near the end of George's life we were all together one night, and I caught my mother looking at George with a gaze that spanned the years and melted the cool reserve that characterized their relationship. She was seeing not an old man with a weak heart but a smiling cadet with a jaunty walk, heading off to war, lovable enough to marry.

It was an echo of the days when their Louisville friendship had matured into courtship. "I think he always loved me," Mother still says today, "at least from the time I was eight." After teenage dating, as George prepared to join the air force late in World War II, they decided to become husband and wife. "He was going off to war, so we got married," says Mother. "That was just what you did in those days and under those circumstances. It wasn't an issue of much deliberation. Our families were friends. We were friends. It was a friendly wedding. Everyone thought it was for the best."

The genders suffered no confusion of roles in 1940s Louisville. Men worked. What women did, from making soap to making babies, was not work; it was something else. Men went off to war and became heroes; women stayed home to care for the children, unheralded and unheroic. Decisiveness and creativity were traits admired in men, but women were best when they were feminine: not too quick with mind or tongue. So George and Mother married because "it was just what you did." Then he went into the military, where he could pursue hopes of heroism. And Mother, an art student, joined in the war effort to draw maps for the U.S. Army Map Service.

Mother had talent. She could design clothing. She could sketch. When she sang, relatives wondered if Broadway was too big a reach. When she wrote, she won praise for her gifted expressions. But Mother was, and is, unconventional. And to freely express ideas that challenged the conventions of the time and place, to creatively exercise her mind as a writer or her hands as a designer—such notions might have been tolerated but were not to be encouraged. She was, after all, a woman, in a time and a society dominated by the whims and egos of men.

Creativity and flair were family traits. The Switows were known as "characters." Their ideas were unpredictable, their business dealings sometimes shrewd and sometimes comical, and their integrity was unquestioned by all who knew them. Childhood memories are full of Switow relatives—in the house, in the yard, up and down the street, hollering to one another, hoisting plates of aromatic foods, hugging around a piano. Such characters: grandparents, uncles, aunts, cousins, friends—and Lucille, my grandmother's housekeeper, who kept her heart well concealed beneath a stern and inflexible exterior, at least whenever we children were involved.

The Switows of Louisville were entertainment impresarios by profession, and they took their work home. Evenings and weekends were filled with endless stories and jokes told by a constantly replenished multitude of adults. My grandfather—"Papaharry," one word—played the piano. My uncles and aunts, all comics, would make up lyrics for silly parodies sung to familiar melodies. When evenings grew late, Papaharry grew bold. Eventually, one of his lyrics would culminate in a dirty word and my grandmother would roar out of the kitchen scolding, first in Yiddish and then louder in English: "Harry, not in front of the children."

Other elements of life at Papaharry's house also belonged out of range of the children. Only later did I hear uncles and aunts whisper stories about "bathtub gin" during Prohibition. In an album somewhere I have a picture Papaharry sent to me not long before he died. It's me, maybe one year old, clutching a Kentucky whiskey jug large enough to lubricate a weekend of parties.

Beyond his zest for life and his love of family, Papaharry had one characteristic that especially distinguished him in his time and place: He believed in the absolute equality of all people. Religion was important, because it shaped one's values—but each religion had something of value, and deserved respect. Black and white were different colors, not different classes. He despised discrimination of any kind. Flohoney worried that he would say something "dirty" in front of the children, but Papaharry taught his family that any term that demeaned others was truly filthy.

Louisville offered a charmed environment to Phillip and me—we never ran out of playmates, never wondered if we were cherished. And Papaharry's house sits in the middle of my memories as once it sat in the middle of the neighborhood, host to a little bit of vaudeville, a little bit of burlesque, and a lot of joyful, noisy relatives. It was a madcap house, where a child could hide in the backyard bowers or scamper up a tree next door and come back to a place that felt absolutely like home.

George and Mother moved to Bluefield, West Virginia, after he came home from the war. He took charge of building an outdoor drive-in theater as part of his family's business. But Mother thought only coal, Bluefield's commercial lifeblood, belonged in West Virginia. She belonged in Louisville. No child of hers would need to endure the stigma of having "Bluefield" on a birth certificate—not when Louisville stood nearby, glowing with culture and understated Southern charm. Mother moved home to Louisville. There, at high noon on April 6, 1948, I was born in Jewish Hospital: Lizabeth Davis Frehling.

"Lizabeth" was short-lived. My great-grandmother, Mary Davis Matz, died when I was ten weeks old. She had been, according to family legend, a woman universally praised for kindness and wisdom, and her passing occasioned a name change that evidently had been contemplated. On June 27, 1948, my mother entered into my baby book an account of the religious ceremony at which the change of my name was formalized in the name of God. I was Lizabeth no longer. Now my name was Mary.

In a ninth-grade writing project, I focused a surprising amount of attention on my name change and the departed ancestor I scarcely knew. "I do not remember her (Mary Davis Matz) but I am told that she and I used to play together before she became too sick to receive visitors," I wrote, evidently unaware that she had died before I was old enough to have played with anyone at all. "Everyone loved her and I suppose they hoped I would grow up to be like her. Now when I visit my great-grandfather he always tells me, with tears in his eyes, how much I look like her." I was at an age where I wanted roots, even if I needed to create them with exaggeration; I wanted to belong to some family.

Mother never truly left Louisville again during her marriage to George. She visited Bluefield, but she lived in Louisville. I have only the vaguest memories of Bluefield; I remember a train trip. And I remember that Mother was not happy. But mostly I remember green: green trees, green grass, green wallpaper in, I think, an apartment. Eventually George moved back as well, taking up temporary residence with us in my grandparents' home. But there was more that separated Mother and George than taste in geography. By the time Phillip was born, in the summer of 1951, the strain on their marriage was pronounced.

My mother tells me that, after Phillip's birth, George grew more distant. He had little to do with the new baby, perhaps because he did not know how to get past my mother's family and their increasing acceptance of his absence, or past my mother's conviction that he had too many other places he enjoyed spending his time, too many other things to do.

I, on the other hand, could not get enough of my brother. When he cried, I was the first one at his crib, leaning over, soothing him with, "Don't cry. Me here."

I was four when George left. Mother says she asked him to go. I was playing blindman's bluff in the backyard of my grandparents' house, probably one of a batch of cousins. I noticed when he began to pack some things in his car. I remember being blindfolded with a handkerchief and cheating, lifting the corner of the cloth, watching my father shuttle between the house and his car.

At first I thought he was just moving some things. But he kept going back for more, carrying out boxes and bags and I couldn't tell what all. At some unremembered point I must have sensed that this was not an ordinary coming and going. I ripped off the handkerchief and ran to him. "What are you doing? Why are you loading the car?" I cried. "Where are you going?"

"Ask your mother" was all he said. And he kept packing.

I watched him carry out his drawing board and gently lower it into the back of the station wagon. He was working for a design firm at the time, and the drawing board was his professional lifeline; but his board was more precious to George than his career. His drawing board—I now imagine, having retreated so often to my own studio to take comfort in my own art—was a touch point for his emotions, the "canvas" on which he splashed his heart. This was as close to "home" as George had.

I remember hearing him drive away although I can't recall seeing it; strange memory. I remember running into the house to find Mother. She was changing Phillip's diaper. I knew, although I don't remember how, that she was upset. "Where's Daddy going?" I wanted to know. "Why is he going?"

She was amazingly calm when she told me: "Well, Daddy's leaving."

"Why?" I persisted.

"Because he likes football and I don't," she said. And then she told me to be a big girl, so I could take care of her and my baby brother.

I remember Mother crying. Some nights, she would crawl into my bed, wrap me in her arms. I'd hear her sob softly and feel her body heave until finally she would cry herself to sleep. Perhaps I thought it was all my fault. I knew it wasn't about football. And I certainly took to heart her injunction that I should be a big girl and take care of Phillip and her. I knew my stomach hurt.

Flying from Miami to Louisville for George's burial, this was the one scene that I replayed. I can recall no other episode from early childhood with such clarity. I was too old to blame anyone by the time George died. I had tried and failed at marriage myself. But I could not shake the sense of lifelong absence that had been created. Even at forty-two I could feel the little girl in me who wanted Daddy to come back, who wanted not to be abandoned.

CHAPTER 3

"Starting Over"

The sun shone lavishly on Papaharry's big white Louisville home on Village Drive. Every unlocked house along the drive held a relative or someone we knew only as Aunt This or Uncle That. I did not know the difference between neighborhood and extended family; it was for a child's purposes all the same.

An Italian-style villa with imposing dignity, Papaharry's home had nothing of the stuffy elegance sometimes associated with such houses. Evenings and weekends the place belonged to the adults, eating and singing and drinking and joking—Papaharry's cabaret featuring a supporting cast of dozens. Weekdays, it was the children's domain. A second-floor sunroom was our clubhouse, a playroom that we could make messy as long as we picked up before moving on to another part of the house. It was Lucille's inflexible rule. Lucille was the plain-looking and plainspoken housekeeper, stern to the edge of meanness. She kept a spotless home. And every day she attended Catholic Mass to rebuild her spiritual strength, which was being constantly sapped by Papaharry and his R-rated songs.

My mother's parents, Harry and Florence Switow—"Papaharry" and "Flohoney"—adored their grandchildren. I was the first of the brood and therefore first in line for affection. One summer Papaharry built a wading pool in the backyard. While the cement was still wet, he gently pressed my hands and feet into the gooey stuff to leave my prints. I can still feel his strong hands on mine, and the wet cement.

There was no doubt that I belonged here. They fussed over me as a toddler, and I paid for their attention with Shirley Temple curls and curtsies, dancing and singing on cue when the adults were gathered. Because I was the firstborn grandchild, I was the child

star, belting out "It's a Sin to Tell a Lie" and "Down by the Old Mill
Stream," sentimental Switow family favorites in which everyone—
including my cousins Johnny and Barby Burkoff—would blend
voices on the choruses. The only time I remember the adults being
serene was during reverent renditions of Stephen Foster's "My Old
Kentucky Home." When the final chord was sounded, there were
glistening eyes all around. I now suspect that ample drinking
helped loosen their emotions. But as a child, such moments seemed
to be nearly religious experiences.

Despite the playful and hilarious times, I was growing pensive.
George's leaving had raised grave doubts about security and adult
trustworthiness. The rupture in my parents' relationship had been
an emotional earthquake for me; now it was followed by absolute
silence. No one would discuss it. And who could I ask? Not Lucille.
Not Papaharry and Flohoney, who'd rolled on with life as if my father had never existed. And to ask Mother the hard questions, I
quickly learned, was to bring on tears; one or two experiences with
that, and a four-year-old takes responsibility for her mother's tears.

And so I sang and I danced and I smiled when my extended family applauded. I loved their approval. But how could one be secure
in a world where half your parents could walk off in a single afternoon, never to return, because they liked football? Left alone or
with Phillip for a little while, my stomach would tie itself into a
tight knot. I wondered whether Phillip and I could stay in Papaharry and Flohoney's house forever. And what about Mother—was
this her house now too? What I wanted was simple: I wanted to go
back to being a family again, with my daddy back and smiling
again. What could be so hard about that?

I'm told that I would suddenly become quiet and reflective those
days. Sure. Onstage, I entertained; offstage, I worried—everywhere,
even at the Humpty Dumpty College, a preschool in Louisville. But
I tried never to ask questions that made Lucille look away or
Mommy cry. I tried to be a good girl. And in the quiet moments of
worry, I felt like a tipped-over Humpty Dumpty, broken into teeny
pieces that all of Papaharry's songs could not put together again.

The divorce was final on November 12, 1952. Two weeks later, to
assure some joy in her Thanksgiving holiday, my mother was

invited to spend the weekend with her cousin Carolyn Alexander in Detroit.

"I warned her that I was in no mood for a party," Mother now recalls of that invitation to go north to Michigan. "But she put one together anyway. She invited seventy people, fourteen of them bachelors." And one of them was Max Martin Fisher.

Max Fisher was emerging from a time of mourning. While he'd been gaining prominence in business and national affairs, his wife of nearly two decades—Sylvia Krell Fisher—had been disabled by heart disease. Six months earlier, she'd died. It was time for the forty-four-year-old widower to be invited to parties again. And at this one, he was curious to meet the slender, dark-haired beauty he'd never seen before.

Mother recounts the meeting as one in which she coyly played hard to get. "This was twelve days after the divorce, mind you, and I'm at my cousin's house walking down a staircase," recalls Mother, who was inconspicuous as a peacock in a crimson dress. "And this tall man walks up to me and says, 'Hello, Scarlet.' And I say, 'Hello, Rhett.'

"He asked me for a date," she says, "and I told him right away that I'd never get married again. I meant it. But he was persistent and kept calling and visiting Louisville until I relented."

Mother still claims she had virtually no idea of Max's financial station in life, but no one—including Mother—confused him with a man of modest means. Their courtship set Louisville tongues wagging. Max routinely arrived at the city's Bowman Field in his private airplane. And what really drew attention was his habit of sending his pilot to pick up Mother in the afternoon at Bowman, flying her to Detroit for dinner at the elegant London Chop House, and then returning with her to Louisville around midnight. Even today, this might be an item of note. In the early 1950s, it was the stuff of fairy tales for adults. But as a four-year-old, I saw it differently. When this man showed up at Papaharry's house not once but several times, and when Lucille and Flohoney made me get all dressed up to meet him on one such occasion, I knew something was up. Here at last was a chance to get a question answered. So I pulled myself up to full four-year-old height and cut to the chase: "Are y'all gonna marry my mommy?"

The answer, eventually, was yes. During the last week of June

1953, Phillip and I were dressed up—I was decked out in a navy blue suit with white trim—and taken to the airport with Mother to see her off for the wedding and honeymoon. I must have expressed some sharp disapproval to Flohoney, because her directions included the prohibition that I was not to cry "until Mother is on the plane." I waited, and then I cried.

Max and Mother were married July 1 in New York City, eight months after their Rhett-and-Scarlet meeting. It was a small, private affair, in keeping with the style of the day for remarriages. Max's then-teenage daughter from his first marriage, Jane, whom Phillip and I had never met, was in attendance. So were a few of Max's friends. After a Hawaiian honeymoon, Mother and Max stopped in Louisville to pick up Phillip and me on their way to life in Detroit. I held Phillip's hand as we stepped onto Max's plane at Bowman Field and waved good-bye to Papaharry, and to Flohoney, and to life as we had known it.

Max Fisher had graduated from Ohio State University in 1930 with a degree in business administration, a $5 bill in his pocket, and a 1916 Ford roadster acquired with a borrowed $100. A football star until injury ended his athletic career and scholarship during his junior year, Max never feared risk. In the teeth of the Depression, he rejected a guaranteed salary selling clothes for Richman Brothers in Cleveland and moved instead to Detroit to join his father, William, who had failed spectacularly in a string of businesses.

William Fisher had a new venture, reprocessing waste oil. Max became the firm's salesman at $15 a week when there was money enough to make payroll. By the close of 1931, Max had designed a way to convert his father's plant into a crude-oil refinery, vaulting the company ahead of competitors and creating the foundation for Aurora Gasoline Company. By the time we moved to Detroit, Aurora was the largest independent oil company in the Midwest, technologically sophisticated, known in the industry for its commitment to the environment, and headed by young Max Fisher.

Max grew a business by the same methods he used to woo my mother—dogged determination and remarkable timing. He had an uncanny ability to focus on a problem until it was solved and the quick mind to make solutions more likely. The barons of Detroit business—the Fords, the Hudsons, the Up-and-Comers—all were his friends. Incumbent and aspiring power brokers of the Republican party and all the champions of the new state of Israel learned their way to our door. A pragmatic and broad-minded strategist, his success at business positioned him to become a trusted behind-the-scenes confidant of American presidents and Israeli prime ministers.

The health of Max's first wife, Sylvia, had never been robust, and her heart condition—rheumatic mitral stenosis—made Michigan winters especially trying. When it became clear that warm weather and clear air brought her comfort, Max bought her a home in Tucson, Arizona. During holidays and school breaks, Max would visit Sylvia along with their daughter Jane, born in 1938—until 1952, when Sylvia died of congestive heart failure while visiting Detroit. It was to Max and Sylvia's home, and Jane's, that we moved in the summer of 1953.

Detroit was definitely not Louisville; this was "the North." Detroit of the 1950s was a union-organized, lunch pail–carrying, workingman kind of town, full of factories and smokestacks and neighborhoods crammed with bungalows and corner taverns. They made cars here, not whiskey. The house itself was a four-bedroom, red-brick home near Seven Mile Road and Parkside, in the Sherwood Forest area beyond the industry of the city. By comparison to the rollicking stage of Louisville's Village Drive, this place was quiet, almost austere, dark. From my upstairs corner room, resting my head against the pillow on my bed and looking out the window, I would fall asleep watching the cycle of the traffic light at the intersection of Seven Mile and Parkside—green, yellow, red, green, yellow, red, painting the dark night sky.

Jane was fourteen when her father first married this other woman—this beautiful, smart, Southern, and overwhelmingly healthy twenty-nine-year-old woman—and then brought her home with a not-quite-three- and a five-year-old in tow. I could invent a new reality for my missing father, George, precisely because he was gone. In Jane's life, invention cured nothing: The three Louisville migrants were very present realities.

On good days in the house on Parkside, Jane and Mother maintained an uneasy peace. Jane, a gifted pianist, found comfort at her mother's Steinway baby grand piano; I always imagined that when she closed her eyes and her fingers caressed the keys, she was still playing for Sylvia. A year and a half after we moved in, Julie was born (February 9, 1955). Less than three years later (December 30, 1957) came Marjorie Martin Fisher—the child with Mother's first name and Dad's last two. As more children took more of the house from Jane, and from her mother's memory, she tried to dominate the house with her teenage rage. And when her anger turned to physical attacks on Mother, who was much smaller than she, I literally feared for my mother's life. Peace finally descended on the family only when Jane went away to school.

Apart from Jane, Mother was beginning a quieter battle of her own. Drinking had been a way of celebrating life in Louisville; in Detroit, it would become a means of coping. We were all in the North now, where we had to cope, had to adapt. When other children heard us speak, they told us we talked funny. I hated the way they talked in this place with clipped words and brittle phrases. They said "Dad" with the force of a sledgehammer, with the tongue hitting the consonant so hard that the affection found in the vowel *a* never came through. Most days Mother encouraged us to make the changes. But sometimes, feeling her own distance from home, she would take us into her bedroom and help us practice our Southern accents, or pull us to the piano to play a Papaharry song.

The most joyful place in my life those years was Brookside School, a private and somewhat exclusive school a long bus ride from our house on Parkside. Mother dressed me like a little Southern belle, with pinafores and petticoats as the order of the day, frequently with "Mary" stitched in large lettering across my chest. To my stinging embarrassment, no one had to wonder if my name were Mary. To my even greater embarrassment, the gentle rocking motion of the school bus evoked a bout of daily nausea. I was soon known as "the one who gets sick." Other riders learned to stay out of range of my seat. It was not pretty.

Once at school, I excelled. Grown-ups told me exactly how I could please them and rewarded me with praise each time I did it. It was perfect symbiosis: a child desperate to make adults happy and adults who adored such a child. Miss Canberry, my first-grade teacher, praised my neat penmanship and clean, orderly desk. Mrs. French, my second-grade teacher, wrote glowing notes about my conduct and my reading. Art class was my favorite in third grade. By then Dr. Casey, the music teacher, was also letting me spend time with him as he tuned the school's instruments to the notes of a piano. In fourth grade I began ferrying a cello between home and school every day. I loved being in the orchestra, especially when we played "Edelweiss," in which the cello had the melody and the solo.

At home there were the babies, Julie and Margie—and Phillip was always "mine." When Mother's pregnancy with Margie became complicated and nearly terminated much too early, she let me help care for her and heaped praise on me for being her "big girl." I felt very needed, very grown-up.

My notions about family were shifting. With a ninety-minute flight to Detroit, Phillip and I had inherited a new batch of relatives who were not like the relatives we'd known in Louisville: They did not live down the street, did not howl at Yiddish jokes or pour whiskey from a treasured jug, did not spend weekend evenings cooking up a party. My new grandmother, Max's mother, noting my un-Jewish looks, said I was "the family's shiksa" (Gentile girl). I imagine she meant it affectionately, but to me it carried tones of disapproval— that I wasn't really, sufficiently, Jewish.

I had, at best, a somewhat muddled view of my own identity. When I wrote a letter from camp to my parents in 1957—I'd turned nine in April of that year—I signed my letter "Elizabeth [sic] Mary Davis Frehling Fisher." And the "Fisher" part was a wish, not yet a reality. My mother had become Marjorie Fisher on the way to Detroit. Years later, I was still Mary Frehling, and I hated having a last name that was different from hers. It did not occur to me that it was Max's name I wanted. It was Mother's. Since she was now a Fisher, I wanted to be a Fisher, too.

Max had offered to adopt Phillip and me, but George would not consent. On Phillip's fifth birthday, August 19, 1955, George wrote Mother a curious letter containing obscure objections based on advice from "a doctor in Louisville." His real objections were never clear, but some arrangement was finally approved by everyone. I know that Max told Mother, as soon as they were married, not to cash checks for child support sent by George. And I know that I was twelve before the adoptions were finalized in 1960. But whatever additional concessions were needed to satisfy George or others, no

ar Mommi SAYS
    I bet you a
ing a wonderful
ida. I know th
not very good
it gets much better
sake.

        I am going

orge and tell with our
ns will you
I tell me th

    Love y

Eliz'bth Mary Davis Frehly
                    Fisher

parent has ever disclosed—although Phillip and I have asked on a number of occasions.

By the time the adoptions were a matter of public record, George had married Joyce Spiegel in Chicago (1956) and started another family. Their son Joe was born shortly before Julie, and Lisa was added while Mother was pregnant with Margie, so their Chicago apartment offered me, when Phillip and I visited, another chance to be a big sister. Our visits were rare but comfortable, and Joyce made sure that we knew we were welcome in their world. But George himself was a fading reality in our lives. In September 1957 he explained his summer of absence by writing Mother about his "yearly back trouble . . . just got back on my feet this week." He "had missed Phillip's birthday because I thought he would be with us and would give him something at that time. . . ." He hoped for a visit later in the year. George was better at living on wispy promises and thin hope than were his children.

In the summer of my tenth year, 1958, we left the Parkside house and moved a few miles farther out of the city to Franklin, Michigan, a largely affluent community north of Detroit. It was then a Midwestern dream community wrapped around country clubs and private schools and social comfort. My greatest joy was not arriving in Franklin but leaving the Parkside house.

The two happiest memories I took from Parkside were Odie and Randall. Randall Martin and Mary Oden (known in our home as "Odie" because I had prior claim on the name Mary) had joined the great black migration to Detroit years earlier. Odie, who was slight, and Randall, who was generously proportioned, were the gateways in our home to food.

The sound of Odie closing the refrigerator door could pull us out from under the covers on a snowy day. By the time we slid through the kitchen door, Randall had bacon sizzling, filling our world with the sweet, smoky aromas of a winter morning—pancakes and syrup, freshly squeezed orange juice, and perking coffee—all inhaled as we bent our young noses over a mug of steaming hot chocolate.

And food was only the final blessing; before the food came the laughter. Odie would start into a story, and then into a giggle, and soon she'd be bent over, knees squeezed together, tears streaming from all our eyes not for the story but for her inability to finish it. If Phillip wanted to know what was in a boiling pot, Randall would hoist him toward the ceiling and lower him, squealing, toward the steaming kettle. Breakfast was prepared to the sounds of love, and we never left that kitchen without hugs and kisses.

As the Parkside kitchen had been Odie and Randall's, so the Franklin kitchen belonged to Emmett. Emmett Stowe was a big man—big in body, big in knowledge, big in reputation, big in affection, big in character. When Emmett spoke, he roared. Dad loved his cooking as much as we did, and the two of them, nearly the same age, started swapping stories the moment Dad came into the kitchen.

Emmett had gimpy knees and a citywide reputation for his chicken. Using Emmett's recipes, and on weekends his supervision, flocks of birds laid down their lives to satisfy customers of "The Chicken Club" in Detroit's African-American community of the 1950s and '60s. Weekdays in our kitchen Emmett laid claim to a rolling stool on which he would half-sit, half-lean, propelling himself around corners and between counters as quickly as anyone else would have walked.

Emmett's kitchen became my place of refuge. Emmett was the man in my life who was always there to feed and protect me. When I was certain that I was too short and too fat, it was Emmett who would scan my thirteen-year-old frame and say, "You're beautiful, honey," in tones that settled the question. When grief broke out for reasons real or imagined, Emmett would gather me into his arms with a reassuring, "It'll be all right, honey . . . it'll be all right."

The sound of a piano playing honky-tonk can still today return me to Papaharry's big white house on Village Drive in Louisville. And in the quiet of an early morning, I can still hear Emmett setting silverware on a table, his low voice humming a bittersweet spiritual, "Burden Down, Lord, Burden Down."

CHAPTER 4

"Making It Okay"

Smoke darkened the skyline south of the Franklin Hills Country Club as Detroit burned. It was the Summer of Riots, 1967. On television, Detroit's reporters stood on streets whose names we knew to chronicle a scene that was surreal—the burning and looting and, soon, the dying. A grim-faced George Romney, my father's friend and the governor of Michigan, looked into the camera to announce a call-up of the National Guard.

Injustice and militarism, inequity and racism—these were agenda items for the American cultural revolution of the sixties. But they caused scarcely a ripple in my sealed-off world of suburban sensibility. I sipped vanilla Cokes with friends at the club, after tennis. We spent another Saturday afternoon cruising nearby Birmingham shops and restaurants. Someone said, "Looks like the smoke's heading over the border into Canada."

Decades of seething anger had exploded in nearby Detroit, and I saw only a distant haze drifting over a border into someone else's world. It was not real to me—not like algebra was real, or Friday's date was real. I could watch civil outrage blacken the sky; I could hear contempt screamed at "the system" or "the establishment." But it was possible to believe—because I did—that the anger had nothing to do with me.

I've heard friends claim that if you can remember the sixties, you weren't there. They may be right, because the sixties were my era but not my time. I was present, but I wasn't fully there. I was one of the compliant teenage spectators in a suburban world secured against riots and rebellion and revolution. We tested the rules but rarely mustered the commitment needed to break them, or even bend them severely.

Our indiscretions involved beer, not LSD. Our crimes were forged excuse notes from parents buying us an afternoon's freedom from school. We smoked only tobacco—Newports were my brand. If we ventured into the nearby City of Detroit it was for a reason: a game at Tiger Stadium, a dinner downtown, a cruise around Belle Isle. But we were careful where we parked because we were responsible teenagers, good teenagers. Economically, we were pampered. Culturally, we were indulged. Politically, we were Republican.

The music of the sixties—the Beatles, the Rolling Stones, Marvin Gaye, Smokey Robinson and the Miracles, Diana Ross and the Supremes—is still my music. When the Beatles played the old Olympia Stadium in Detroit I was there, cupping my hands over my ears to reduce the pain caused by screaming, stomping, hysterical fans. I loved the Beatles but hated the noise level. The stage and the audience were so far apart that the Beatles appeared in miniature. I watched a tiny Paul McCartney—the doe-eyed, gentle Beatle—on a platform too distant, but he still appeared as handsome to me as he did in the collage of photos I kept on a bulletin board in my bedroom. I could tell which song the Beatles were singing by reading his lips. I wished everyone would be quiet so I could hear his soft, sweet voice.

Time and *Newsweek* magazines recently ran retrospectives on the sixties. They described a world I never knew. I'd spent the revolution at home fighting a hopeless battle against my self-image (seeing myself, always, at any weight, as overweight), negotiating around my mother's drinking, wondering about two fathers—one constantly traveling or on the telephone, one just plain missing.

At school I made sure all the girls' needs were met. Need a class project planned? See me. Need a friend? Here I am. I was rewarded with four consecutive terms as class president. At home I filled the blank spaces left by others. When Dad was gone and Mother was lonesome, I became her companion. When the younger children needed care and Mother had been drinking, I became the responsible adult. Even the household staff, when they saw a crisis building— usually around Mother's drinking and Dad's frustration—would signal me into action. At school and at home, I was the responsible one, the organizer, the caregiver, the good girl wanting—desperately—to make things okay.

• • •

Kingswood is a private, all-girls school (boys attend Cranbrook, just across the lake on the shared campus). The campus is safely nestled into Bloomfield Hills, a half hour's drive north of Detroit. Students naturally divide between "boarders" and "day students" (commuters), but my friends came from both groups. Molly Mc-Graw, Chris Huebner, and Susie Swan were boarders; Terry Lerchen, Mary Weir, Karin Christianson, Martha Cross, "Cram," and I were all day students.

I graduated in 1966. Paging today through that year's *Wood-winds*, the Kingswood yearbook, I see my picture. I'm surprised to see that I'm thin; in my memory, I'm still fighting teenage fat. Six lines of fine print recount my extracurricular activities, including my stints as class president (1962–63, 63–64, 64–65, and 65–66). I'm described as "our organizer." No surprise there. "Sensitive and sincere . . . an unending wardrobe . . . U of M next year." That was me. And then, the clincher: "To be liked by all who know her is the highest compliment we owe her." It was my specialty: pleasing.

Cram—Judy Conrad (now Sherman)—remembers me as "the kid everybody trusted, the one who treated each of us as if we were the only friend she had . . . never nasty, never tried to steal your boyfriend . . . totally unpretentious, terribly careful not to expose her family at school."

Kingswood was perfect for me. The curriculum emphasized writing and personal communication, encouraging me to find ways to express my feelings. Teachers and staff had close, often nurturing, relationships with students. But most of all, the curriculum was built around achievement, founded on the conviction we "enter to learn," we "go forth to serve." I was a good student, but not exceptional. I remember once persuading my parents that Kingswood's grading system peaked at a "four" (the actual equivalent of a B in most systems), only to have my little sister Julie come home later with a fistful of fives.

Math was by far my favorite subject. I loved it in every form, from basic arithmetic to geometry and advanced algebra. The beauty of math was that it always had one and only one right answer; nothing was ambiguous. And I liked the fact that the outcome was in my control: I was right, or I was wrong, but the results were mine.

In contrast, dating was a world of uncertainty over which I felt no control. It never even occurred to me that I could accept or reject invitations when offered. When I dated someone, I just assumed our relationship was his to control. If he wanted to continue the relationship, we continued; if he wanted to stop, we stopped. I never imagined that I could have any decision-making authority in the matter.

It was at Kingswood that I discovered weaving. One of the options for eighth-grade art was Miss Lillian Holm's course with the looms. From the beginning, I loved the process of weaving: physical, hands-on, both muscular and delicate. I loved feeling the soft fabrics and hard tools, using hands to shape something that came from the soul. The weaving room at Kingswood was the closest thing I could imagine to absolute serenity, filled with the smells of wools and wood and the gentle, strangely maternal sounds of the shuttle clacking back and forth. It was okay to be vulnerable here; it was safe. If life turned mean, an hour in the weaving room could offer healing. My last hour as a senior at Kingswood was spent alone in the weaving room.

The school was private, not parochial, but maintained a loose connection with the Episcopal church. My Jewishness meant little to me or anyone else. There were regular chapels on campus and weekly worship services at Christ Church Cranbrook down the street. Like my friends, I complained about them, and attended them, and developed a sense of quiet spirituality in them. When, as junior class president, I was slated by school tradition to carry a tall mounted cross into the seniors' commencement ceremony, everyone agreed to make a simple shift. I carried an American flag, and somebody else hoisted the cross. Being Christian, being Jewish, whatever—it was not a big deal.

I finished Kingswood as a young woman proficient at math, able to communicate effectively, in love with weaving, and skilled at pleasing. The latter skill was most apparent: I knew how to study others so I could meet their needs. And when I made them happy, I was happy. Sort of.

We came to expect the unexpected from my father Max in those years. When the telephone rang in the big white house in Franklin, it could be my friends Cram or Susie or Molly calling for me. Or it could be Golda Meir or Richard Nixon calling for Dad.

His first major foray into electoral politics was George Romney's

bid (and win) in Michigan's 1962 gubernatorial race. I always thought they were an unlikely pair: a shy, behind-the-scenes Jewish entrepreneur and a square-jawed, outgoing Mormon corporate executive. But they trusted each other and rose together to national prominence in the Republican party during the sixties. Toward the end of the decade, Dad helped rehabilitate Richard Nixon's image and interpreted Israeli security issues to him before his 1968 presidential run while lining up Jewish support for his campaign.

Dad merged his oil business with the Ohio Oil Company in 1959 (it took the name Marathon in 1962), shifting his focus away from corporate management toward investments and philanthropy and international affairs. There may have been some talk about his "slowing down," but it was—then as now—only talk. He was a blur of constant motion, away from home days at a time and, when at home, a commanding, even intimidating, presence surgically attached to the telephone. (A prized family photograph caught him, glasses on and tie in place, asleep on the couch with his hand cupped to his ear, as if he were still cradling his beloved phone.) When he entered the house, everyone in it snapped to attention. I don't remember ever asking, "Is Dad home?" You knew.

Dad was neither a mean man, nor especially gruff, but he exuded (and still does) power—the kind of sheer personal force that can inspire fear. This is in part what makes him a potent businessman and political advisor. It's also what makes some memories especially funny. Although the incident actually took place some years later, I remember the terror that broke out the night Dad came home late, greeted my friends standing in the kitchen, chatted for a few minutes, grabbed three brownies off a heaping plate, and headed for his room. A friend, who had stopped breathing when Dad came into the room, turned to me and said, "Do you realize that the straightest man in America just left Richard Nixon's Oval Office to fly home and go to bed eating a fistful of marijuana brownies?"

While Dad was holding court in the corridors of commerce and power, Mother held court in her bedroom. Friends from high school days still recall times when she would summon us to her room where, with dramatic flourishes as colorful as her robes, she would regale us with hilarious stories. She's a phenomenal storyteller with a memory for detail and timing that would qualify her as a professional. And beyond the humor, sometimes hidden beneath it, is a

woman of substance and ambition. Guests visiting my parents'
home expect to see the gallery of photographs showing Dad with
world leaders, but they're often surprised to find a library full of
Mother's books exploring science, philosophy, and religion. Dad's
jokes about Mother's spending—and her response: "Your stocks
went up, Max; let's go to the drugstore"—mask the considerable
skills with math and logic that make her a potent gin player.

The topic about which Mother and I tangled most during those
years was college. She, who had once longed for a liberal arts education, couldn't understand why I wanted to go to Paris and study
French before attending college.

Robert Goldstein—then head of Twentieth Century–Fox in Europe, one of Dad's associates and a longtime family friend—was a
regular visitor at our home. During his stays Mother began subject-
ing "Uncle Bob" to lengthy reviews of my dancing and theatrical
abilities. Perhaps she considered Broadway an acceptable alterna-
tive to college; perhaps she knew that nothing gave me a more
heightened sense of being alive than mounting a stage and dancing;
perhaps she merely remembered her own unfulfilled fantasies.
Whatever the reason, one evening I watched her raise the stakes in
her conversations with Uncle Bob. She asked him, flat out, to use
his influence to get me into the Royal Academy of Dramatic Arts in
London, where I could hone my artistic skills and live with the
Goldsteins. She was—as she can be when the cause is one of her
children—assertive beyond reason.

After a series of batterings on the topic, spread over several visits,
Uncle Bob began to take the matter seriously. He discussed in
somber tones the demands of the theater and the high expectations
of the Royal Academy itself. He delivered an extended lecture on
the rigors of the stage and the sacrifice required, then turned to me
and asked earnestly, "Are you really ready, Mary, to give up your
entire life for acting?" Before I could clear my throat, Mother
blurted out, "She is!" I wasn't. Or, if I was, I didn't dare.

What I wanted most was "normal." A normal weight, instead of sizes
that demanded diet pills. A normal height—when I hit five feet one, I
peaked—instead of thyroid and pituitary prescriptions. I hankered for
a "normal household" with evenings of homework on the living
room floor, and bowls of potato chips and Lipton-onion-soup-mix chip
dip, and both parents present and aware that I was present, too.

When normal didn't happen, I invented it—just as I had invented a "good George" who hadn't really left us. Friends invited me for Friday night visits; I wanted to go but said I couldn't "because Mother has plans for me on Friday." There were no other plans; I just thought that, if we were normal, we would have had some. And if no one else—like Mother—could make it happen, I could.

My father George made his last memorable appearance in my life the day of my confirmation. I was fifteen. When he left, he kept going for a very long time.

Mother and Dad had planned a wonderful celebration, my first "big event" at the Franklin house. I told Mother that I wanted to invite George and his new wife Joyce. She was skeptical, and I suspect it was Dad who carried the day with logic like, "It's her party, and if it's important to her . . ."

I remember when planning the party that I didn't know what I was going to call George or Max when they were together. I hadn't faced the challenge before. I didn't want to call Max "Dad" and hurt George's feelings, but I couldn't switch titles in front of Max to make George feel better. So I decided I wouldn't call Max anything at all, and I would call George "George." I rehearsed my lines.

Everyone I loved came to my party. Phillip and the girls were all dressed up. Friends from Kingswood and Temple Beth El were in one room, and Uncle Bob, in from London, was telling stories to Dad in another. George Primo was playing the piano in the garden room with Papaharry working the crowd around him and Flohoney worrying about off-color jokes around the children.

I didn't see George and Joyce arrive. But when he came out of the den, I ran to meet him with a hug. As my arms went around his neck, he said, "Let's get out of here; let's go to the hotel." He had already had a fight with Mother.

"I can't leave," I told him. "This is my party."

"It's not your party," he said. "It's your mother's party, Max's party—it's not your party."

We went halfway up the stairway toward the back of the house and hid on the landing, where I tried to explain again that I couldn't leave. But he wouldn't listen. When I finally left him sitting there to head back for the party, he followed me, still insisting that we leave. I was torn between people who were congratulating and embracing me and George, who was tugging at me to leave with him, making me cry.

When George followed me into the den, Mother started up with him again. Max tried to calm the conversation and to move it away from the guests. I ran into the garden room to do a promised dance. The guests were still applauding when I went back into the den to catch the final rounds of the fight. I remember saying, over and over, "Stop this, George," and "This is my party." And crying.

I saw a side of George that day I'd never seen before: demanding, unreasoning, unfair. He was trying to make me feel guilty for not going with him, as if it were I who were deserting him.

I was hurt and confused, and I did not see George again for a very long time. Some years later, during one of my spring breaks, I went to Florida, where he was living. I looked up his number in a telephone book at the Miami airport. I made a few calls to wrong numbers, and then I scored. I was excited just to hear his voice. After a few moments of pleasantries, I was ready to ask where we could meet when I heard him say, "Well, I'm really busy right now." He wondered if I could call later. I stumbled through some explanation about taking off soon anyway. He hung up. For a long time I sat in the phone booth, first in shock and then in tears, again.

I did what I could to let George go. The confirmation party was a turning point. Before, it had been his absence that inflicted pain; this time it had been his presence. I gave up writing him letters and took up the latest fad of Kingswood School students—girls wearing men's fragrances. English Leather was really "cool." I wore it every day.

Shopping in Birmingham with friends one Saturday, we were all trying men's colognes. I splashed on Old Spice. It was clean and pungent, and I was converted. This, I announced, was "my" fragrance. It smelled good. It felt good. It was even faintly familiar. And then I knew: It smelled of George.

Years later, well into adulthood, I kept Old Spice in a cabinet in my bedroom.

Drinking, at midcentury, was a feature of the good social life of Louisville. Early May, when Derby Time rolled in, mint juleps—and every family's secret recipe for them—were hoisted with the same reverence and appreciation reserved by marines for the flag. Midway through the twentieth century, drinking was a requirement, not a vice, in Louisville, Kentucky.

Mother drank lightly, socially, in Louisville. She held that pattern in Detroit. But in Franklin, beginning during my high school years, her drinking escalated almost imperceptibly until the trouble it produced was inescapable.

Mother felt trapped. She'd left Louisville, where relatives and friends were largely the same and the absence of any one person was, if noticeable, not catastrophic. What attracted her most to a home in Detroit was Max Fisher. And now, increasingly, Max Fisher was not home. He was in Washington, arguing for a change in national policy; he was in Israel, looking for a narrow path to a broader peace. Even when he was in Detroit, his days were devoted to rebuilding the city or revitalizing a sagging economy. Mother was lonesome. Worse yet, her lonesomeness seemed like selfishness: Max was pursuing noble goals, higher goods, human welfare—how could she be so selfish as to hold him back? The answer was: she couldn't. And sometimes a drink, perhaps two, made the lonesomeness less painful.

When I came home from school I would check in with Emmett, or whoever was in the kitchen. If Mother was drinking heavily, they would point a finger toward her bedroom. I'd round up Phillip and Julie and Margie, if they were home, and try to come up with some excuse to keep all of us out of range. I'd organize.

But when Dad came home and Mother was in her bedroom, not in good shape, tension mounted to an instant boil. Weeks might have elapsed since Mother's last episode, encouraging me to believe they were over, so I was unprepared; I couldn't organize peace quickly enough. First there was an ominous silence, then Mother's voice, hostile and belligerent. Dad would say something short and low and walk out of their room. She'd follow him, shaking her finger, accusing, shouting. He'd stop in the hallway and turn around to look down at her, saying nothing, seething. When she finished her lecture she'd go pour another drink—dropping ice cubes loudly into the glass so he would be sure to hear her. He'd take refuge on the telephone, his voice calm and controlled as if nothing had happened, nothing at all. And we would hear her head back to her bedroom and close the door.

Then it would be dinnertime. We had to come out of hiding. Mother's chair at the end opposite Dad's would be empty. The four children would take our appointed spots, looking down at our plates, saying nothing. Daddy would clear his throat and try a math game. "Go ahead, ask me to add any string of five numbers." He could add faster than we could talk. After he'd proven himself a human calculator, we'd fall silent again. He'd ask questions, trying to coax one or two complete sentences into the room; we'd say, "Yes," or "No," or just shake our heads. Phillip would fidget. Julie couldn't eat. Margie would start to cry.

And all the while, I would be thinking of ways to protect Mother. Dad would ask me where she'd been during the day. If I didn't know, I'd say, "I don't know." If I knew, I'd say, "I don't know." I didn't want to get between them, but neither did I want them to collide so wildly that one of them would say "divorce" and the other one would say, "You've got it." I didn't know how to organize it, how to regulate it, how to make it right.

By the time I was a senior at Kingswood, Mother was drinking heavily. I was uncomfortable bringing friends home directly from school—I needed to get the lay of the land before anyone came in. Instead of retreating to her bedroom as she had always done, Mother had taken to drinking in the library. I'd come home to find her alone there, with no lights on, a fire lit, a drink on the mantel. "Bye, Bye, Blackbird" or "Am I Blue?" would be playing as she stood near the fire, softly mouthing the lyrics, swaying as if in a slow dance, hugging herself, crying.

It was a time of enormous contrasts. When Mother was not drinking, she was my closest friend. I remember the night of my first real kiss—his name was Johnny Goodman. I'd stayed out later than usual, and Mom had waited up. But when I ran up the stairs with stars in my eyes, she knew instantly that I had found love, and she celebrated the moment with me. She sat on my bed and we talked. She helped me get undressed, still talking, and finally hugged me good-night. No one had a mother who was wiser or more loving.

And I remember Mother and Dad coming down the stairs like Hollywood stars, ready to go out for the evening. Mother would be stunningly beautiful, the image of glamour; they both smelled great. She would have a drink before leaving and look enviously at her favorite meal, which she'd had prepared for our dinner: a breakfast, usually ham and fried eggs. Playfully, she'd take a bite from Phillip's plate; she'd wink at me, sigh, and turn to take Dad's arm to leave. I can still see them, younger, as if it were yesterday.

But I can replay the same scene in my memory, and it is all different. I hear the ice cubes clinking loudly into an empty glass. I see myself sitting quietly in the kitchen with Phillip, Julie, Margie, and usually whoever had cooked the meal. There is a quiet, sullen mood—no glamour, no one talking. It's ham and eggs and silence again. I have never, ever, heard a silence as piercing as the quiet of those meals, or felt more alone in the company of others.

The question of my college attendance finally needed to be answered. Miss Goodale, Kingswood's headmistress, had once explained that "you do not *not* go to college." My parents agreed. And so I did what all my friends did: I applied for admission to the University of Michigan. For most of us, U of M was a "backup" application—the place they could attend to satisfy family needs and personal ambitions if preferred first or second choices were not approved. For me, it was my only application. I'd heard stories of Michigan's admissions standards and thought if I wasn't admitted I could still argue for Paris. A week after I mailed my application, I received the congratulatory message welcoming me as a student at the University of Michigan.

I arrived in Ann Arbor the following fall in the company of friends from Kingswood. After orientation and class registration came "rush," the annual tour of (mostly) freshmen women through sororities that alternately sold themselves as the one to join and asked newcomers to sell themselves as candidates for membership. We visited four or five sororities each day, inspecting and being inspected.

My Jewishness at Kingswood had been neither an asset nor a liability, just a fact. Despite Dad's pro-Israel politics, family friends came from all religious traditions, and I'd never heard either parent use religion as a wedge or as a club. But during rush, I noticed that several sororities assigned one "host" for all the Jewish girls; I'd heard of anti-Semitism, and I could survive it. But at a "Jewish" sorority, eight people talked to me, and no one tried to woo my

Gentile friends. I couldn't imagine that "we" would do this. I got angry, an uncommon emotion for me. I let it be known that I was committed to my friends. We were joining Kappa Alpha Theta—which had no Jews before but was about to have one now.

Then I called home. To my absolute disbelief, I heard my father insisting that I belonged in the Jewish sorority. I was stunned. Religion had always been a point of our life, but never a dividing point. We'd spoken of Jewish roots and Jewish politics, but never in exclusive terms.

Dad was adamant. When I argued, I expected him to say, "We'll talk about it this weekend." He didn't. He said, "Your mother and I are coming to Ann Arbor, now. We'll have dinner." I could see the scene before it unfolded: Mother would be upset about Dad being upset. She would drink, Dad would be unbending, and I would wind up crying.

I was right on all three points. It was an ugly discussion. Dad let it be known that I would never—"Never!"—be a "Theta."

Dad was prophetic. I never moved into Theta with my friends. In the weeks following our Ann Arbor dinner, I retreated first from friends and then from classes and eventually from the campus itself. By Thanksgiving, I was looking for someplace to live near home. Sometime over the winter holidays I told my parents that they could have their way. I would not join Theta, because I was never going back.

I'd been overzealous in my course selection to begin with. My academic advisor disliked women in general and saw me in particular as a pampered rich girl who needed a "coming down." He pressed me to enroll in a series of advanced classes that would have challenged me however hard I studied. And I wasn't studying rigorously. I was finding parties on campus, not just on weekends but after a while nightly. I was drinking and playing and watching my grades slide, causing anxiety that was most comforted by another drink or two at another party. To the delight of my advisor, I was experiencing my first taste of academic failure.

I left college less certain than when I had entered it. I enrolled again, later, in other places, for short-term runs, but never with the motivation needed to carry me through to graduation.

A few days after Christmas I visited Kingswood to walk into the weaving room, to feel the old comfort of the place before students returned. I was surprised to find Robert Kidd there. Mr. Kidd had taken over the weaving program a few years earlier, and we'd become friends during my last two years at Kingswood. He was youthful and creative, handsome and sensitive. He would kneel next to me as I sat at the loom, and he'd spin an idea full of patterns and textures and colors that I could fill hours creating. He was at the school during the holidays because he was doubly busy: Besides teaching, he'd opened his own weaving business in a barn near the campus. In fact, he needed a weaver. Any chance I'd be interested?

By evening I was inhaling the familiar mix of wood and wools in Bob Kidd's business studio. There were patterns to be followed for place mats and wall maps, and free-form projects ranging from afghans to rugs. The loom on which I worked was a beauty—massive, solid, responsive. Early in the morning I would sit at the loom with coffee, and I'd weave. In the afternoon, to the strains of classical music and the sight of dust wafting through streaks of sunlight, I'd weave. Into the evening, sometimes into the night, I would step on the pedal, throw the shuttle, pull the beater, and feel the wool race through my fingertips.

My parents reluctantly accepted the fact that I was not returning to college. By spring, Dad had forgiven me enough to ask me to help him with a speaking trip to San Francisco. As Israel prepared for the war that broke out weeks later, the American Jewish community was evaluating its traditional ties to the Democratic party. Dad was going to present the Republican case.

His speech was wonderful; the trip was zany. This was a major speech for Dad, and he was actually nervous. So was I. I clucked about like a mother hen. Within hours of our arrival at the St. Francis Hotel, Dad's room became the gathering place for all his friends. At first they talked about Jerusalem and its security. Then they talked about Washington, D.C., and its politics. Then, somehow, they got around to San Francisco and its nudity.

San Francisco was the only American city in the sixties that had topless and bottomless clubs as accessible as bagels in New York. Dad's friends wanted to see what they'd only heard about, and they wanted Max Fisher's company for their escapade. There was a lull in their conversation, and then each head turned toward me. What were they going to do with Max's underage daughter? They'd never get her into a club. The room grew quiet.

"Well," someone suggested, "then how about a shoe shine?"

Two blocks from the hotel, in a cramped shop with glaring lights, one by one the old men climbed into high black chairs. They looked like a odd Jewish jury lined up in their suits and hats. Each tucked his head behind the day's *Wall Street Journal*, then raised his paper just high enough to have a clear, close view of his wing tips being buffed by women with large, bare breasts. I stood wordlessly nearby, a raincoat pulled over my fashionably short dress, saying to myself, "Someday I should write a book."

Back in Detroit, Dad encouraged me to become ever more active in philanthropies. "If you're not going to school, do something for the community." If business was Dad's vocation and political policy his avocation, philanthropy had always been his abiding conviction. For him, this has never been charity; it is responsibility. "We should give back." We were raised hearing him say it, and we had all taken our turns at every charity and charity event he supported. Now he encouraged me to pick up the pace.

I had time. I knew what I did not want to be: a student. But I did not know what I could in fact do, other than weave. So I took Dad's advice and poured myself into work with the Detroit Symphony Orchestra, the Police Athletic League, the Children's Orthogenic School. Between volunteer activities, I indulged my love of theater. The "Fisher Theater" (no relation) was in the "Fisher Building" (no relation) where Dad had his office. Family friends, the Nederlanders, ran the splendid theater and were bringing wonderful Broadway productions to Detroit. They gave me a personal key to the theater, and I'd often visit Dad's office late in the day so that when we were through, I could slip into the auditorium during rehearsals or performances. I'd sit, alone and unseen, on decorative floral pots at the edge of the orchestra, escaping into a world of unapologetic fantasy.

My passion for theater led to another passion; it pitched me, headlong and without a moment's reservation, into the arms of an actor who'd come to town in *How to Succeed in Business Without Really Trying*. The substance of our relationship was, like his profession, mainly fantasy. I was half starstruck fan and half local celebrity; first we were sort of a couple, then we were sort of engaged, then it was sort of over. What was enduring had little to do with our relationship; it had to do with the creative energy of the theater. I loved it more than I loved him.

And with each passing day, in the background, the smoke and noise of Vietnam was becoming more and more undeniable. Friends were now being shipped off to fight, and some were being shipped home in boxes. Phillip and his friends had draft numbers on which their lives depended. But I was no activist. I was busy—very, very busy—being Miss Socialite, Miss Philanthropist, Miss Pleaser.

By the time election year 1968 rolled around, I was Dad's preferred advance person. Among other trips was one to Los Angeles. Before we left, Mother called me aside. She'd arranged a makeover for me by a stylist who had left Detroit to take Hollywood by storm. He did all the stars, performing miracles at $200 an hour—although Mother had mentioned only the miracles to Dad, not the price. She wanted me to enjoy the makeover, take notes on everything done by The Genius, and come home modeling his work and ready to teach her his secrets.

The Genius himself wasn't yet available when I arrived at his salon wearing my short pink dress and a smile, but an assistant had me under a faucet in fewer than sixty seconds. "My hair is naturally curly," I warned him. "It'll need a cream rinse." All I heard, as he squirted shampoo into my eyes and wrapped my face in a towel, was, "Oh no, no, no . . ." As I protested he wheeled me, still sputtering, under a dryer. Moments later I emerged with a full-blown, luminescent blond Afro.

Then came The Genius himself. Wanting to find some connection between us, I said, "I understand you're from Detroit, too." He looked wounded. "Detroit!?!?" He was indignant. "Oh no, no, no . . ." He began setting my hair, dry. I said meekly, "You'll have to wet it a little," and again I heard his favorite litany: "Oh no, no, no . . ." Genius knew no bounds.

Then came makeup, beginning with a pancake so heavy you could shape death masks with it. "I'm going to make your eyes bigger," I heard him say, as he glued on two massive (think ostrich-feather fans) eyelashes. Before the glue could dry, he was back to my hair, which he now cut to the edge of baldness. The few remaining strands stood on their ends like taut little springs until he doused them with hairspray and molded them down with his hands.

When The Genius finished, he spun me toward a mirror. Someone in my short pink dress was looking at me—Betty Boop with her finger in an electric socket. I paid for the damage, slipped my scarf over my head, and fled.

Dad was conferring in our suite with key players of the United Jewish Appeal. The only way to my room was through the crowd. I pulled the scarf down tight and ran the gauntlet, hearing Dad's voice behind me as I slipped into my room: "Who was *that?*"

Mother would pay only if I left the work in place for her inspection. I couldn't cry, or it would wash off. It was a sleepless night, since The Genius had glued open both eyelids with the giant fake lashes. But none of it mattered: By morning, my face was melting. My deepest fear, that Dad would explode over the extravagant cost, proved groundless. He was greatly relieved to discover that my "skin condition" was curable.

Once home, I had more to do than worry about my hairstyle. I needed to make some decision about who I was and what I was going to do with my life. The thrill of escaping college had long since passed. Weaving was a respite, not a career. I would always contribute to the community, but I did not want to become a "professional volunteer." I loved traveling with Dad and helping him, but trips ended and he went back to work—an option I did not have. I'd become adept at ruling out options. But I had no idea how to rule in one that would be satisfying.

CHAPTER 5

"Searching for Mary"

Two years after high school grad-
uation, in the spring of 1968, I was still working on a loom when Dr.
Martin Luther King was assassinated in Memphis. I was visiting the
Fisher Theater after a Detroit charity board meeting when Robert
Kennedy was gunned down weeks later in Los Angeles. That summer, the "Chicago Police Riot" broke out during the Democratic
convention. Hubert H. Humphrey was eventually nominated, but
the process of nomination was a sideshow for the main event starring Yippies and Cops in nearby Grant Park. I remember wondering—between dates and community events and an occasional trip
with my father—what made people believe so passionately in something that they would take to the streets.

My causes were pretty tame by comparison. I was a builder, a
worker, a supporter, rarely a critic and never a protestor. Community projects and fundraising events, these were the places where
"Max Fisher's daughter Mary" (as each clipping in the *Detroit Free
Press* or the *Detroit News* reintroduced me to its social page readers) was becoming known around town.

But for me, the summer wasn't about political protests. It was
about Israel, and a search for a sense of who I was.

Author Roger Kahn, best known for his *Boys of Summer,* also wrote *The
Passionate People,* about the lot and lives of Jews in America. Somewhere in that book he said of my father, "On the way to his fortune, Max
Fisher became a devout Zionist." I still don't know all the forces that
shaped Dad's ferocious commitment to Israel, but his zeal for that

nation is unrivaled. Mother once said that "Max loves, first, the Jews of the world, then the people of Detroit, and then the political arena. I'm fourth. But I don't mind; he could have had three mistresses."

I've never heard my father, then or now, enjoy a moment of self-congratulation about his public stature. He enjoys his politics the way Mother enjoys a good game of gin or bridge, or other men relish golf. He focuses on politics and philanthropy because he believes he needs to "give back," and because he loves it. Mother may have been a little sharp in ranking herself fourth; but she wasn't wrong about the fact that her husband adores Israel and politics.

By the summer of 1968 my father was arguably the most recognized and influential Jew in America. At the time, I did not know it, and I don't think he cared. But looking back now, as an adult, I see how obvious it was. Over a twenty-four-month span beginning in 1967, he was elected president and then chairman of the United Jewish Appeal, named to the Board of Directors and Executive Committee of the American Jewish Joint Distribution Committee, awarded the first honorary doctorate from Bar-Ilan University (Israel), elected chairman of the National Executive Board of the American Jewish Committee, presented the Humanitarian Award of the Federation of Jewish Agencies of Greater Philadelphia, elected president of the Council of Jewish Federations and Welfare Funds, and appointed advisor to the president of the United States. And these notations only begin to scratch the surface of two of Dad's nearly ninety years. No wonder so many places in Israel bear his name (from a community center in Ramla to a park in Jerusalem).

When the Six Day War broke out in early June 1967, Dad had just finished raising $65 million as chairman of the United Jewish Appeal. It was, especially then, a tidy sum. But in the aftermath of the war, he immediately went to work raising additional pledges for the Israel Emergency Fund. An eye-popping $100 million rolled in during the first month. By the end of the summer, the figure rose to $180 million, with another $100 million of Israel bonds purchased. In June of 1968, Dad was returning to Israel, and I was going with him.

Dad and I had collided over sororities and Jewishness at the University of Michigan, and the damage of that collision had never been fully repaired. We'd walked away from our differences, not settled them; as so often happened in our family, conflict was finally sent off into silence, rarely into understanding or compromise.

In fairness to both my parents, neither had ever insisted that their children become "Jewish jewels" for them to show off, either in public or private. We went to temple from time to time, and I was regularly dispatched to Sunday School until I was confirmed at the age of fifteen. We observed the Jewish holidays, learning the traditions, but often with as many Christian friends as Jewish, and never with the duty-bound grimness I later encountered in Orthodox homes. Judaism held my roots, and I saw it as interesting and distant family history, but I had not been seized by a vibrant spirituality, and while I enjoyed the stories from the Old Testament, the religious trappings of Judaism had never become a part of either my self-identity or my lifestyle. I never devalued religion, but neither had I incorporated Jewishness as *the* defining characteristic by which I identified myself.

But, at the age of twenty, asking harder questions about who I was, I began to rethink this part of my identity. "Maybe," I thought, "who I really am is *Jewish*. Maybe this is where I could uncover roots planted more deeply than Dad and Mother, or George Frehling, or even Papaharry."

My father had welcomed me to come along to Israel, and I knew that this would not be a family holiday. He was going to be holed up in conferences with Israeli officials and world Jewish leaders. I didn't care. I was going to Israel to dig out my own roots and discover a clearer sense of who I was, who I could become.

On our arrival in Israel, I was committed to the tender mercies of Miriam Eshkol, wife of Israeli prime minister Levi Eshkol, with whom Dad was spending much of his time. It was made clear to me that Dad's assignment was "business" and my duty was to take in the sights of Israel and stay out of his way. I was given a schedule for each day's activities and a full escort of interpreters, tour guides, and security forces.

For a day or two, being "toured" was fine. Then I asked Miriam if I could visit with my father for a little while to discuss some plans I was considering. She thought he might be too busy to see me. After several more days of touring Jerusalem—we never left the city—I was beginning to feel more like a prisoner than an explorer. I was being shuttled around Jerusalem not to discover my roots but simply to stay out of my father's way.

The adult part of me was frustrated at being treated like a child, and I suspect the little-girl part of me was missing her dad. I wanted to know that I counted, too. And it was true that I was wondering more deeply about myself and my Jewishness. I was considering joining the thousands of young adults who were moving to Israel, but I wanted to see the countryside—not just Jerusalem—before making a commitment.

It was clear that Israeli officials did not want my father to be distracted from his business. I couldn't interrupt him just to say hello. I'd need to have a reason to bother him. I told the person responsible for my security that it was imperative: I had to see my father, alone, for just a few minutes. With phone calls and much commotion, the meeting was arranged. We were to go to the Knesset, the Israeli parliament building, and my father would be taken from a meeting to visit with me in a hallway.

Dad emerged from a side conference room and strode down the hallway toward me. He was accompanied by important-looking officials still talking to him. And I wasn't alone either, because my bodyguards wouldn't leave. I felt very small and very lonesome; what I wanted most was to crawl onto Dad's lap, throw my arms around his neck, and hug him. But I never dared to do that, even when we were at home.

Instead, I marched up to ask Dad the question I had taken most of a week to think up—a question I had promised was so critical it could not wait. My mouth was dry and my lower lip quivered as I leaned out of range of the others to ask: "Daddy, are you a Jew first or an American first?"

He barely paused. "What do you think?" he asked. "What are you?"

"I don't know," I replied. "That's why I asked you. I'm wrestling with whether or not I should stay in Israel for a while."

He was impassive. "When you decide what you are," he said, "I'll tell you what I am. Is there anything else?"

No, there was nothing else. He returned to his important business. And I had a tour waiting.

The Knesset interlude had not satisfied either my longing for a hug or my desire for self-understanding. But Dad's answer touched off a very real struggle within me. I resolved to begin a serious soul search: Who was I? And what was I? Had I been redefined as nothing more than "Max Fisher's daughter"? Who was this "Mary" person?

My father's time in Israel was scheduled to last six days, and then he was headed back to the States. I did not fully appreciate at the time his role as "quiet diplomat" (later chosen as the title of his biography by Peter Golden) between Israel and the campaign of Richard Nixon already building toward a November victory. At least in part, I didn't understand these things because it was my identity, not my father's diplomacy, that occupied my attention.

Shortly before he was scheduled to leave, I sent word to Dad that I wanted to stay in Israel, at least to tour the country for a week or two and perhaps to stay even longer. Miriam Eshkol suggested that if I wanted to understand the country, I needed to understand the language. She proposed that I consider studying Hebrew at an Ulpan—a residential school for adults and immigrants who wanted an immersion in the language and culture of Israel. In short order, I was in residence at the Ulpan Akiva in Netanya, near Tel Aviv, the only Ulpan in Israel that would also admit non-Jews. I was one of 160 people at the Ulpan. We ranged in age from seven to sixty-five, came from thirty-five different countries, and were all enrolled in a crash course in Hebrew.

It did not take me long to get a heavy dose of Israeli nationalism. Zionism was in full flower a year after the Six Day War. I had chosen Akiva because I did not want to be in a place that was exclusive or excluding; I remembered my distaste for the "Jewish sororities."

The Ulpan was everything I had hoped for, and more. I met a generous and gentle non-Jewish American family at Akiva. They first befriended me and then invited me into their family. The Campbells had been inspired to sell their Pennsylvania farmstead and uproot their family in the aftermath of the 1967 war, explaining that even though they were Gentiles they felt strongly that Israel must continue to exist.

No one at the Ulpan was more committed to Israel than the Campbells. He was a farmer who saw ways he could improve agricultural life in the rocky and dusty terrain that characterizes much of Israel. She was a teacher, ready to devote her career to educating Jewish children. They'd gambled the lives of their five sons and their own hopes in America on Israel's uncertain future.

I was sorry to see Jack Campbell and his family preparing to leave the Ulpan before my time had ended. I was struggling with basic Hebrew as they packed. But then things slowed down for them;

their plans weren't materializing as quickly as they'd hoped. Finally the reason for the delay became clear. Everywhere they looked for land to farm and put down roots, they were rejected. They were honest, hardworking, and committed. But they were not Jews.

It was, it seemed to me, the most blatant case of discrimination I had ever encountered, violating people I loved in the name of an identity I was trying to embrace. I was outraged. How could the people who had suffered the unspeakable inhumanity of Adolf Hitler respond in such a way to people who were "different," particularly when they came as friends and allies? I took my question to the home of the prime minister and to the office of the chief of police in Jerusalem. They both heard me out, and soon thereafter the Campbells were settled as emigrés. Even so, I could not fully celebrate their success; I had a mouthful of the bitterness of prejudice.

Besides, I had a toothache, throbbing and demanding. Ulpan Akiva had provided a rich experience, but it had been relatively hard living. The compound itself had been hit by mortars and bombed during the Six Day War, the buildings reduced to rubble. The ruins had never been fully restored or replaced, and sanitary conditions were passable but not ideal. Midway through the summer I'd developed a skin rash. I supposed it related in one way or another to our living conditions. Eventually, whatever was turning patches of my skin into painful blotches took a turn and attacked my gums. I was shuttled to offices of oral surgeons. I couldn't sleep or eat. I was sick. I missed my family and my friends. I was ready to go home.

I returned frequently to Israel over the next five or six years, as part of a mission or a group. But I never went back to "find myself" again. If I was unsatisfied when I came home from this first search for roots, I was also a step closer to the goal of knowing myself. I had learned to ask, "Who am I?" Even if I had no answer, I had learned the right question.

Politics and politicians had become mainstays at the house in Franklin by the time I returned from Israel. I had always shared my father's interest in people, but not in politics. Dad loved them both. Mother enjoyed the repartee—the sparkling conversations that

opened doors for her wonderful stories, the quick wit and fast humor at which she excelled. Besides, she was photogenic, a marvelous addition to any political pose.

Max Fisher had not always been a Republican. He cast his first Republican vote in 1940 for presidential candidate Wendell L. Willkie, on the principle that no one—not even Franklin Delano Roosevelt, whom he much admired—should serve more than two terms. "I thought it was a mistake for the Jewish community to be locked in by the Democrats because they were taken for granted," Dad later told his biographer. "Every election the Democrats knew they could count on 75 or 80 percent of the Jewish vote. They didn't even have to go out and listen to the concerns of [the Jewish community]. They didn't have to work for it. This was one of the big arguments I made [to Jews]."

My father never appreciates being taken for granted, not by anyone. His success in business made him a player to reckon with, and his desire to have an impact on history made relationships with strong politicians all the more likely. He'd been a delegate to the 1964 Republican convention in San Francisco when Rockefeller was swamped by Barry Goldwater, and it was in the Cow Palace where Dad refined his distaste for right-wing extremism.

In 1966 he agreed to chair the finance committee of the (Michigan governor George) Romney for President campaign. At first it was thought that Romney's status as a Mormon elder might be a political liability. But it never was. Instead, Romney's candidacy became one of Southeast Asia's strangest casualties when papers reported his too frank, or too colorful, assertion that he might have been "brainwashed" during a fact-finding mission to Vietnam. With Romney out, Dad's allegiance swung to the next centrist candidate: Richard M. Nixon.

Dad had liked Richard Nixon the first time they met, in 1959, when Nixon was Eisenhower's vice president. Nixon was a Quaker from small-town California, and Dad was a Jew from Salem, Ohio, but both had been driven to succeed—and had succeeded—in part by holding on to privacy and control. Pragmatic, reserved almost to introversion, both were drawn to power. And both spoke frequently, with great reverence, of their mothers. When his mother died in 1969, Dad was especially moved by President Nixon's condolence letter, which had said "She must have been very proud of you."

There was one clear difference between my father and the president, and it only served to strengthen their relationship: Dad did not want the limelight that Nixon seemed to crave. They had nothing for which to compete. Over the years, it was this difference that kept my father buried in his business and philanthropic interests, clinging to his personal privacy, firmly turning down each offer of cabinet posts or ambassadorships.

I returned from Israel after the 1968 Republican National Convention in Miami Beach, where Dad had proven to be one of Nixon's most persuasive supporters. By the time I arrived in Franklin, the house was full of the sound of campaign conversations and emerging strategies. When Nixon won in November, Dad was slotted into a position as White House advisor—both on and off the record—on matters ranging from Israel and the Middle East to business and economic issues.

Dad's network of acquaintances and power is impressive. But it isn't only whom he knows that has made him valuable to this and other presidents; it's also *what* he knows. My father is, to say it plainly, both smart and wise. He can reduce the most complicated set of circumstances to a few understandable options. He's not afraid to make or to recommend decisions. He likes to get his way, but when decisions go against him, he neither pouts nor quits. He comes back the next day friendlier and stronger and more convincing than ever.

All of this was becoming evident during Nixon's first two years in office, when Dad's global reputation was rapidly enlarging. By 1970 Max Fisher was the most powerful Jewish Republican in the known universe, and the universe in which he was known best was the power circle of "insider Republicans."

I don't recall Dad ever inviting the children into matters of political intrigue. Neither do I recall ever wishing he would. But occasionally his political and my social interests would intersect. Without his connections, I'd not have been at Nixon's inauguration and ball.

And if I'd not been at the inauguration, I wouldn't have been invited back in July 1970, when Tricia and Julie Nixon threw a dinner bash for Prince Charles and his sister Princess Anne. Dad paid the tab for a first-class round-trip ticket from Detroit—a less than princely sum, even then, of $88. His friend Henry Ford II arranged to have a car pick me up at the National Airport to whisk me to the Jefferson Hotel to change clothes and then to the South Lawn of the White House.

It was a magical party under a massive tent festooned with Italian lights. We danced, serenaded by the Who ("Won't Get Fooled Again") and Gary Puckett and the Union Gap ("This Girl Is a Woman Now" and "Lady Willpower"), bands calculated to make young hearts race. Formal escorts for the evening were assigned by the White House social office. My escort turned out to be a lean, lanky son of a Republican Texas congressman. I'd not have predicted, based on our brief time together, that my date that evening would one day be governor of Texas, where he owns the Texas Rangers baseball team, and where his father retired shortly after leaving the White House: George Bush, Jr.

I was home from Israel, and staying home, in the fall of 1968. Despite an August *Detroit Jewish News* article (headline: MARY FISHER FINDS 'SHALOM' IN ISRAEL) in which I said I was home only briefly and "then I'm going back," I wasn't. I was home to stay. But it was clearer to me than it had been before Israel that I did not have a good grasp on either my identity or any clear purpose in my life: work, calling, vocation. I had no defined career, and when I had "business cards" printed to leave with job applications, I stammered to find the right name and finally settled on a conglomeration: "Mary Lizabeth Davis Fisher." I felt that I had failed at Israel, that I had gone away to make life's most critical discovery—myself—and come home more uncertain of who I was than when I'd left. I'd come home unfulfilled.

It was probably as much a hope for fulfillment as a desire to be charitable that led me back into community service, working hard and raising money for causes, especially those that had to do with children. By October, there were stories in both the *Detroit News* and the *Detroit Free Press* about my efforts to pry contributions out of my father's friends for causes ranging from ALSAC (Aid to Leukemia Stricken American Children), to adman and friend Fred Yaffe's "Drugs Are Dumb" campaign, to the well-regarded Children's Orthogenic School.

These were not leisurely days. I don't think I had until that point

ever worked harder in my life than I did then, probably in part to
show my parents that I was no failure and had not grown lazy. I was
up early in the morning and off to breakfast planning sessions,
stopping by the house late afternoons to change clothes for dinner
meetings and evening events. Perhaps I was too busy; perhaps I was
hiding in the busyness. Perhaps. But I did not want Max or Marjorie
Fisher or anyone else to think that Mary Fisher was a freeloader.

Then came one of the telephone calls that changed my life.
Margie Levin, wife of the doctor who'd spent my adolescence pre-
scribing pills for whatever ailed me, called to ask if I'd help with an
auction to support local public television.

Public television wasn't very public in the late 1960s, or very
much television, for that matter. Most people who'd heard of it
called it "educational TV." These were, comparatively speaking,
the Dark Ages of television—no cable, no satellite dishes, no remote
controls, and much mumbo-jumbo about the benefits of "UHF,"
with its strange circular antenna, over "VHF."

Public television in Detroit was "Channel 56." It was more idea
than reality; "Sesame Street," which almost single-handedly made
public television what it is today, had not yet arrived in the Motor
City. Like most public television stations across America, Channel
56 was built on impossibly high hopes and improbably low budgets
in loaned space filled with used equipment. Public television in the
late 1960s was, at its best, a promise.

By late fall of 1968 I was part of a Detroit delegation to Chicago,
studying a successful auction that had been established by WTTW-
TV. Back in Detroit, I took on the role of "Auction Celebrity Chairman," contacting every well-known name in the city for the
springtime 1969 Channel 56 Auction. By the time the first Channel
56 Auction was finished, we'd raised a little more than $90,000 and
I was addicted. Public television in Detroit had become my passion.

Nothing interfered with my commitment to public television in
the spring of 1969 except my twenty-first birthday party. Jack
Tucker, then the "Free Press Society Columnist," told all of Detroit
about the double-decker bus we rented to ferry thirty-five guests—
and two live karakul lambs given as a gift by Cleo, one of Mother's
unusual astrologer friends, because I'm an Aries and my sign is a
ram—from one nightclub to another. It was a kind of progressive
party, ending at Arthur's disco. My scrapbook still gives evidence

that in 1969 local papers really covered these things: "Mary and mother Marge both wore white pajama outfits." Good grief.

The crass reality was less appealing. My date that evening, Fred Yaffe, could not have predicted the destruction two lambs would wreak upon his car. The backseat was covered with a thick, aromatic blanket of lamb droppings when we returned, and the animals looked—I'm not making this up—sheepish. I compounded the misery by taking the beasts to the Franklin house, where they set upon my mother's prized vegetable garden. She still remembers those critters.

By fall I'd been named general chairman and producer of the 1970 Channel 56 Auction. I threw myself into the work; I organized. I had lists for every category of interest: celebrities, contributions, financial goals. I had schedules for every day of the weeklong, on-air auction and for every day of the four months prior to that week. When not organizing lists and projects, I was organizing people. I inducted friends and relatives on behalf of the cause on weekends, having them do everything from licking envelopes containing requests for corporate sponsorships to picking up contributed merchandise from local stores and companies. My mother discovered I was using her address list to get the home listings of all her friends. And every time my father called an acquaintance in the city, he'd say the same thing: "Hi, Max . . . just talked to your daughter."

We went on the air the morning of June 1, 1970; I'd not slept in more than two days. We continued on air through June 6. When the tally was finally announced, we'd raised an unprecedented $275,800. "Sesame Street" was on its way to Detroit. We'd convinced Detroit merchants to part with 4,035 items (total estimated value: $365,282), which were auctioned off, on air, by celebrity auctioneers. All told, more than four thousand names of people involved—from telephone installers to catering services, General Motors executives to Henry Ford II—had been logged in my personal book: names, roles, addresses, and telephone numbers.

It was exhilarating. I'd brought my skills at organizing to a job that needed above all else organization. My family's network of friends and acquaintances—which I regularly hid from potential dates lest they start into the "poor little rich girl" routine—was a resource I could access night and day. Even my love of theater was satisfied here, from publicity shots with Bozo the Clown to on-camera conversations with celebrities who stopped by.

By spring 1971 I was so identified with the Channel 56 Auction that I needed to do little more than get on the phone and say, "Hi, this is Mary Fisher." Merchants knew I wanted a contribution, "maybe a little larger than last year's?" Volunteers knew I needed their time, or their cars, or their family members. I worked out of an office-trailer parked behind the mall where goods for the auction were warehoused with Aggie Scott, who had begun as a volunteer but was by now a Channel 56 staffer. When it was over, we'd raised more than $300,000. Everything was bigger and better than the year before. In seventy-plus on-air hours, broadcast from "chaos central" at the Tel-Twelve Mall in Southfield, 1970's rookies proved that they had become 1971's veterans, including us.

The 1971 auction was my last, and my involvements were limited. The work had become more than any volunteer could shoulder. It needed to be staffed, and staffed with excellence, which it was. They had another "bigger and better" show in 1972, broadcast from a new studio paid for by proceeds from earlier auctions. But I was already looking around for full-time work. I had a clearer sense of what I could do. And I knew where I wanted to be: in a commercial television studio.

CHAPTER 6

"Daddy's Shadow"

F resh from her chairmanship of
the Channel 56 Auction," noted a columnist in the May 29, 1972,
Detroit News, "young socialite Mary Fisher may have found herself her
first job. . . . This week she'll produce the Bob Hynes' Morning Show,
standing in for producer Perry Krause, who's on vacation. Word
from station officials is Mary's 'done a helluva good job for us' so far."

I knew the Detroit television producers, all of them. I'd been on
every one of their shows for the Channel 56 Auction. Since public
TV accepts no advertising, it was a "rival station" that never
evoked any feelings of rivalry among commercial stations. And all
of Detroit's on-air talent from radio and television had been either
cajoled or co-opted into appearing with me on the auction itself. We
all knew one another.

What they did not know at WXYZ was that I wanted a job. I
didn't resent getting up in the morning to be at my post on time,
doing the work anyone else would be expected to do, without airs
and without attitude. Everyone had so frequently heard the words
"Mary Fisher" connected to the word "socialite" that they didn't
imagine I was anything else. Silently, intensely, I hated the word
"socialite." It was an elegant way of saying "freeloader."

It was true that my family had wealth, but it was also true that in
professional circles I was living in my father's shadow. It was not
something he intended. But to be Max Fisher's child in Detroit was to
be the object of a set of assumptions, not all of them fair or accurate.

Henry Baskin has been one of Detroit's best-known attorneys
and, since public TV days, one of my best friends. Henry set up an
appointment for me with Arno Marcaccio, then the executive pro-

ducer of WXYZ (Channel 7), one of five ABC-owned-and-operated stations in the nation. "Be bold," Henry told me. I marched in boldly and handed over my résumé, which prominently featured my three years at Channel 56. Marcaccio looked at the résumé, then at me, and said, "You haven't got any experience, young lady."

"Three years," I said.

"Didn't get paid," he said.

There was silence, broken when I finally said, "Okay, give me anything. Anything."

He gave me a one-week, fill-in shot as the "Morning Show" secretary when Gail Pebbles went on vacation, and I jumped at it. I had suspected that work isn't really *work*—isn't really valued—unless you're being paid for it. I had felt this way even while working terribly hard for no money to do things people said were important. But now I discovered that this wasn't merely my feeling about work, it was a social standard. I learned it, hard, in that first interview.

In 1972 there was no ABC's "Good Morning, America" filling time slots from 7:00 to 8:30 each morning. ABC's local stations needed to go head-to-head with the king of morning programming, NBC's "Today Show," while fending off "Captain Kangaroo" and "Bozo's Circus." It was a tough assignment in Detroit, one of the nation's top five markets.

I was serving as secretary at ABC's Channel 7 when I got word that I'd be a stand-in, fill-in, just-for-a-week producer for Bob Hynes's "Morning Show." After years of producing the Channel 56 Auction, here at last was my shot at glory in commercial TV. I got on the telephone and turned the next five days into a Mary Fisher "sweeps week." I called every big-name talent I'd met over the past five years and asked if they'd do me a favor. Then I called my father's list, starting with Henry Ford, who did not do local interviews. He agreed to come "whatever morning you want, honey."

If they were big names in Detroit business, entertainment, and industry, I was lining them up for Bob Hynes. My first Monday as producer, we had more local celebrities slotted to be guests for the week than we had airtime to use them. When my week ended, I was called in and given the title "associate producer." As it turned out, I wasn't associate to anyone else because they resisted naming a producer—I did the show alone. But in the beginning it didn't matter to me. I had a job that looked like a stepping-stone to a real career.

I was on the payroll. My work finally mattered. And if my work mattered, well . . . I must matter, too.

For sheer, heart-stopping excitement, nothing compares to live broadcasting in television. Bob Hynes stayed at Channel 7 just long enough for us to become friends, and then Tom Shannon—who'd been working in Windsor, Ontario, across from Detroit, at CKLW radio—became the morning host. Mornings when Shannon was feeling well were chaotic, funny, sometimes nearly brilliant. But Shannon, to put it mildly, was not a morning person. Quite often he'd let me know just before airtime that he wasn't entirely awake, and I'd go charging off to find our newsman, who would need to do the final half hour.

The crew and director I inherited were mainly people left over from the Soupy Sales days, when the comedian had launched his popular show from the Channel 7 studios. These were guys with names like "White Fang" and "Black Tooth." They had literally arrived with the first cameras and never left. They contributed to an easy camaraderie at the station with a laid-back professionalism that provided a needed counterweight to my frenetic, tightly wound demeanor. They became my mentors and my friends.

In live television, disasters happen on a regular basis and near-disasters even more frequently. I died a thousand deaths in live TV. Sets fell in. Guests showed up drunk. Ten minutes before the morning's featured headliner was scheduled to arrive, he called to say he'd been grounded by fog in Boston or a blizzard in Minneapolis.

Everyone who's worked in live broadcasting has his or her own stable of stories ready to be trotted out at a moment's notice. Much of the humor surrounds pranks staged while the cameras are rolling. One of Detroit's best-known anchormen during my years at WXYZ had more than his share of vanity. He always wanted to look tall on camera, so he sat on pillows. I couldn't count the number of times he rushed onto the set, still primping his thinning hair, to discover that I had both lowered his seat and stolen his pillows. Additional silliness took place after the shows ended, including ankle-cuffing people to their chairs and putting discreet dollops of shaving cream on telephone earpieces.

Because Channel 7 was owned and operated by the ABC network, we had special access to interesting guests. One was Kitty

Carlisle, the well-spoken, utterly proper, and somewhat assertive panelist from the popular prime-time network game show "To Tell the Truth." She didn't walk onto the set; she possessed it.

As it happened, I'd already booked for the same show Marilyn Chambers, a young actress and model not best known for her speaking roles. Chambers had modeled for the photograph on the label of Ivory Snow ("ninety-nine and forty-four one-hundredths percent pure") and had then gone on to star in pornographic movies like *Behind the Green Door.* I thought she would make a good interview for Tom Shannon, and I set it up. Kitty Carlisle, the woman of literature and grace, was already on the set when Chambers arrived. Carlisle wanted to stay. One did not say no to Carlisle, so she stayed.

Shannon had introduced Chambers and asked her one question when Carlisle took over the interview. She questioned Chambers with intense curiosity, asking everything any proper woman would want to know, greeting each answer with a sort of stunned you've-got-to-be-kidding-me amazement.

"How do you *do* that?" Carlisle wondered of the porn goddess. "I mean, really! How do you *do* that?" Miss Manners was confronting the Happy Hooker. Shannon never got back into the interview; he watched Carlisle throw questions and Chambers swat back answers as if he were watching a Ping-Pong match.

After fifteen minutes of back-and-forth between his guests, Shannon announced a commercial break. In the tiny pause before the director could make the switch from studio to tape, Carlisle squeezed in one more question to Chambers: "Does your mother know what you do?" It was great television.

One of my most memorable bookings at WXYZ was Muhammad Ali, then heavyweight boxing champion of the world. Shortly before airtime I went into the "green room," where guests wait to go on the air, to introduce myself and warm him up for the on-air interview. I was cheery and pleasant and a little awed to meet him. He stared at me, yawned, and looked away.

I didn't know if I was personally unimpressive to him or if he just intended to be a bored, even hostile, guest. But I needed to bring him to life before he went on camera. I'd been assured by sportscaster Howard Cosell and others that he had a great personality and incredible magnetism. He was hiding it brilliantly this morning. I asked questions and he muttered one-word answers. He yawned.

Two minutes before Ali was due to be interviewed on the set by our host John Kelly and our sportscaster Dave Diles, the champ appeared to have fallen asleep. I nudged him—cautiously—and led him to the studio.

Earlier I had arranged for a surprise live telephone hookup from New York with Howard Cosell, then at the apex of his career. When I got Cosell on the line that morning, just before Ali went on the air, he said to me, "Don't worry about a thing, young lady. Just put me on the air with him, and I'll assure that you have a sterling guest." I thanked him profusely; it was clear that I needed his help.

The red light of the camera flashed on, and so did Muhammad Ali. He was effervescent, charming, funny, outrageous, even bantering and showing boxing moves to kids from the Police Athletic League in Detroit's inner city. He was everything you want in a television guest. I couldn't believe it. This wasn't the same man who had just responded to my charm with yawns. I wondered what it was about me that had so bored him.

Then the "surprise conversation" with Cosell began. But something was wrong. It was going badly. At first Ali was merely irritated. But then, out on the floor, I could hear him telling Cosell things that were taboo on family television. Cosell could be heard over the speakerphone, shouting insults at the champ. Suddenly Ali stood up, eyes flashing, ripped off his lapel microphone, and threw it across the set. He exploded, "I don't have to take this!" and stormed out.

I stood, openmouthed, as the camera followed the champ off the set and through a studio door, which he slammed shut with heavyweight ferocity.

In the quiet that followed Ali's tirade, all eyes turned to me. Oh. I'm the producer. We're still on the air, live, with no guest, no explanation, and no way to just sign off. We cut for a commercial. I was about to fly out to find somebody—anybody—to do something—anything—when it began—the sound of laughter. First it came bubbling out of the speakerphone, from Howard Cosell, then rumbling out of people on the set. It rolled out of the shadows of the studio, where Ali was standing, laughing, pointing at me. It had all been staged as a prank. I'd had no clue and no control. Cosell said something self-congratulatory over the speakerphone—something about a sensa-

tional stunt to pull on Detroit at the beginning of a new day. I had
been had by Ali, Cosell, and company on my own turf.

Every weekday morning I was up before sunrise and charging off
to the studio. By the time Rita Bell was on camera after our show,
introducing the feature film of WXYZ's "Million Dollar Movie" of
the day, I was congratulating hosts, thanking our crew, and heading
for the telephone to spend another long day solving crises and
booking guests. The days were long but interesting. I knew what I
needed to do, and how to do it: I organized.

I never knew if it was because I'd been a volunteer before, or
because I was a woman then, that WXYZ wouldn't give me either
the title or the pay of "producer." Maybe it was just that they knew
I'd work without either, so they withheld both.

I had the duties of a producer, plus the duties of people who usually assist a producer. The four other ABC-owned-and-operated
station morning shows—in New York, Chicago, San Francisco, and
Los Angeles—had full-time producers, and each of them had full-
time staffs to help. From all the feedback I received, and from the
show's results, the work I did seemed more than adequate. But the
message I received, sometimes explicitly, was that I was not worthy
of the title or the pay.

John Kelly, a consummate professional with a playful sense of
humor, took over the hosting duties of the "Morning Show" about a
year after I arrived. We renamed it "Kelly and Co." It was going
well, and ratings were exceptional. It seemed like the right time for
me to make a move.

I asked the powers that be if they would consider giving me an
assistant so I could reduce my hours or concentrate more on features and investigative reports. They had little motivation to add to
their costs, but they agreed.

If they would give me an assistant, might they also consider giving
me the title of producer? No. Well, then how about a raise, something
to recognize that I'd actually increased our market share while
working alone? No. Why not? Because "you don't need the money."

It wasn't about money, of course, even if I didn't know how to say
that. It was about dignity, about self-worth, about being valued. I
knew how I felt, but I didn't know how to respond.

Henry Baskin says of those years that "it wasn't a woman's time. You did the work of a producer, but they weren't willing to give you the title—they just couldn't imagine doing it. They had all been raised in, and had risen to the top of, a male-dominated society." Henry is probably right. Most of the men with whom I worked in television had never seen let alone worked with women executives.

During the summer of 1973 I was wearing down and I knew it. I did not feel valued at WXYZ. The truth is, I did not feel valued anywhere. I wanted to know that my father approved of me and of what I did. For all I knew, he might have been very approving—but I didn't hear or feel it.

Worse, I didn't approve of myself. I had grown tired and heavier at the same time. Being a woman was hard. At work, years of social patterning justified a form of sexism that most of us didn't even know how to name, let alone fight. Now it was helping block my own sense of worthiness, of value. And at home, I had taken refuge in eating. I'd added pounds and I hated my shape. I wanted to be feminine again: slim, attractive, sexy—like Mother.

Mother has always been drop-dead beautiful. Always. Her sister, my aunt Joyce Burkoff, used to go horseback riding with Mother in Kentucky. "You *had* to ride in Kentucky," she will still drawl, and then launch into the line I've heard since childhood: "And your mother, she was always the gorgeous one. She'd fall off her horse, and all the men would run over to see if she had been hurt. She'd stand up and ask me, 'How's my hair?'"

When I looked at my mother, I saw beauty. When I looked in the mirror, I saw short and fat. It wasn't a new battle that I was fighting. During adolescence I'd been given pills to reduce my appetite, to reduce my weight. They were probably amphetamines. Whatever they were, they helped me avoid both food and sleep—which led, of course, to the need for sleeping pills, too.

No matter what shape my body has taken over four-plus decades, I've always had a chubby self-image. At any moment I can hear the voices—countless voices over the years—of people looking at me, and then saying to one another, "Isn't it a shame; such a pretty face . . ."

In the spring of 1974 my professional energy was disappearing, my body was ballooning, and my self-image was crashing. I needed to change my life. And I did not want to go back to prescriptions.

I left WXYZ and, a few weeks later, headed for Duke University for a special eating disorders clinic that featured a rice diet. I moved into a motel in Durham, North Carolina, not far from Duke's campus. My entire life consisted of eating three "meals" constructed largely of rice—no salt. Between meals and weigh-ins, occasional group sessions and five-mile walks, I sat in my motel room, watching the Watergate Hearings, wondering if I really was valueless, losing weight and losing hope.

I went to Duke five feet, one inch tall, weighing about 135 pounds. I headed home for the summer holidays at the same height but under 100 pounds in weight.

While at Duke I'd considered returning to work at WXYZ, which was possible. But by the summer of 1974, back in Detroit, the morning format had shifted and ABC's "Good Morning, America" was being introduced. I returned to my apartment and spoke of finding the job that would give me financial independence. I made guest appearances at the Channel 56 Auction.

But Detroit belonged to my father in those days. I imagine that was part of the appeal of television for me: Producing television was one thing that he did not know how to do. When we both came home from long days, we could talk to each other about people we'd been with, about issues being discussed. The television studio was, in some ways, a platform on which I could stand and be lifted up to his height so that I was nearly, for the first time in my life, toe-to-toe with my father.

Eventually, of course, such tactics fail. We are who we are, not what we do. While Dad's accomplishments had set the stage for my own success, they also made it impossible for me to know what success was due to his stage setting and what, if any, was owed to my own performance. When I achieved something, was it I who had done it— or Max Fisher's name, or his reputation, or his power? When I was denied a promotion, or even a job, because a man looked me in the eye and said, "Mary, you don't need the money," was he telling me I was undeserving or merely explaining why he didn't want to grant the request? When someone wanted to hire me, or date me, or have lunch with me, was it me they had in their sights, or my father?

I wanted to be neither a full-time volunteer in the community nor a full-time charity case at home. I wanted a job, a career, a sense of my own worth. And I wanted to get it on my own, as a result of my own reputation (not my father's) for hard work and proven ability. So I decided to leave Detroit and visit every television network and studio in New York City to find work based on my own merit, my achievements. New York was far enough away from Detroit that I could be Mary Fisher—not Max Fisher's daughter.

After two months of pounding Gotham's pavement, looking for any position in any arena that was television, I had learned two things: First, there were a lot of gifted people in New York City looking for work and I was just one of them. Second, when my application arrived on the desks of men with enough corporate power to actually decide to hire me, they always asked me the same question: "Are you Max Fisher's daughter?"

Vice President Ford, previously West Michigan's Congressman Ford, became President Ford in August. The Michigan Republicans were planning an event to salute William Milliken, the state's popular governor, and President Nixon had earlier promised to deliver the keynote address. When Nixon flew home to California following his resignation, Michigan's event appeared to lack a keynote speaker. But within days, President Ford had agreed to keep the date at Cobo Hall in downtown Detroit.

Whether it was confusion over the president's appearance or other factors that left local organizers of the event a little disorganized, I don't know. But I do remember getting the call in New York from Dad, asking if I'd be willing to come back for a few weeks to help put the event together. I was happy for the diversion and glad for the excuse to be doing something productive, something I knew how to do, in a place where I knew how to do it.

I'd never before worked on a major event with the White House, but I was made the White House's "key contact" in Detroit and all the Secret Service and advance team people began calling, asking questions and arranging details. In the days just before the event itself, carloads of handsome young men began arriving. What had previously been mere voices attached to Secret Service codes or advance team titles were suddenly translated into what Mother described as "gorgeous young men with things in their ears."

When White House advance chief Red Cavaney arrived in Detroit to head the preadvance team and lead our meetings, I told him I was

enjoying my work with the White House staff and that I'd be willing
to help out with other trips if I was needed. He said he might call me.

The event itself was a huge success. Dad introduced President
Ford in what became in subsequent years a near-standard introduction. It always went something like this: "President Ford and I
have a lot in common. We both went to college on partial scholar-
ships. We both washed dishes to earn spending money. We both
played center on our respective football teams, he for the University
of Michigan and I for Ohio State. He went on to become president
of the United States, and I went on to become rich"—pause,
smile—"betting with him on Ohio State–Michigan football games."
It's true that they bet on these games each year—and still do. And
the amount of the standing bet has never changed: five dollars.

What I remember most is not the crowd of five thousand or Ray
Bolger's entertainment, but President Ford's personal, even intimate, comments about his absent wife. Mrs. Ford had just had
surgery for breast cancer, and breast cancer was a topic rarely discussed in public during those years. But President Ford spoke of his
wife and her illness as only a loving husband can speak. His voice was
muted and gentle as he described his fear of losing her; and he was so
respectful, so full of pride in her courage, that I've never forgotten the
emotion of that moment.

White House advanceman Red Cavaney did remember me, and
he called not long after. There was another Michigan event on the
schedule, this one in President Ford's hometown of Grand Rapids.
The event was a presidential visit as part of the campaign then
being waged for the president's old congressional seat. Paul Goebel,
Jr., a loyal Republican and popular civic leader, had been a "shoo-
in" candidate for the office until the president announced his pardon of ex-President Nixon. Suddenly the shoo-in had become a
toss-up and threatened to become an embarrassment. I headed for
Grand Rapids to organize a massive "balloon drop" at the Calvin
College Fieldhouse as part of a get-out-the-vote pre-election drive
to undo some of the political damage done by the pardon. The balloon drop went off with great fanfare and success, but the election
went to the Democrats—a quiet foreboding of what would follow
for the president two years later.

I was back in New York, following the Grand Rapids trip, when
Cavaney called again. I'd imagined, frankly, that I had been turned

To Mary Fisher,
in grateful appreciation and
with best wishes.
Jerry Ford

MICHIGAN REPUBLICANS

SALUTE

THE PRESIDENT

October 10, 1974
Cobo Hall
Detroit, Michigan

into their "Michigan volunteer." But Cavaney had more in mind. Advance teams were in a state of flux, with some people left over from the Nixon presidency and others coming in with President Ford. They needed someone to help with a trip to Scottsdale, Arizona. Was I interested? Yes. Was I free? Yes. "Great. Meet us at Andrews Air Force Base at the end of the week."

I was frankly thrilled to have this opportunity. Advance work seemed like the perfect blend of things I knew how to do and did well, from organizing detail to organizing people to managing large events. When I'd worked with the advance team in Detroit, it all seemed perfectly natural, even easy.

Besides, it was dramatic, important, to be doing something directly in service to the president of the United States. I'd met President Ford for the first time at the Detroit dinner, and he was utterly charming. But his charm did not detract from the fact that my palms were dripping when I went to shake his hand, or that all those "gorgeous young men with things in their ears" were ready to exchange their lives for his in a heartbeat. I had dreamt of being an "advanceman," of flying on *Air Force One*, of coming down red-carpeted ramps to throngs of reporters and banks of cameras—of crowds wondering who I was, and what I'd ever done to merit flying with the president. It seemed almost magical, too good to be true.

I was at Andrews Air Force Base in the darkness before "O-dawn hundred," wearing an especially elegant white pantsuit with an orange turtleneck sweater. There were several planes on the tarmac, all looking like *Air Force One* to the untrained eye. I assumed that I would be flying on the presidential plane. When I ventured into the appointed holding area in the terminal, it was full of guys standing around in jeans and sweaters. They didn't look like the men who'd been at dinner in tuxedos and earpieces. These were ordinary guys, carrying duffel bags and jogging outfits, reviewing the previous night's ball scores—until they saw me and the room went quiet. There I stood, a woman, in my pretty white pantsuit and gold earrings, with my best luggage, ready to board *Air Force One*. And there they stood, looking quietly in my direction.

When an advance team goes to a city where the president will travel, the team flies in a C-141 air transport, one of the huge blue and white machines with the seal of America on the side, often with two of the president's cars in the hold. It's common to have two or even three planes going at one time—so that the cars and the people, the security resources and the communication equipment, are all ready when the president arrives.

Advance trips are not caviar flights. You are ushered aboard by air force loadmasters wearing green jumpsuits, heavy headphones, and harnessed equipment. Travel is noisy, bumpy, and dark on airplanes designed to lug machinery, not people. There are no windows, no movies, no flight attendants, and no comfortable seats. There is, in fact, no finished floor and no ceiling; wires are strung everywhere. My luggage was heaved into stowage without regard for its delicacy, and my pantsuit was never again white.

Because the demands of their work often put them at odds with each other, agents (Secret Service) are not always fond of advance people, or vice versa. When you meet the teams in public, these feelings are well disguised; when you're flying together in cramped quarters, not many feelings are masked. And I was on board a flight with mainly agents and military personnel—not only as an advanceman but worse, as a woman. There had never before been a woman advanceman.

During the takeoff, I watched what others did—how they found a place to sit and held on, what sounds they accepted as normal and which got their attention. Someone passed around little wads of something. Before I noticed what others were doing with the substance, I popped it in my mouth and began chewing. This did not appear to be the preferred usage. I saw everyone else massage the soft substance in their hands, break it into two smaller pieces, and then stick it in their ears to block out the noise and compensate for the leaky cabin pressure system that made ascents and descents uncomfortable. My embarrassment increased.

We were probably in the air an hour when I noticed that one by one guys were heading toward the back of the plane. Someone had a deck of cards, and a game soon broke out on the hood of the president's limo. I thought to myself, "It's now or never."

I got up, took off my jacket and earrings, pulled the clip out of my hair and whisked it into a ponytail, slipped off all my other jewelry, and bounced to the back of the plane, steadying myself against the massive metal containers that lined the walls. When I approached the card game, it stopped. Everyone turned and looked at me.

I've never known whose voice it was that finally broke the silence. "It's poker—you wanna sit in?"

"Yeah," I said. I leaned over the car hood to take my first hand. I played poker, whose rules and strategies I did not fully understand, all the way to Phoenix.

It was not a stamp of universal approval, not of advance people by agents, not of a woman in a world that had known only men. But it was a nod in the direction of acceptance, and I was grateful for it.

My father had invited Phillip to go with him to Israel early in 1971. They were aboard a flight from New York to Tel Aviv on January 23, 1971, when William Fisher, Dad's father, died. They learned of his death the next morning, when they came off the plane at Lod Airport.

William Fisher had not been an easy man. He was especially hard on his son Max. No matter what achievement or recognition came to Dad, his father was singularly unimpressed. When his father was financially stressed, Dad supported him. When he was physically spent, it was his son Max who saw to his care. But the one thing my father could never achieve was his father's bold, clear, public, and unambiguous approval. Either it wasn't there or it was always hidden.

Phillip still remembers that Dad kept each of his scheduled appointments in Israel with Prime Minister Golda Meir, Defense Minister Moshe Dayan, and President Zalman Shazar. Personal loss, deep as it might be, did not justify failing to do one's duty. Only when Dad's work had been satisfactorily finished did they fly back to New York and on to Detroit, arriving the night before the funeral.

The following noon, in the Ira Kaufman Chapel in Southfield, Michigan, before the service began, Max Fisher stood next to the open casket and stroked his father's hair. Dad said nothing for a time, perhaps remembering other places, or recalling his father's voice, or wondering why he could never do enough to satisfy his father's wishes—why he could never quite please him.

When my cousin Sherry approached and saw Dad quietly caressing his fallen father's hair, she did not ask. But he offered an explanation anyway. "Dad always liked that," he said.

Even in death, he was still trying to please his father. I understand.

CHAPTER 7

"The Advanceman Is a Woman"

I never meant to break the gender line, to become the "first woman" this or the "first woman to do" that. Only after I became associate producer at Channel 7 in Detroit did I discover that I was ABC's only woman producer at any of their owned-and-operated stations. My entire response, I think, was, "Oh." I'd wanted a job in which I could succeed, and I'd never wondered whether I was the first woman or the hundredth to take on the work.

When told at WXYZ that I couldn't have a raise because "you don't need the money," I resented it. I thought this discrimination was aimed at my family's wealth, and so I wrongly felt as much resentment toward my father, whose wealth was "the problem," as I did toward the boss who was denying me equal status or a fair wage. It did not occur to me then that gender might also have been involved.

At age twenty-five or twenty-six, I did not understand the power of male-dominated American society or the principles of sexism. I felt injured. But I was not sure whether these were merely feelings—feelings of, perhaps, a spoiled child—or whether they were the justified conclusions of an offended woman. If I couldn't understand what had happened, neither could I figure out how to fight back.

Those of us raised in the fifties and sixties suffered the consequences of gender stereotyping, men and women alike. If men defended a male-dominated society as a just world, we eventually labeled them chauvinists, but my own beliefs were not much different. If some nineteenth-century African-Americans were convinced to their souls that they were inferior to American whites, women like me a century later were equally convinced to our souls that we were inferior to American men. If we weren't June Cleaver, full-time nurturers, then we might be

"Our Miss Brooks" or "Lucy," comediennes. Women like my mother could be funny. But they couldn't be boss. Men were in charge.

I've gradually learned the value of what Gloria Steinem (*Revolution from Within*) calls "the importance of unlearning," of contradicting the major definitions of ourselves that we women assume early in life. Such "unlearning" is needed because, as Steinem recalls the words of Mona Caird, "We are governed not by armies and police, but by ideas." I grew up in a generation of women needing to develop a new idea—and certainly a new understanding—of who we are and what we could be.

I see this now, as a woman approaching fifty. But I did not understand it, even if I felt it, when I left ABC or when I ventured into the Advance Office of the White House in the mid-1970s. Had I known then what I know now, it might have changed how I saw myself, even how I defined myself. There would still have been blame to assign, but I would have given myself, and my parents, a good deal less of it.

When the call came from Washington, D.C., sometime between Thanksgiving and the holiday parties at the end of 1974, I pinched myself. I'd been invited to interview for a paid position on the White House advance team.

My trip to Arizona had convinced me I could do this work. It also apparently had demonstrated to Red Cavaney that my competence wasn't limited to events on my home turf in Michigan. The job required organization of people and public events, precise attention to detail, some social grace, reasonably good humor, and enough stamina to handle sleepless nights and grueling days—all this, plus a sense of loyalty and a desire to please. This was me!

I needed to interview for the job, first with an attorney in the White House Office of Personnel and then with Red Cavaney himself. I wanted the job; my goal was to not blow it.

I'd learned my lesson about clothes. This time I bought a tasteful outfit, not too dressy and not too casual. Makeup and jewelry were modest. I completed the entire FBI security form—nearly fifty pages asking for details I couldn't even remember, let alone imagine important—before I appeared at the White House to begin the interviews. I was ready not only to be interviewed but to be interviewed at the White House.

At the White House Office of Personnel, forms were waiting in a file for me to complete. A picture was taken for a security badge. The attorney assigned to interview me was courteous and thorough.

The critical interview was Red Cavaney's. He already knew I would work hard, but up until now I'd been regarded only as a "volunteer," not a paid colleague. I needed to pass muster now as a professional, to walk beyond the boundary of being "Max Fisher's daughter," thus qualified on matters of social poise and political pedigree, to being "Mary Fisher," a competent young woman who was no pampered socialite. I needed to impress Red not with my father's status but with my skills, with what I could do for the president and the White House.

I walked slowly from the White House Office of Personnel to the Executive Office Building (EOB) where, in room 348, Red Cavaney and the Advance Office staff were housed. I used the walk to rehearse the things I would say to impress the man who held my future in his hands. I tried different sentences to see if they were too modest or too familiar. I honed my language as well as my ideas.

I arrived at the EOB early enough to stop by the office of Leonard Garment, one of my father's friends who'd been counsel to President Nixon and had stayed on to serve President Ford, as well. It was strictly a courtesy call, one I wouldn't mention when I got to the Advance Office.

Leaving Leonard's office a bit later than I'd meant to, I wasn't quite sure where I was going. After trying one direction, then another, I realized I needed to hurry. How could I be trusted to get the president of the United States to the right place at the right time if I couldn't find my way to an interview on time?

With less than a minute to spare, heart pounding, I put my hand on the knob of room 348 and swung open the door to an office full of advance people and secretaries. Stepping into the glare of bright sunlight pouring through the office windows, having come out of a dark hallway, I was blinded. I tripped over the threshold, sprawling headlong across the floor of the Advance Office for the President of the United States. It was, for me and all the assembled witnesses, a memorable entrance.

Red Cavaney did not mention my entrance, or chat with me about my father. He spoke about the presidency, about the stress of the position and the need to make travel as stress-free as possible.

He talked about human limits stretched to unbearable lengths by long days and hard decisions, and about the fact that a half dozen people in the Advance Office could make a critical difference in the life of any president. When I left, I believed Red knew I could do the work, but I also had a higher view of what the work meant.

I got the job. During the holidays, I found an apartment in the Watergate Complex and moved what I needed from New York to Washington, D.C. I made a quick holiday trip to Palm Beach, Florida, where my parents were spending more and more time each winter. I left my dog Angel with Mother, since I would need to leave home for extended periods with little if any advance notice.

The background check was still being completed by the FBI, so I was officially a "volunteer" until mid- or late January. But I was working in a job I loved and could do, on the staff of the president of the United States. And I had gotten this job myself. My father had not won it for me.

My own convictions in this regard may not have been widely shared in other quarters. Not long after I started work in the Advance Office, the *Detroit Free Press* did a hometown-girl-makes-good feature entitled ADVANCEMAN IS A WOMAN. The title announced the plot. What made my appointment interesting was my gender. "Mary Fisher, 27, in January became the first woman appointed a presidential advanceman. . . ." It was an innocuous little story.

But if I had forgotten how others might see these things, I was soon reminded. A letter, signed "Mona Carter," arrived at the White House less than a week later:

Dear, Dear Sweet Mary:
    The enclosed article . . . made me want to throw up.
    You're the spoiled brat daughter of a rich daddy who "bought" you this plush job as "advanceman for the President," that's who you are, besides being an "obnoxious and overbearing kike. . . ."

It closed with some unprintable suggestions.

I sent a copy to Red Cavaney with a note attached: "Thought you might like to take a look at this—lovely, isn't it?"

He sent it back with a question: "Admirer of yours?"

•   •   •

For each presidential gambit outside the White House, an advance team is formed that's responsible for planning a detailed, minute-by-minute itinerary. Everything's included, from which car the president is in to who shakes his hand when he reaches his destination. If the president once met someone who'll be present, he's given a reminder. If it's a dignitary's birthday, the president will know. Each team has a "lead person" responsible for overseeing the process, chairing staff meetings, and taking charge during the trip itself. Nothing is left to the imagination, or until the last minute.

Details need to be coordinated with the Secret Service. The White House Advance Office is concerned to have the president see and be seen by the public; the Secret Service is concerned to keep the president alive. Advance team members consider good crowd views; Secret Service agents point out that if a crowd has a good view of the president, so does a gunman.

People in the Advance Office, all of whom are political appointees, may occasionally have higher ambitions, or may use their work as a stepping-stone to other positions. Those in the Secret Service tend to stay within the service, no matter the occupant of the Oval Office. Although we often tussled during planning sessions, agents with whom I served in the White House were exceptional people.

Larry Buendorf, one of the funniest agents in the White House, had the sort of quick wit that would turn a straight conversation into spasms of laughter. He was also the man who, on September 5, 1975, never hesitated when Lynette "Squeaky" Fromme attempted to shoot President Ford. Buendorf plunged through the crowd, toward—not away from—the gun and grabbed it out of her hand. He then refused all interviews for fear someone might think his actions were "heroic or something."

Buendorf was typical of those with whom I worked. David Carpenter, who's since returned as special agent in charge (SAIC) of President Clinton's detail as I write this, was just as loyal, just as courageous. And I've never admired any man more than Rutgers graduate Ashley ("Skip") Williams, who guarded the president not merely out of loyalty or sense of duty but out of affection for the man and respect for the office, with a gentleness and commitment that made me love him all the more.

The agents all were men during my years at the White House;

there were no women on the detail. They were, to a man, extraordinary. And when they saw a woman in the Advance Office, they had their doubts.

My first out-of-town trip was to Atlanta, Georgia. The president was scheduled for an overnight visit, coming in on Monday, February 3, 1975, and leaving Tuesday morning, February 4. I arrived in Atlanta the Monday before the president's planned arrival to do on-site staff advance work. Every other planning team—communications, press, transportation, Secret Service—had their advance there, too.

The lead person for our office was a volunteer, John Gilday, a good guy. My assignment was the hotel, the Hyatt Regency, and all events connected with it: getting the rooms ready for everyone, arranging the logistics of the president's moves, making sure everyone would be comfortable.

Things went well the first day. I quickly learned that I was the only "Indian" on the assignment and everyone else was a "chief." But I took orders well and kept things moving by negotiation and consensus.

On Tuesday, things got bumpier. It seemed that every member of the entire advance team in Atlanta was calling his or her respective bosses in Washington, each trying to get his or her own way, setting up warfare between home offices. In my naivete, I had not expected to see White House personnel engaged in power plays over such seemingly petty issues.

For example, a set of elevators ultimately became an irresolvable bone of contention—the Hyatt's glass elevators scale the walls of an atrium surrounded by floors of rooms like a huge, multilayered cake with a hole in the middle.

The Advance Office wanted the president to ride in the glass elevators. Dick Smith, the Secret Service advance agent in charge of the hotel in Atlanta, said, "No way." He'd compromised on everything he was going to compromise on. He wasn't going to expose the president to that many floors and rooms; there was no way they could protect him. That made sense to me, and I agreed. No president in a glass elevator. Strike the glass elevator, move him to the freight elevator.

When I reported to Red Cavaney that the atrium elevator ride had been canceled out of concern for the president's safety, Cavaney was irritated. He'd taken the position that "the president isn't going to ride in a freight elevator again." While we had been negotiating elevators in Atlanta, he had been at war with his Secret Service counterpart in Washington. When I told him I'd yielded, he concluded that I wasn't tough enough to stand up to the Secret Service and others. All along he had told me, "Don't let the agents tell you how to do your job." Now I'd given in on a point that he was still defending.

All the powers that be—and all the powers that wannabe—soon boarded airplanes for Atlanta. By Wednesday evening, Dick Smith ("Smitty" to everyone who knows him)—who had already let me know that he'd had "a bellyful" of my suggestions—was trying to deal with all my superiors, each of whom came to Atlanta believing that I'd let Smitty trample all over me.

From Thursday morning on, it was all downhill. First I got orders to make it work this way; then I got countermanding orders to reverse it all. No matter how I arranged the details, someone was angry and vetoed the plan.

Toward the end of a grueling day, I was following Smitty as he climbed a stairway and headed across a landing. I could tell from his walk that he was seething. But he just kept walking while I badgered him about letting the president use an escalator at some point in the visit. I didn't know he'd reached his breaking point until he stopped. Then he wheeled around, face red and gun drawn.

"Goddamn it!" he roared, pointing the pistol toward my face, "that's it!"

I assumed he wouldn't shoot me, though I might not have blamed him. But I also knew that no matter what Red said, we'd definitely reached an impasse. I was not negotiating from a position of strength. I was unarmed.

By Sunday night, things had degenerated unmercifully. The only woman on staff—me—drew the assignment to type the final room list. This was, of course, before computers. Any error meant a retyping. And the typewriter I was given had a loose *n* key. Robert Hartmann, President Ford's counselor and speechwriter, of course needed his name on the list. But each time I typed "Hartmann," the second *n* would hit the paper a little higher than the first. Red and all the other chiefs would see it, hand it back to me, and tell me to type it over. I was up all night typing a room list.

By the time the president arrived, I felt like the trip had ended. He was as always accompanied by a full entourage. David Hume Kennerly, the official White House photographer—and Pulitzer Prize–winner for heroic work done in Vietnam and Cambodia—had a special guest: Candice Bergen, amateur photographer and admired actress, who was shooting pictures of President Ford for some publication. Dignitaries were everywhere, and the trip was finally under way.

I'd been given directions to have every hotel room ready with keys in the door. By the time I put my earpiece in place, turned on my radio, and double-checked everyone's name and room number on the final list, the motorcade was arriving. Every room was ready and even special: flowers, fruit, all the amenities. It was good to know that the worst was over.

As the presidential party unloaded at the hotel, luggage went to each person's room. Most people followed their luggage up to their rooms, while I greeted the president and walked him to his first scheduled event. I had just left the president when over the radio I heard some confusion.

"Fisher, Fisher. Cannonball. Where are you?" It was Cavaney, identifying himself by his code name. But before I could respond, other voices were barking over the radio. "How do you get back in here?" came one voice, and then another: "I'm locked out!"

By now I was in the middle of the atrium looking up toward the rooms of the presidential party. People were scampering all over up there, some pulling knobs and some pounding on doors. I knew I'd better call Cavaney.

"Cannonball. Fisher."

"Fisher, what'd you do to the doors? The keys don't work!"

Before I had time to figure out what I'd done, my earpiece blared, "This is Hotshot—somebody get me a hotel engineer." "Hotshot," I was told when I innocently inquired, was Kennerly. Hotshot's cameras and film were locked in his room; Hotshot's appointment with Candice Bergen and the president was going to smash; and Hotshot was a deeply distressed and impressively articulate man.

He wasn't alone. Somehow my adjustments of deadbolts in every room had triggered some thingamajig that offset a whosamacallit and, well, there you have it. When their doors closed, they locked, and keys no longer worked. By now a crowd of White House staff and quite a few dignitaries were locked out of their rooms, screaming into the atrium, down the hallways, to anyone who would listen.

I did the only reasonable thing. I pulled out my earpiece, turned off my radio, went to find a hotel engineer, and stayed out of everyone's way until the crisis passed.

It was a long, trying evening. I fell asleep not long before the alarm would have awakened me, if it had. But it didn't. Which is why I was still unconscious Tuesday morning when the president appeared at a breakfast for governors of the southeastern U.S. area, the final event in Atlanta, and why I didn't greet the president when he left his suite, and why I didn't accompany him, as planned, to his breakfast speech.

I arrived, breathless, as the president and his guests were concluding a reception and sitting down for breakfast. My mind was whirling. I was focused not on the organization of details, not on the schedule that had been my Bible, but on one simple prayer: "Please, God, let this trip be over. Let them leave now."

I was at the president's side as he left the room. I accompanied him through the underground passage, out of the Hyatt Regency, to the waiting motorcade. Everyone was scheduled to leave with the president except two of us: Smitty, who hadn't spoken to me since our confrontation with the gun on the landing, and me. One by one, I watched each person find the right car; one by one the doors to each car closed until, at last, they were all behind steel and glass.

There was just a momentary pause before the motorcade revved up. Then the pause grew longer. And longer. Then the front door of the president's car flew open and an agent jumped out. Dick Kaiser, head of the president's detail, shouted to Smitty, "The president doesn't have his newspapers!"

What papers? What are they talking about? With the motorcade on hold, I learned what no one had told me: When the president gets into his car in the morning, he wants to see papers to review coverage of world and domestic events.

I looked over at Smitty, who pointed to me. "My job?" I asked. With a sorry look, he nodded. I patted my pockets; no change. Smitty ran by me, calling, "I'll take care of it," clearly wanting me not to screw up anything else.

I ran into the hotel behind him and saw him disappearing up the down escalator, running full tilt, two steps at a time. I headed for a newsstand just behind the escalator, assuming he'd missed it in his haste. When I tried to beg a paper from the lady—"It's for the president!"—she looked me in the eye and said, "Somebody else was just here and tried that one already." She was out of papers anyway.

By this time Smitty had come back into view, riding the down escalator, furiously trying to assemble the sections of an *Atlanta Constitution* that he'd found in pieces in the men's room, hoping that nothing critical had been lost.

We ran together back to the motorcade, handed the paper through the rear window of the president's limo, and stood silently as the procession pulled out.

When the last car rounded the corner and rolled out of sight, I collapsed. "Oh, Smitty," I cried, "my first—and certainly my last—out-of-town trip!"

The only man who ever pulled a gun on me reached out to give me a hug. "Oh, it all went fine," he lied. I've always loved him for that.

CHAPTER 8

"Sand in My Shoes"

$\mathbf{M}$y work as the first woman advanceman eventually settled into a hectic but satisfying pace. I discovered President Ford's likes and dislikes, including the little things that could make his travels less stressful, like the fact that he could sleep somewhat restfully, despite chronic back pain, if a board were inserted under the mattress in his bed. I did not make a big deal out of it, but he never again slept in a board-free bed on a trip that I advanced.

My scrapbook of these years has page after page filled with memorabilia of cities and events. Some of the sites were relatively small: Pekin, Illinois, the hometown of President Ford's longtime congressional ally Senator Everett Dirksen and "Marigold Capital of the World"; Milwaukee, Wisconsin, where I became such a regular—I always drew Milwaukee when a trip was scheduled there—that I could organize events with bratwurst and brew as if I were a hometowner; picturesque Traverse City, Michigan, where during the "National Cherry Festival" one July I helped raise a crowd of 300,000 people for a presidential visit while Anne Compton, ABC's White House correspondent, amused herself by doing a story on me (slant: woman's work in a man's world). Other venues, in addition to weekends in Washington, D.C., were large: Chicago, Atlanta (again), Houston, St. Louis, Baltimore, New York City, Cleveland, Boston, New Haven, northern and southern California, and Norfolk, Virginia.

Norfolk was memorable for the commissioning of an aircraft carrier, the USS *Nimitz*. Thousands of sailors were standing ready on the *Nimitz* when "the president's representative" came on board— and to a man, they were surprised to discover that she was a blonde. Because aircraft aren't allowed to land on a carrier before it's actually commissioned, and aircraft are "waved in" by the deck crew wearing yellow jerseys, the commissioning becomes the inaugural for wearing yellow shirts to bring in the first wave of jets. Before I left, the officers and the crew made a formal presentation to me with a special gift: When I opened it, it was a yellow turtleneck bearing a customized message. It read "Wonder Woman" on the front and "USS *Nimitz* CVAN 68" on the back. It still occupies a special place in my home.

On the Fourth of July weekend, 1975, I was with the president in Cincinnati. The trip was my first as lead advance and included a dedication of the Environmental Protection Agency's research center in that city. We needed to organize a large and happy crowd for the event, despite the weather: broiling, steaming, stifling heat that enshrouded the city, suspending in midair every particle of manmade pollution. The opening of the nation's premier environmental center was about to be marked by "air quality alerts" being broadcast on radio and television, warning people to stay indoors or risk their own longevity.

By then, I'd been on staff half a year. My mother had begun my tenure, she once confided, concerned and saddened about "all those gorgeous young men with things in their ears." When I explained that they were Secret Service agents who wore earpieces to maintain communication, she was greatly relieved. She'd feared they all had hearing defects. She was similarly confused about other aspects of my work. To comfort her with the knowledge that I could always be reached, I'd mistakenly given Mom the White House number needed to contact me when I was traveling. It involved calling through the military switchboard at the White House and using "SIGNAL," the communication system typically reserved for matters of substance.

The night before the president arrived in Cincinnati, I was chairing my first ever countdown meeting, the on-site conference reviewing every detail and contingency. I'd encountered the usual skepticism about "a woman doing a man's job," and I was proving that I could do the job as well as any man. We were grinding through a minute-by-minute itinerary of the trip, resolving problems, when the phone rang. "Mary, it's for you," said an agent. I asked if it could wait.

"It's your mother."

"I'll call her back."

"She says it's critical, some kind of emergency." By now the meeting had stopped. Everyone was watching me reach for the phone.

"Hi, honey," said my mother, not a hint of distress in her voice.

"I'm in a countdown meeting," I said, turning away from the table and lowering my voice as I added with urgency, "Mom! I can't talk now."

"Well, okay, honey, but your dog Angel has been missing you and needs to talk to you for a minute."

Before I could protest, I—and whoever was monitoring SIGNAL at that hour—heard the distinctive sound of a dog licking a telephone receiver. I must have turned eleven shades of purple.

The following day, the president gave a mercifully brief outdoor address to a sweltering crowd. They were seated on folding chairs in the research center parking lot—we'd arranged the seating out of fear that fainting would otherwise fell the crowd. As a way of thanking them for coming out, the president came offstage at the end of his remarks and headed into the crowd, shaking hands. There was a predictable surge toward him, but the heat was so intense that when people stood to greet the president, their chairs stuck in the hot asphalt and couldn't be nudged aside. The crowd began tripping over what they assumed were portable arrangements, now made permanent by the combination of temperature and soft asphalt. Eventually, the president was among the few left standing.

International travel presented unusual challenges to the advance team, from temperamental translators to indecipherable menus to serious security glitches. In Rumania, state officials offered us a new itinerary each evening that was supposed to outline our advance activities for the following day. Yet each morning we would wait to be picked up, and no one would arrive. This was no accident. Rumanian officials had no intention of letting us see anything until the president was actually in the country, and they controlled all the variables.

General Larry Adams, from the White House Communications Agency (WHCA), was with us in Rumania. Early in the trip he pointed out that we'd all been assigned rooms on one side of the hotel, probably, he said, because only that portion of the hotel was adequately "wired" to eavesdrop on our conversations. To make his point, he located the crude listening device installed in his room's radio and removed the "bug" so we could talk freely. Within minutes, two "hotel engineers" were at his door to "fix the radio."

"It's working just fine," the general said with a smile, turning up the volume to our delight.

"Ah, but no," they insisted. "There's a loose wire—very, very dangerous."

It took them five minutes to replace the bug, and General Adams thirty seconds to remove their newest installation.

Many of the stories about my years as the White House's first "woman advanceman" are more amusing than important. On one trip to the West, we were at the Sheraton Hotel in Portland, Oregon, when the president needed to make a few taped remarks—and no one could find a tape recorder to send up to his suite. I finally located a recorder and then discovered that no one except me knew how to use it.

It was a hectic evening, and the fastest way to get everything done was simply to do it myself. I ran up to the presidential suite, past the agents, and interrupted an informal conversation the president was having with Bob Barrett, his military aide, and Chief of Staff Dick Cheney.

"We can do this quickly," I said apologetically to the president, while looking for an electric outlet. His day had already been difficult and tiring. "Do this," I said, "and then you can have a break." It was then that I noticed he'd begun the break already, with a hot shower, after which he'd not dressed. I backed out of the room, maintaining discreet eye contact, saying, "Oh, I'm so sorry, Mr. President." It was not a good moment, and it was not yet over.

Twenty minutes later, all of us fully dressed, I needed to escort the president and his party to an event downstairs. We were on the elevator when Bob Barrett delivered a well-aimed jab: "Mary, is it your usual custom to walk in on the president when he doesn't have any clothes on?"

Though I was at least a foot shorter than every man behind me, there was no place on that elevator to hide. I was moved almost to tears when out of the back corner came the voice of President Ford: "Bob, why don't you pick on somebody your own size?" My hero had come to my defense.

Two decades later, giving a keynote address for the Betty Ford Center's tenth anniversary celebration, I'd recovered enough from a similar embarrassment to tell the audience:

> President Ford made me the first woman advanceman in the history of the White House. I retaliated by subjecting My President to occasional indignities so he could learn the ancient truth: "No good deed goes unpunished . . ."
>
> It was early in my White House career. I'd been up three nights straight trying to keep peace between stubborn Secret Service agents, balky hotel managers, and even more stubborn advancemen.
>
> It was now late afternoon and hot. During My President's fourth speech of the day, I may have dozed off for just a second or two. Suddenly the speech was over, the agents were moving him toward me, we were late for the airport, people were shoving papers at me, and My President leaned down and whispered, "I'd like to use the men's room before we leave." So I led him to the rest room, turned around, leaned against a wall, and saw the faces of agents, mouths open, all aghast. Just as the door swung shut I heard a scream from inside—clearly, a woman's voice.
>
> Twenty-seven years of habit had helped me send the president of the United States into an occupied women's bathroom.

Dr. Henry Kissinger, who remained secretary of state under President Ford, was famous for having his way while traveling. I discovered the truth of his reputation when he arrived in Bucharest with the president. Everyone, including the president, was in a motorcade ready to visit the Tomb of the Unknown, but the man whose code name was "Woodcutter" (Kissinger) was missing. Advance people inside the palace were trying to persuade the secretary to keep the schedule, but "Woodcutter" was happy to keep everyone— even the president—waiting.

"Fisher," came the order over my radio from Red Cavaney, "get him." I did. His tie was undone and his irritation was showing.

Even so, I retrieved him from his room unceremoniously and pointed him at the motorcade in the circular drive out front just as the president's car was pulling out.

"Stop that car," he bellowed.

"I can't, Mr. Secretary," I replied. "That's the president's car."

"Stop that car," he insisted even more loudly. "I must be with the president."

I stopped, turned, and explained reality to him in simple terms: "If you want to attend this event, get in a car. Otherwise, stay here." I walked away, and he took another car. And when we arrived at the tomb, I hid behind Red Cavaney.

Everywhere I stood near the tomb, I could hear the secretary asking, "Who is she? Who's the blonde?" Eventually Brent Scowcroft leaned over and said, "Henry, that's Mary." When I heard Kissinger say back, "I want to meet her," I was even more resolved to keep Red safely positioned between the secretary and myself.

The next evening, while I was getting ready to escort the president to a formal state dinner, two agents found me. One of them said, in a tone slightly mocking of Dr. Kissinger's German accent, "Dr. Kissinger vants to meet vit you, now!"

"I just met him last evening," I told them. "I don't need to meet him again." But throughout the trip, at every stop, the secretary was asking for me. Finally, with a day or two left in Bucharest, I happened to have access to a SIGNAL phone, and I called my father. "Your friend Henry is coming on pretty strong, Dad," I told him.

"Does he know who you are?"

"He doesn't know I'm your daughter, if that's what you mean."

"Good," said Dad. "Don't tell him."

The day I was scheduled to head back to the States, Secretary Kissinger was going on to Belgrade. We were gathered at airport departure ceremonies when he announced that I would accompany him to Belgrade, that it had all been arranged.

"It's a nice city," he said. "You will like going with me."

"I don't think so," I said. "I'm already committed to a trip to Fort Smith, Arkansas."

Several weeks later we were all back in Washington, D.C., when my father paid a call on his friend. "I understand you met my daughter a few weeks ago, Henry," he said as he entered the secretary's office.

"No, no, I'm afraid not," said Kissinger, sorry for the confusion. "I'd remember, I'm sure. Where did you think that was, Max?"

"In Bucharest."

Kissinger looked troubled. "What does she look like?"

"Oh," said Dad, extending his arm at the height of his shoulder, "she's about this high. Late twenties, blond hair. Some people think she's pretty. . . ."

There was a pause. Then a look of amazement worked its way across Kissinger's face.

"Max, Max," said Kissinger, "that wasn't *your* daughter—why, she doesn't look a thing like you!"

I was at the White House during America's Bicentennial Year, 1976. The July Fourth weekend was full of presidential participation in the national celebration, and I was assigned New York's harbor where the Tall Ships were sailing. It was a case study in the management of egos belonging to a variety of dignitaries, real and imagined, from the City of New York, the United States Navy, "Operation Sail 1976" (the Tall Ships sponsors), and the White House itself. But no one had accommodations to rival mine. Everyone on the advance team was based on board the USS *Forrestal* for the last night, where my male colleagues had to bunk with the sailors. Because I was a woman, I was assigned the "admiral's quarters," with its queen-size bed and glorious bath, and two marine guards were stationed outside my door for security. It was, I was told, the first time a civilian woman had spent the night on board. Gender had some benefits, as well as some liabilities, that I'd never imagined.

It was midday on July 4 when the president arrived to ring the bicentennial bell thirteen times at 2:00 P.M. on the USS *Forrestal's* flight deck. After the bell-ringing ceremony, the presidential party transferred by helicopter to another, smaller carrier where the president viewed the passing of the tall ships in the harbor. We had just landed on the second ship when a vicious storm blew in, darkening the sky and battering the ships and all of us with dangerous hail. There was talk of "getting the president out of here," but the storm was too intense, with too much lightning to risk a takeoff. By the time the president was safely in the captain's quarters and everyone

else—the press, visiting dignitaries, and other members of the presidential party—was under cover, I was a waterlogged wreck. When the storm had passed, my coiffed hair and bright green pantsuit had been transformed into a jumble of curls atop a now deep green rag sopping up a steady flow of mascara.

When I was told that a takeoff would be safe, I found the president and announced that he could go. He took one look at me and, glancing around, said, "Does anyone have a comb for Mary?"

"It's all right, Mr. President," I assured him, not wanting him to feel as if he needed to take responsibility for me. "We really can't help this today."

"We could try," he said, to everyone's amusement but my own.

I flew back to Washington that evening with the president aboard *Air Force One*. Crowds were gathering for bicentennial fireworks as we broke into the capital's airspace, which is cleared of other planes as a security precaution during a president's approach to the field at National Airport. We stayed aloft an extra fifteen or twenty minutes, enjoying the special splendor of the occasion.

The first skyrockets were just bursting in the cool summer sky when we stepped off the plane. My hair had dried in an unusual formation, my suit was a disaster, and I was carrying a coin and bicentennial stamp, canceled in Philadelphia, signed by the president. I was bone weary from months of strenuous work. But I was proud of My President and grateful for my place in his life during that incredible, historic evening.

Sometimes being a woman in the White House Advance Office was neither amusing nor triumphant. The hardest part was not the crises, but the daily grind: the incessant need to prove that, contrary to expectations, and sometimes contrary to beliefs, a woman could be just as good at this job as a man.

I rarely objected to the many jokes about my being a woman. But there is a weariness that grows with constant teasing, with relentless joking, when it is based on one's identity. It reminds me of the African-American friend who said, only partially in jest, that he was going to "break the fingers of the next white guy who runs his hand through one of my kids' hair to see how it feels." It's the sort of innocent thing that shouts no intended indignity; it merely whispers, over and over, "You're different from us." It's the knowledge that, no matter what, you will never be "one of us."

Sometime midway through 1976 a man celebrated the bicentennial by walking all the way across America. An interviewer on one of the morning news shows asked what had been the most difficult challenge: Delinquents hurling insults and potentially lethal bottles from passing cars? The tornado that nearly ended his walk? Snakes and scorpions in the desert? No, it was none of those.

"The hardest thing," the walker said, "was that sand kept getting in my shoes." Precisely.

Sometimes my place in the Advance Office was challenged by outright discrimination and its twin, stupidity. I was the lead advance assigned to Providence, Rhode Island, for a late 1975 private dinner for the president. When Agent David Carpenter and I were introduced to the mayor of Providence—his name, I believe, was Vincent Cianci, Jr.—the mayor looked me up and down with disgust, then announced to Carpenter, "We're not starting our meeting until an advanceman gets here."

I said, in the cheerful tone I'd learned to affect in such moments, "Advanceman? That's me!" The mayor replied, in impolite terms, that he was going to wait "for a man."

Cianci then made a blustering telephone call to Washington and issued some silly threats. Before long, Carpenter had had enough. He quietly and firmly explained that I was the advanceman, the real advanceman, and the only advanceman that would ever work the trip to Providence. "Talk to her," said Carpenter to the mayor, "or you scrub the trip. Pick one."

He talked to me.

As time wore on, the incidents that most grated on me came not from outside but from within the Advance Office. Small incidents, but persistent ones—"sand in my shoes," mainly. What drew those incidents together was my discovery that, although being asked to train new advance team members (men), I would not be considered for a merit review or a raise. My salary was $17,500; new men were being hired at a starting wage of nearly twice that amount.

Red Cavaney had been my mentor and my protector. But as I grew less dependent on him, our relationship grew strained. After discussing a promotion or raise with Red on several occasions, I finally made a formal petition. In a déjà vu moment, I heard Red say,

"You don't really need the money." Then, as if it provided his rationale, he added, "You're a girl, and you have no family." And he sat
back to see how I'd respond. I was angry, and expressed it. His response: "You don't like it? So sue me."

He knew I wouldn't do anything that would cast a poor light on
the president. He had me. But why? Did I have some quiet gene inside me that had programmed me for failure? Was I failing at this
for the same reason I'd failed at Channel 7? What made me so
inept, so unable to prove my worth—if, in fact, I had any?

In 1976 the Advance Office staff and assignments were being shuffled
like a deck of cards to accommodate the needs of the presidential campaign. Everything done within the campaign for Candidate Ford
was, of course, strictly segregated from everything done in our official
capacities for President Ford. I enjoyed serving the president, but the
campaign was a new challenge. Some people who drove the campaign,
and the ambitions that some of them harbored, were not as noble as
the president himself. And by August 1976, I was weary of fighting with
Red Cavaney. I worked the Republican National Convention for him
in Kansas City, handling arrangements for the president's cabinet
as well as some VIP accommodations. But I knew my time as an
advanceman was coming to an end.

The night of the convention, as the presidential ballots were
being counted, every cabinet member's need had been (temporar-
ily) satisfied. The president, of course, was not there—he'd not appear until he received the nomination. Standing on the floor, I
looked up toward the president's skybox and happened to notice
that only one person was in the box: Mrs. Ford. No children, no
staff, no reporters.

I took the elevator to the secured skybox level, walked into the
president's box, and sat down next to Mrs. Ford. We chatted for a
long time. I had always admired and been drawn to her. Here, in
this improbable place, it was just the two of us.

When the cameras were on her—and she had the instinct to tell
when the red light was on—she brightened and smiled, her eyes
twinkling. When people passing below waved, she rose energetically
from her seat to return their greetings with laughing, cheerful eyes.
But in between cameras and cheers from her fans, her eyes did not

sparkle. She looked tired, and her eyes looked distantly sad. In the largest and happiest crowd of Republicans in the world, watched by people across the globe, the wife of the president seemed terribly, terribly alone.

Less than a month later (September 6), I penned a handwritten letter of resignation to the president. "I'm resigning effective September 11," it said. "Although I will no longer be a member of the White House staff, I will always be at your service."

The man who will always be My President responded with characteristic grace. I went to say good-bye to him on my last day—Saturday, September 11. I wanted somehow to tell him that I loved him, and wanted to help care for him, but just couldn't anymore. I was worn down, exhausted.

It was a good visit, although I didn't get very much of that said. But he listened kindly, puffing one of his favorite pipes and finally coming over to hug me. "I understand," he said. "I understand."

I left the White House absolutely drained. I lacked the stamina to keep up the pace of a campaign while simultaneously fighting daily with Red and his other advancemen. I was not even sure why I was fighting anymore, or for whom. Me? Women? The president? I wanted to stop.

I'd hoped to go back to New York, but my apartment—for which my father had signed some years earlier—had been given in my absence to Gayle Taubman, daughter of one of Dad's Detroit colleagues, Al Taubman. I couldn't get it back. So I returned to Detroit, a decision made less by choice than by default.

When a *Detroit Free Press* reporter did a local-angle story on me during the August '76 convention, she opened it with the observation that I was "twenty-eight and tired." I wasn't hiding it well.

"Whatever happens in the November elections," I had told her, "I will be looking for something else." I even admitted that "sometime I want to get married and lead a normal life."

But that wasn't why I was leaving. I was leaving because I was unbelievably weary of being "the first woman" anything. The novelty—if there had ever been any—was gone, and with it my energy had disappeared. I felt defeated, by nothing more stunning than sand in my shoes.

CHAPTER 9

"Trying Out Normal"

My return to Detroit was less a happy homecoming than a reluctant retreat. I had no plan for my life, nothing to organize, no one in my life to please except myself, and I didn't matter. I was exhausted, both wanting and dreading isolation. I didn't know how to explain my last few years to people. What was I to say when people asked, "What happened?" That the White House wouldn't give me a raise?

The presidential campaign was in the homestretch when I arrived back in Michigan and moved into the Claymoor Apartments in Southfield. President Ford was narrowing Governor Carter's early lead, and my father was deeply immersed in the effort, devoted both to the Ford campaign and to the man himself. I watched the November election results alone in my apartment. When the president conceded, I wept, and I heard in my father's voice an agony I'd never heard before, or since. "It was," he later recalled, "the most disappointing moment in my life."

I needed work, even if I had little appetite for job hunting. I put out the word through all my working friends that I was available; no one called. Paging idly through the *Detroit Free Press* one morning, I noticed my name: "Previous experience as a member of the presidential advance team just doesn't seem to have greatly brightened up Ms. Fisher's resume: Job-hunting efforts so far have been unsuccessful." Thanks for noticing.

President and Mrs. Ford were preparing to leave the White House when their new chief of staff called. Would I like to work with them in California? I was flattered but needed to say no. I needed a "regular" job. I wanted normalcy.

I had friends from high school who were normal: They were married, had children, played tennis, took piano lessons, and were perfectly content not to be working for a paycheck. I wondered: Maybe if I were married with children and had hobbies, I'd be normal, too. I could hear what sounded like the ticking of my own biological clock. I was turning twenty-nine in a few months, approaching the pivotal thirty. I wanted children. Having a husband first would be a good idea.

I'd dated more or less regularly, but rarely seriously. Aside from the now-we're-in-love, now-we're-not relationship with a visiting actor, no sparks had ignited talk of marriage. Some men were uninterested in commitment; some were, I discovered, already committed to others, or to careers, or to other interests. I fell absolutely in love only once, with a man then separated from his wife; we'd agreed, in one of the hardest moments of my life, that he should go back to salvage the marriage if he could. And he did, with both my support and my love.

So here I was, back in Detroit, pushing thirty, wondering why I couldn't be "normal" like other women. In social circles, I excused my lack of a marriage on the busyness of my work. Privately, I assumed I didn't really know how to please a man enough to make him want me as a life partner. And I could hear my mother wondering about my weight, which was edging back up again. (Once I thought the problem might be my *height:* I was dating a divorced man when we took his children to an amusement park; the attendant let me in for half price because I was "shorter than the laughing clown," the standard for setting prices.)

I couldn't manufacture a husband any more than I could manufacture a job. The only part of normalcy really within my reach was the cultivation of hobbies. I started playing the piano again, taking lessons with John Williams. I dusted off my golf clubs. And I took up racquetball, big time, at the Franklin Racquet Club.

By the spring of 1977, my life was filling up. I "advanced" several trips for President Ford; it was healing to spend time with him again. I helped some Detroit community groups. And I was seeing a lot of my brother Phillip. We'd always been close but rarely had the chance to spend time alone together as adults. Now I was fresh from the White House and he was freshly divorced. We both had that time.

When Phillip was a few weeks old, his head had somehow become caught between the railings on his crib; he was turning blue when I found him and got him out. That was the moment, I remember, at which I began to think of him as "mine." When he was in trouble, I defended him. When he was hurt, I rushed to comfort him. What I discovered now, during our first extended time together as adults, was that he brought a joy to me that no one else provided. Whether he was telling jokes, sharing a secret, or just listening to me ramble on about some notion, there was and still is a magic between us that brings to life the idea of "brother-sister."

Phillip was not an "easy" child. He struggled with school, and several schools struggled with him. He was smart, quick-witted, easily bored. Being a boarding student at Cranbrook hadn't worked particularly well, nor had being a day student, nor had enrollment in a nearby public school. He finally found an academic home at Detroit Country Day, a private school (where twenty years later he became a trustee).

Phillip has always been very loving, and very funny. As children at home we'd sit at formal dinners, dressed up, with guests and candles and people serving us. In this "be seen and not heard" context Phillip would invariably say something funny under his breath. I'd giggle, draw a sharp look from Dad, and duck behind my napkin. Phillip would say something else, and grins would spread across the faces of our sisters, while under the table Mother would be kicking both Phillip and me.

He always knew just how far he could push. He was eighteen when he wanted a motorcycle. Dad said absolutely not. Phillip promptly came home with a used cycle and brazenly parked it in the garage. "Are you crazy?" I asked him. "Dad will have a stroke when he sees that thing!"

"Dad'll never see it," said Phillip. "He's never gone into the garage in his life, and he's not likely to start visiting it now."

He was right. Dad never saw the bike.

Phillip and I both liked Howard Arnkoff. I'd met him through friends, Dick and Linda Rosin, who were convinced that Howard and I would be great for each other. On the Fourth of July weekend, 1977, they arranged a blind date for us.

"When you have been single as long as I've been, it's really strange to meet someone and just know he's right." That's how I was quoted six weeks later. I didn't explain that Howard, an attorney in nearby Troy, was more reclusive than outgoing, or that arranging details of a large wedding gave me something to do.

Wasn't this a bit sudden? I didn't think so. "We both want to have a family," I explained to a reporter. "We both want to marry." Besides: "You could be engaged for two years, you know, but that seems silly. There are no guarantees. . . ." Not only that, but: "We both like to laugh a lot. We both play golf. We both like music—I play the piano and he plays the guitar." This was the stuff out of which I was going to build a lasting foundation for a strong marriage?

On Sunday evening, October 2, we were married at the Franklin Hills Country Club in (by one account) "a sea of orchids." The dress came from Brussels; President and Mrs. Ford came from California; relatives and friends came from all over. It was a spectacular wedding according to the standards of the time and place.

The marriage, by contrast, was unfortunately lackluster. Howard was as casual as I was formal, as relaxed as I was intense. The more I pushed, the more he retreated, and the more he retreated, the more I felt sorry for both of us. Golf clubs and guitars and pianos offered momentary diversions, but they were no substitute for loving respect and commitment to each other's values. We wanted to have our ways, both of us. We were better at avoidance than compromise, at silence than communication.

Six months into the marriage, I concluded that whatever else this was, it wasn't normal. I told my friend and attorney Henry Baskin, "I've got to get out." He wanted to know if I'd discussed it with my family. I hadn't.

The next morning I explained to Dad that the marriage was hopeless and I was going to file for divorce. "Let me think about it for a few days," he said, as if I'd proposed trading cars. Mother was still in bed. "Mom," I told her simply, "I'm getting a divorce." She pulled the covers up over her head and said, "Oh, God, I can't deal with this—it's like your first father all over again." I left her beneath the blankets, went to the nearest phone, called Henry Baskin, and said, "Do it." The divorce was filed, and we separated.

Even after a misbegotten and brief marriage, divorce produces a

DETROIT FREE PRESS • Wednesday, April 6, '77 — 5-A

Gerald Ford is flanked by Secret Service agents and aide Mary Fisher as he leaves political science class at Ann Arbor Tuesday morning.

To Mary Fisher
With love and
warmest wishes
to a very
dear friend
Betty Ford

Henry Ford 2nd and Mary Fisher

peculiar and enduring pain, an emotionally lethal mixture of real failure and imagined hopelessness. Public embarrassment stings, but the long thoughts when you're alone—about your inability to love and be loved—are much worse. I saw it all in Howard's eyes the day we settled the divorce. It was August. He'd chosen to defend himself, and Henry Baskin was methodically, clinically, disemboweling his claims. I'd come to court feeling defensive. As Henry took apart Howard's case, I'd begun to feel smug. But just before the decree was issued, Howard looked directly at me. I saw grief deeper than any emotion I'd seen in him during our months of marriage. Decades later I still remember that look, and I remember feeling sorry for Howard and for Howard-and-Mary.

Normal people had houses and jobs. The ink was still drying on my divorce when I bought a small, picturesque, century-old home in a quiet neighborhood of Birmingham. This would be my "Michigan home," my base until I found the job I needed—probably in New York City. I made job-hunting forays into New York and occasionally thought I was on the verge of finding the right position. But if normalcy was a home and career, I couldn't get the second half in place.

Dad had been chairing Detroit Renaissance, a public-private partnership to rebuild the city following the 1967 riots, and had sold Detroit as the site for the 1980 Republican National Convention. He wanted the convention to showcase the city's new image, an urban center rebounding from poverty and violence. I suspect he also hoped that Michigan would be a favorable setting for President Ford's possible bid for the presidency.

I signed on as head of the convention's transportation committee—lining up volunteers and professionals to manage the schedules and travel of four thousand delegates, alternates, and assorted VIPs. Press tours and National Republican Committee visits began in November 1979 for a convention slated to open the following July.

Dad was ready for a return to the glory years when the Republicans ruled the White House. His banishment from the presidential circle during the Carter administration was powerfully symbolized when, at the White House signing of the famed Camp David accords in 1979, a huge tent was erected on the lawn of the White House. Room was reserved for every dignitary even rumored to have a desire to attend. Dad was assigned a place at the outer edge of the tent.

At the same time, the Republican party remained a bit unsettled. Many of those close to President Ford during the 1976 campaign believed that Ronald Reagan's primary challenges and, after the convention, his restrained endorsement of Ford had cost Republicans the election. And the so-called religious right was beginning to emerge within state organizations. I never heard Dad blame (then) Governor Reagan, but his friendship was clearly with President Ford and his distaste for—and mistrust of—hard-line, right-wing politics was never masked.

The 1980 National Republican Convention belonged to Ronald Reagan even before he landed in Detroit. The only real drama centered on Reagan's choice of a vice presidential running mate. Most party leaders believed a Reagan-Ford ticket was unbeatable. Governor Reagan had greeted all such suggestions with a smile and a nod and a promise to let everyone know when the time came. President Ford had stayed noncommittal. But the suspicion between the Reagan and Ford camps remained evident.

The evening of July 14 belonged to President Ford. It was his sixty-seventh birthday. I grew teary when the convention audience rose to sing "Happy Birthday" to him. In his keynote address that night he recalled for the delegates that "elder statesmen are supposed to sit quietly and smile wisely from the sidelines," adding, "I've never been much for sitting." Then he said what many had been waiting to hear: "When this convention fields a team for Governor Reagan, count me in."

We all sat around the garden room at the Franklin house later that evening—President and Mrs. Ford, Ambassador and Mrs. Leonard Firestone, Mom and Dad and me—eating coconut cake and telling stories. It was a strangely intimate time after the noisy whirlwind of the convention. The next morning, Dad and the president spent several hours in the upstairs library discussing the pros and cons of a Reagan-Ford ticket but in the end, the discussions were moot: George Bush was Ronald Reagan's choice for running mate.

The 1980 convention was my last hurrah in Detroit. A month later—August 26—I was off to New York, with a farewell party in downtown Detroit. I never moved back to Detroit. A reporter who described the party devoted nearly half her column to my weight loss. I came to the party at a trim 105 pounds.

John Williams, my piano teacher, played the piano with me for hours that night. John died of AIDS some years ago, but I still hear him playing with me that night, still see him smiling.

Papaharry and Flohoney were in New York City a week after I arrived. All of us, including Mother and Aunt Joyce Burkoff, were ensconced in the Regency Hotel for the long Labor Day weekend.

Papaharry's heart had grown weaker over the years, giving him material for an endless set of off-color jokes about sexual feats that he'd happily perform were it not for the fact that he'd die in the act, even before getting to the really good parts. Flohoney had aged but had not given up her role as censor and disciplinarian, doing what she could to "make Harry behave."

I'd gotten tickets to see Larry L. King's rollicking *Best Little Whorehouse in Texas* on Broadway. Papaharry dressed to the nines for the night, and he was my date. He was as bawdy and boisterous as ever. The show, with its vaudeville-like themes, prompted a deluge of Papaharry anecdotes that kept me on the edge of hysterical laughter through most of the night.

Before the weekend ended, Papaharry began to complain of chest pains. Mother decided to fly back to Louisville with him and Flohoney. He died shortly after returning home. He'd suffered a massive coronary.

Papaharry's funeral was anticlimactic for the family, because weeks earlier we'd all been together in Louisville for the only Switow family reunion ever held. It was a weekend of catching up with Michael Saag, Barby Dale and her brother John Burkoff, and other cousins, telling stories we'd almost forgotten, all culminating in a Switow dinner show at which original poems were read with hands clamped over the ears of younger children, songs were sung, skits were performed, and the sounds of Papaharry's old piano could be heard again.

We all knew Papaharry wasn't well. At evening's end, a funny and tender tribute was read to him. He'd been seated, uncharacteristically, in the back of the room throughout dinner. When the tribute ended, he was invited to come forward. He rose from his seat as his family stood up, turned toward him, and began to applaud, then whistle, then cheer. As the crowd parted, Papaharry came forward—not shuffling like a weakened old man, but grinning like a young dancer, one hand raised above his head, pumping the air, leaving an enduring image as he made his last run through an adoring crowd.

The week before Papaharry died, I'd taken a job in partner relations for Securities Groups, an investment and banking firm in New York City. My work assignments were tolerable. Most had nothing to do with the financial side of the business, for which I was thankful when the firm later sank in a hailstorm of indictments. I was good at event planning and one-to-one contacts. But I felt that if I was strong enough to tackle these tasks for this business, I could take on the White House again. At one point, after the November elections, I sent Dad a letter asking if he would try to open a door for me to work for President Reagan. He wouldn't. I stayed in New York.

My routine came to a crashing halt in May 1981. Dad was in town for business, staying at the Regency Hotel at Park and Sixty-first Street. We'd had dinner, and since my apartment was only a few blocks away on Fifty-ninth, I told Dad I'd walk home. "Take a cab," he said, worried. I argued that it was a perfect summer night; he guessed I didn't have any money and gave me five dollars.

The Yellow Cab I took from the Regency swung hard and fast around the curve by the Plaza Hotel before plowing into a car that had been stopped by the police. I flew out of the backseat, headfirst, into the metal partition behind the driver, ricocheting hard into the passenger door before coming to a painful rest in a crumpled heap on the taxi's floorboard. The cabdriver pulled himself up in the front seat, turned around to look at me, and wheezed, "Oh, Jesus . . ."

I remember thinking that I couldn't pass out because I had no identification with me. I could feel blood streaming from my face, and I couldn't talk very well because my teeth were all rearranged and my lip had been ripped open nearly to my chin.

The police wanted to call someone for me. I gave them Dad's name and number, and slurred out a warning to be careful not to alarm him. "He's just taken a sleeping pill and he has a heart condition," I remember mumbling.

Dad spent the rest of the night with me at the hospital where I was splinted and stitched back together. When we left, he wanted me to stay with him, so we stopped at my apartment to get some clean bedclothes. My face was by now swollen almost beyond recognition, and Dad was doing everything he could to be nurturing. I needed to keep ice on my face, so Dad sat by the phone ordering ice. Then the phone system broke down, and his nursing skills were at an end. "Dad," I told him, "you need to get some sleep." Without argument he got up and changed clothes.

I went into his room to tuck him into bed, loving him for what he wanted to do even if he could not do it. He had stayed at the hospital, not knowing what else to do; he'd ordered ice, not certain what to do with it when it arrived. He'd been a devoted father all night long. And I loved him.

Only two things worth noting came out of the accident: a small scar on my chin, and memories of a relationship with a plastic surgeon with whom I went from patient to almost fiancée. This time, however, I was in no hurry. I needed to know whom I was marrying. And there had always been a side to my surgeon-turned-lover that was occasionally verbally abusive. One weekend the abuse was not merely verbal, at which point I knew I needed to get out.

I left my job with Securities Groups to chase a dream. I'd never entirely given up hope of doing creative work. Over the years I had moved from weaving to sewing and was designing and producing quilts, place mats, napkins, and handmade fabrics. At first it was a hobby, then a source of gifts for friends. But when people started to ask if they could buy my creations, it occurred to me that there might be a market for craft products from "Mary Fisher Associates." I created a cottage-industry business.

Within months I contracted with Marta Lewis, a gifted seamstress in Detroit, to take charge of production. I fabricated samples and did marketing in New York while Marta hired women to work in their home and her workshop in Troy, Michigan. With the automobile companies laying off workers by the thousands at that time, Marta had no problem finding American women eager to do the work. And my old weaving employer, Bob Kidd, promised to develop a line of yarns and yarn kits; when his promise didn't produce any goods, I stopped marketing the yarn portion of the business and concentrated my efforts on the handmade gift items. By 1983 we had high hopes, with me working in New York to develop a marketing plan for selling the goods Marta was producing in Detroit. We scheduled special openings in both cities to introduce our new product lines in July. When I arrived in Detroit to begin work with the media and buyers, I was met by a process server who delivered a lawsuit from Bob Kidd, claiming we'd stolen his designs.

Because I had thought of this business as blending all the elements of my life—hard work with creative talent, old friends with new opportunities—the lawsuit from Bob Kidd, of all people, devastated me. I was physically nauseated—as if I'd been punched in the stomach. The suit was eventually settled. But it took money from profits to pay for the litigation; worse, it took the exuberance I'd felt for my new business and for myself. What had begun as an adventure and a cause became instead a duty performed under the watchful and skeptical eyes of lawyers and accountants.

We went forward with our planned opening in New York, "Christmas in July," to introduce our products. It was a smashing success, in part because of the creative advertising and display work done by a New York artist and designer, Brian Campbell. I admired his work, and we became friends.

But if normalcy involved marriage and a career, children and a station wagon, I appeared to be going in the wrong direction. I was weary of fighting lawyers for a living. The week the lawsuit with Bob Kidd was settled, I closed my business. My friend Dominique Fourcade, whose family lived in Corsica, said she was planning to spend some time traveling in Europe and visiting her family. Would I like to go? Sure, why not. If I couldn't find normal in work, maybe I could find it in vacation.

I was not happy with myself, or my life. I was good at pouring untold energy into work that seemed destined to fail, and I did not understand this. The obvious explanation—that the problem was me—did little to raise my confidence or hope. I was not leaving for Paris to refuel for the next adventure; and I did not tell people I was going to Paris to find myself, or find meaning, or find anything else. I was just leaving, and calling it a vacation.

I'd never have been aware of Phillip's sense of an absent father had I not seen, at about this time, a copy of a letter he'd penned to

George Frehling, dated July 19, 1969, when Phillip was nineteen. Here was, despite Max Fisher's best efforts, a young man still looking for a father:

> I tried to call you about three months ago but I found that you had moved. . . . I thought that you must have some feelings as far as I'm concerned. Mother is fine and she is a great person. Just because things didn't work out between you two . . . doesn't mean that the hereditary values that you gave me are cut off. . . . I *do* have great feelings for you. I feel that people I like or love can't be cut off from my life. This is one reason that I'm writing you. I want to know what you're doing and what my feelings about our relationship should be. . . .
>
> Most important of all, I want you to know that I'm not apathetic and I care a lot about you and your future. . . . Write me if you would like to. I'm always interested in what you have to say. . . .
>
> I remain, Lovingly Yours, Phil

In 1976, while working in the White House Advance Office, I'd made a quick trip to Florida with the president and called George to invite him for lunch at the downtown Miami hotel where I was staying.

When George came to the hotel, he had with him his daughter Lisa. It was a pleasant visit, strained by our long absence but not unhappy. He said, when they arrived, that they couldn't stay for lunch. I was left with a lingering uncertainty over whether he had come because I was his daughter or because he thought he might meet the president or some other dignitary.

Later, while I was living in New York, both Phillip and I were in Florida visiting with Mother and Dad. We decided to invite George and his third wife, Susan, for dinner with us at the Brazilian Court, a classic old hotel and restaurant that still evokes the kind of glamour where you expect to see Bogart or Clark Gable sitting at the bar.

Mother had invited a group of women to lunch the same day Phillip and I were planning dinner with George and Susan, and just as guests began arriving she sent down word that she'd "taken ill." Would I please take over as hostess? When we left Mother and Dad's house to head for the restaurant that evening, she was still in bed, and I was still irritated with her.

Dinner with George and Susan was wonderful. We were all adults, at last, and we could talk together. I remember Phillip saying, "George, we've never known what to call you—Dad, George, whatever," even though I don't remember George's response.

I had just turned from saying something to George when someone said, "I think your mother's here." My heart stopped.

The woman who'd been too sick to hostess her own luncheon had somehow done her hair and was dressed to the hilt. She didn't walk in; she flowed, wearing a red caftan and a siren smile. With her eyes on George and a cigarette in one hand, she ordered a round of champagne before she got to our table.

The rest of us, dressed in casual summer wear, suddenly looked frumpy. As kind as Mother was to Susan—and she *was* especially welcoming and sweet—it was not Susan Mother was there to see. It was George—and it was for George that she had dressed. She was, despite her years, stunning.

Mother turned what had been a comforting reunion into a party, and I resented it. We were having a conversation that had been needed for thirty years, and she roared in as more than a distraction. She was unbeatable competition, both comedienne and seductress, utterly engaging. She looked across the table at George with undisguised pleasure, and he did not know where to look, where to turn, toward his wife of a few months or toward the wife he had long since left.

I did not want my mother to be Auntie Mame that night. I did not want my mother's competition or her social brilliance. What both Phillip and I wanted was a normal, quiet conversation with a man we did not know, who happened to be our biological father.

But what we wanted, or did not want, did not matter. Mother floated in and stole the show.

CHAPTER 10

"The Many Faces of Mary"

I knew Dominique Fourcade because we shared a diet doctor famous for homeopathic treatments. We alternately swore by his counsel and swore *at* his odder prescriptions. Dominique and I bonded by counting calories and measuring fat grams, all the while discussing our real passions, especially art and tap dancing.

Dominique's family lived on the fabulous French Mediterranean island of Corsica, but she had lived "everywhere." Her skill as a jewelry designer gave her instant professional credibility, plus a decidedly upscale social network, in whatever city happened to be home at the moment. She'd moved into my New York apartment with me and was one of the few guests I'd never really wanted to see leave.

We'd agreed to travel, more or less together, with a good deal of talk about spending time in France. After several days visiting Dominique's family on Corsica, I headed for Paris alone. It was wonderful to be back, to visit favorite cafés and shops. And the "City of Love" kept its famed promise: Within days of my arrival, unescorted by Dominique, I'd met a gentleman who was, above all else, French—from his hyphenated first name (Jean-Michel) to his perfectly manicured poodle. I decided that I should find an apartment, stay awhile, and learn to be like Jean-Michel: very, very French. By August I was immersed in learning the language and inhaling the culture. Berlitz classes in French occupied every morning, and an occasional piano lesson competed for time with tap lessons and practice sessions.

My sublet apartment in Paris was trimmed out in rich purple vel-

vets and located at the center of action, on Rue de Berri near the
Arc de Triomphe. Mornings I would take French lessons and shop
(for groceries, mainly). I'd have lunch with friends—a wonderful
social moment: sitting, watching people, talking, sipping wine, and
celebrating life. Afternoons were filled with errands and lessons,
followed by evenings of socializing with wine and dinner and Jean-
Michel.

Summer faded into early autumn. I was working hard to master
the language—but learning French wasn't a job, and what was I
going to do once I'd mastered it? My relationship with Jean-Michel
was perfectly pleasant—and probably fading along with the heat of
the September sun. Decades after telling people I wanted to live in
Paris and learn French, I was living in Paris and learning French.
But I longed for something no geography could provide: a sense of
my own value, of purpose, of accomplishment.

Then my body began to betray me. My weight was fine, but
something else wasn't. At first I thought I was having irregular
menstrual cycles. But it was more than that: I was constantly hemorrhaging, slowly at first, then more profusely. Several types of prescriptions did nothing to slow the bleeding. The doctors said, "Try
rest," so I rested. And bled. My knowledge of French was adequate
enough to let me know that several of the physicians were talking
about surgery.

In the middle of reviewing the options I had—I could stay in
Paris or go back to New York, have surgery immediately or try
other treatments—Mother called. She was coming to Paris.

This was not good news. Whatever else I might have been longing for, I was not feeling any need for a parent, especially a parent
inclined to tell me what to do. This was, without question, not good
news.

The previous summer I'd attempted to confront my mother about
her drinking. I'd tried to organize a family intervention with guid-
ance from Betty Ford. But others in the family had opted out, and
I'd given up. Now, a year later, in Paris, I wondered if I'd forfeited
my moral right to confront Mother about her drinking. I was drinking quite a bit myself, and more regularly than ever before.

Every lunchtime conversation was lubricated with wine.
Midafternoons I began counting the hours until the first drink before dinner, because the drink was the social bell ringing in the

evening's entertainment and at the same time the relaxant that guaranteed I'd enjoy myself. I wasn't looking to get high, but to get courage—courage enough to, say, try a complete conversation in French.

My wishes notwithstanding, Mother arrived. She was concerned about my health, of course, but even so we didn't turn our backs on Paris. We spent a few days shopping and drinking and eating, in approximately that order. But my condition was getting worse, not better. Something would need to be done, and I didn't want to have surgery in a setting where my language skills were marginal and my support system was one or two people deep. I decided to head back to New York City.

Dominique accompanied me home. Two weeks later, surgery had repaired the hemorrhaging that had been even more threatening than I knew. My greater fear—that I'd never be able to give birth—was relieved. "Good as new," said a satisfied surgeon. "All you need is some rest." Little did he know.

If you have to recover from surgery in November, Palm Beach, Florida, is as good a place as any for recuperation and restoration. But living with Mother soon confirmed my fears about her excessive drinking. We'd go to a restaurant together, and we'd both order a drink. Pretty soon, she'd be having a second drink, and I'd be ordering food. Before my lunch and her second drink were finished, she'd be crying, and I'd be fumbling for keys to get out of the restaurant and back to the privacy of the house.

By the time the whole family began assembling for Thanksgiving, no one (except Mother and maybe Dad) could deny her problem. My brother-in-law Peter Cummings, Julie's husband, joined me in pushing her, hard. I was taking pointers on the phone from Betty Ford, but since my failure to rally family unity the previous year, I was doubly wary of trying to organize another intervention.

With twenty guests scheduled at the house for Thanksgiving dinner, Mother finally broke down. She said the magic words: "I need help." I called to ask about space at the Betty Ford Center. "No problem," Betty told me. "We've got a bed for her; bring her out—but get here before the holiday starts or there'll be a wait."

For reasons still unclear to me—perhaps he didn't know how to ex-

plain his missing wife to twenty Thanksgiving guests—Dad
didn't want her to go. When she heard him resist the idea, she balked
and started to stall. She said that she'd go later, or she'd take care of
this on her own, or she'd join AA in Palm Beach. She wasn't talking
about commitments; she was looking for an excuse to stay home.

I was incensed. I spoke to my father as sharply as I've ever spoken to him about anything. I offered to take her myself and stay
with her. Others may also have spoken to him, I don't remember. I
only know that after a few hours he relented. "Take my plane" was
all I needed to hear. And when Mother heard him say he believed
she should go, she began packing for the trip.

It was a long flight. We had exhausted every topic of conversation
and were sitting quietly, each with our own thoughts. Mother's
thoughts quite naturally turned toward a drink. She announced
that she needed a Bloody Mary. I was feeling like a drink myself. It
had been a grueling day, and we had a long way to go. It wouldn't
hurt to relax a little. Together, we raided the airplane's bar and pol-
ished off several Bloody Marys before landing.

As our plane taxied up to the Combs Aviation hangar at the Palm
Springs airport, I saw that Betty Ford was waiting. She welcomed
us with her usual charm and good humor, telling Mother what a
fine decision she had made.

A counselor with a professional manner met us inside the center.
"She needs to be registered." I hadn't really thought about the
process in these terms. I was ready for my mother to be healed, but I'd
not prepared myself for her confinement in a treatment center. I
stood by Mom as the questions were asked: "Do you have any alcohol
with you? Do you have any weapons? Do you have any prescription
drugs? . . ." For once Mother did not have a single funny response.

Betty had invited me to stay at her home. She was planning to
pick me up as soon as the registration process was complete. But
when the car came, I realized that I was having a hard time leaving
Mother. Papaharry's daughter, a woman who could find the nugget
of humor buried in any catastrophe, was tight-lipped. Mother's eyes
showed fear. She looked tiny, frail. For once I saw no glamour, no
charm, just raw vulnerability. She did not float; she shivered.

I reached out to give her a good-night hug. For an instant I held
her as I had in Louisville, decades earlier, after she and my father
separated. I did not think I could leave her alone and nearly said

out loud what I was thinking to myself: "Dear Lord, what have I done?" Instead I said, "Betty's waiting. I have to go."

I stayed at President and Mrs. Ford's home during Mother's first few days at the center, sharing a room with Pat Benedict, the woman (and nurse) who had helped the Fords with their family intervention for Betty. Evenings at their home were wonderful: The president and the Fords' children and I spent hours playing board games together, talking, laughing. It was so easy to "be family" here.

Betty gave me a book to read. Its point was clear: Take each new day as a new beginning. And both Pat and Betty talked to me about my own drinking, gently urging me to look at myself as well as at my mother. I was grateful for their concern and happy to reassure them that I didn't have a problem. I just needed to get some things organized in my life, beginning with Betty's suggestion to arrange the "family week." I needed to contact people, get plane schedules coordinated—I needed to organize, to manage, to make sure everyone in the family was going to be okay.

Pat never backed down from her advice that I review my own life options to see whether drinking might be playing a negative part in my own decision making. When I hid behind Mother's drinking, as a defense—"My drinking has never done to anyone what hers did to all of us, for years!"—Betty smiled, reached out, took my hand, and said, "You know, sweetheart, you don't need to ride the elevator all the way to the basement."

I flew back to New York to take care of bills and get some clean clothes, but Pat's and Betty's comments had softened, even punctured, my defenses. I was feeling confused, as if the floor were spinning out from under my life.

A few weeks later (December 10) I was back in Palm Springs. Phillip and his then wife, Amy, had already arrived. They were staying for only the first three days of family week, Monday through Wednesday. Everyone else was planning to do the whole week, living in a nearby hotel and spending daytime hours at the center.

The Fisher clan—only Jane was missing—was divided into two groups. Counselor Julie Pettit was assigned to a group consisting of the in-laws (Phillip's wife, Amy; Julie's husband, Peter; and Margie's husband, David) plus Dad and me.

Family week opened with a discussion, led by Julie Pettit, of what it means to live with an alcoholic parent. We read from the book *Adult Children of Alcoholics* to see the most common characteristics of people like me. And when the first characteristic was read, I nearly crumpled: "Adult children of alcoholics guess at what normal behavior is."

Say what? Adult children of alcoholics don't know "normal."

After all those years of trying to figure out what normal was; of trying to create it, feel it, find it; of hiding the truth that I didn't know how to be what everyone else seemed to be—after all those years, here was an explanation. Nothing especially emotional was being discussed. Everyone else was chatting, listening, and I was having a full-blown experience. I felt tears coming, but I did not want to cry. Too late. I began crying softly and thought about leaving the room. Too late. And then the dam broke. I was sobbing. When my mind registered the truth that I had never really known what was normal, and that I'd driven myself to the edge of depression trying to figure it out, my body responded with convulsions of remorse and regret.

Through most of family week, I wept with grief. I stammered out stories about caring for the other kids while Mother drank, and I wept with astonishment. I talked about my absent father, George, and my busy father, Max, and I wept with wonderment. I wept about gaining weight, and losing weight, and hating weight. I wept over hard work that was not valued, and hard relationships that were not secure. Every day of family week, I wept.

Wednesday, the day Phillip and Amy were leaving, we had a special family group session with everyone except Mother. Most of what we (the children) did was "gang up on Father," taking turns blaming Dad for whatever was wrong in our lives. The safety of the setting and the sense of crisis evoked by Mother's treatment encouraged us to tell Dad everything we'd never said before. In retrospect, I wish I'd been more balanced in those moments, that I'd been less one-sided, less ready to blame him—but 20/20 hindsight comes too late to retrieve what's already been said.

Julie Pettit proved to be strong, nurturing, a veteran at dealing with alcoholics and their families. She believed I had more issues to be resolved, especially about George, and she accepted my explanation that I was reluctant to discuss it in front of Dad (Max) out of fear of hurting him unintentionally.

Julie suggested that I work on my feelings about George outside the group, in my own room. She wanted me to learn to recognize, acknowledge, and deal with anger, something I'd never done—after all, how can you please others if you're an angry person?

Alone in my room I went into full-blown rages, ripping apart entire folded copies of the *New York Times* and the *Los Angeles Times*. When they gave me soft clubs with which to pound the chairs, everyone witnessed my anger as I flailed away. I had no idea that I had shoved so much anger so deeply into my soul, and I was in shock when I saw it come pouring out. I'd never dared to be angry before; now it almost felt as if I were nothing but festering, swelling anger.

Julie observed my interactions with my family—my organizing, managing, pleasing. When family members wanted something, I jumped to get it. When they needed details of schedule or transportation, I handed them an itinerary I'd already prepared. In group sessions Julie would ask my father how he felt; when he didn't know, I'd volunteer what it was that he was feeling. "No, Mary," Julie would say, "it's important that he be able to do this himself."

Before I left, Julie wanted me to take the test for indicators of alcoholism. Reading the results, Julie said, "You're probably chemically dependent, if not today, then soon. It's a disease. It's probably genetic. We don't know about your first father, but probably. . . . We know about your mother. Why don't you go home and think about it?

"You've organized your last trip," Julie told me. She was referring to my organization of my family's week, to my calling and arranging and managing everything for everyone. But I was stung: I thought she was criticizing me. I took such satisfaction in pleasing others with my organizing skills, I couldn't understand why she would want to take this service, this gift, away from me.

I agreed to think about her advice and to attend some AA meetings. A new alcoholism center, Hanley Hazelden, was opening in Florida, and I agreed to investigate its services. But I wasn't wildly committed. Mainly, I was confused.

Everyone came to Florida for Christmas 1984 to celebrate the holidays and Mother's homecoming. She was home and she was sober; we partied—in a new way, but no less fun or festive.

Mom and I went to AA meetings together, joking about creating

the newest "mother-daughter 'in thing.'" I was impressed with
Mom's certainty that she would never drink again (she was right).
She was pleased with herself, and everyone was proud of her. I
wouldn't admit it, but I felt some jealousy that she had graduated
and I was stuck, still trying to figure out the lessons.

Mom had changed. She didn't need me anymore—not like she'd
needed me when she was drinking and wanted someone's shoulder
to cry on, or took ill and needed a substitute hostess for her lun-
cheons. Dad didn't need me to organize things for him anymore; he
had his wife back. Suddenly I was no longer needed by either parent, and I didn't know how I would ever please them again. Phillip
and my sisters were all fine, appreciative of all that they'd taken
from the Betty Ford Center; they didn't need me. After the intensity
of our week together in California, during my holiday time in
Florida with my family I felt unconnected, unwanted, alone.

On New Year's Eve, the AA group I'd been attending held a session including family members and friends. I listened first as alcoholics told their stories, and then as family members related theirs.
It occurred to me that I belonged in both crowds. But I thought I'd
prefer the label of "alcoholic" because then, like Mom, I could recover. And if I could recover, like Mom, I could be happy.

On the way home, on the last night of 1984, sitting in my car at a
railway crossing waiting for the flashing gate to go back up, I decided to call Julie Pettit and tell her I wanted to return to the Betty
Ford Center.

When I made the call, I thought it would be a dramatic moment.
It wasn't. Julie thought it would take a few weeks before I could get
in, but she looked forward to my return. "Good for you" was all
Betty said when I called her. She seemed unimpressed. She had a
kind of "of course" tone in her voice, as if she'd never wondered.

Mother had been assigned a sweet woman named Jane Gaunt as her
therapist. I did not know who I would get until I checked in. Would
they consider Jane Gaunt for me? No. Could I, maybe, have Julie
Pettit? No, she was busy with the families.

During the first few weeks of January, on several occasions I had
considered not coming. Every time my commitment wavered, Betty
fortified it again. I arrived expecting a stay of a few weeks—after

Queen Elizabeth 2   Photographed on board 1983

RIBBON CUTTING — Cutting a ribbon dedicating Fisher Hall, Betty Ford Center at Eisenhower's fourth 20-bed patient unit, are, from left, BFC President Mrs. Gerald R. (Betty) Ford, and Mary, Marjorie and Max Fisher. The Fisher family, long-time friends of former President and Mrs. Ford, made a substantial contribution to the new building's construction costs. Fisher Hall, named in their honor, completes the Betty Ford Center's master plan.

all, I'd just finished more than two weeks in the family program, and my elevator hadn't hit the basement level. They said, "Well, maybe six weeks wouldn't be a bad idea." I didn't like it. They called Betty. Betty said, "It wouldn't hurt, Mary. It's a good opportunity to address all your issues, as long as you're here anyway." I gave in again.

They gave me as a therapist an old sailor named Fred Sipe, a career navy enlisted man, a cross between Popeye and Papaharry: solid, balding, tough. He looked like he'd been to war, and he had. In Fred Sipe, I figured I had a man who knew every bar in Korea and Vietnam and most of the ports in between, and a man who would never—never!—understand me: a younger woman wrestling with problems with fathers and bosses and men in general. Since they wouldn't switch counselors, I needed to charm him. I needed him to like me so that he'd help me, so we could get through this.

As it turned out, I was right about Fred Sipe. He was a human atlas of taverns, bars, and blind pigs. The only thing I'd miscalculated was his ability to understand me, or more accurately, his ability to help me understand myself. In some very powerful ways, I owe my life—and any growing compassion and understanding—to Fred Sipe.

After a few days together—me pouring on the charm and Fred listening intently, more like a therapeutic teddy bear than the hard-edged sailor I'd imagined—Fred chuckled and said, "You're really slick, you know that?"

When I thought Fred wanted to hear me talk about being sad, I came up with experiences and a personality that fit "sad." I assumed that's what he wanted, so that's what I was prepared to give him: sad. When I thought Fred wanted me to be angry, I was angry. If I imagined he wanted me to be cute and demure, I flirted. Whatever I thought he wanted me to be, I became. I could show him a face for every mood, tell stories to prove every perspective. This was my skill. These were the personalities I'd honed over the years to satisfy different people—men especially.

In less than two days, Fred had given me a new name: "Slick." He said it with affection, but he meant it. I'd grown expert at keeping people from knowing me, so gifted, in fact, that I did not know myself. When a therapist thought he had pinned me down, I slipped away. When a counselor offered genuine insight, I slid out from under her counsel and hid myself away. Fred was right. I was "Slick." By naming my false identity "Slick," Fred Sipe was able to introduce me to someone I did not know. Her name, my name, is Mary.

"Who are you, Mary?" Fred wanted to know. I told him that I was an organizer. He smiled and said, "Umm-hmmm. Well, I think you're organizing yourself into so many different people we can't keep them all straight, Slick. Let me try again: Who are you, Mary?"

I tried explaining that I was a "pleaser," and I told him about the insights I'd gained during family week. He thought it was all helpful, a very good beginning. "But what would it take to please you, Slick? Who's Mary, and what do we need to do to please *her?*"

I was stumped. I couldn't answer either question.

For as long as I could remember, I had feared that if someone really knew me, they wouldn't like me; so I never let anyone know me. Eventually I didn't know myself. Whatever someone else wanted me to be, I became. If I could satisfy them with the role I played, organizing all the right pieces, they might not judge me, might not reject me, might not leave me. And when I'd perfected the many faces of Mary, I could look directly into a mirror and have no idea who Mary really was. How could I please Mary, or ask others to please her, if even I didn't know her?

"Slick," said Fred, "you've got to stop creating so many Marys in order to discover one. There's a real Mary in there somewhere. Give her a chance to express herself." I couldn't imagine how that would happen. And Fred's answer was very unsatisfying, far too simple: "Trust God."

Fred believed that the Mary who needed to be discovered had never romped and run, never learned to play. So some of my peers and I began playing together. We "tee-peed" (toilet papered) trees outside the Betty Ford Center; we put shaving cream on cars. When I told him about some of the practical jokes we had played at Channel 7—putting a sliced onion on the earpiece of a telephone, taping together chairs that would need to be moved—he lit up. We tried out pranks all over West Hall (where the women stayed on campus).

In the end, it wasn't merely play that I learned; it was freedom. If I could run with my hair blowing in the wind and not worry about tangles; if I could climb trees without worrying about getting my clothes dirty; if I could play pranks without fearing the consequences—Fred believed that then, perhaps, I could taste a sense of release, of freedom. If I could play without alcohol, I could probably live without alcohol. And Fred was right.

His formula for sober self-discovery—"Trust God"—was easier said than done. Trust was not easy for me. And I had no real God-concept, no sense of what or who I should be trusting. I began to meditate, and to take walks, and to listen to the voices within myself, all things I'd never done before. I listened to Fred talk about God, and I read the books he gave me. Gradually I began to understand the meaning of the Serenity Prayer, which is offered by alcoholics everywhere:

> God grant me the serenity to accept the things I cannot change, the courage to change the things I can, and the wisdom to know the difference.

It is not a prayer about an abstract idea named God; it's a prayer about Someone Else in control, about recognizing that we are not in charge of our own lives or the lives of others, about accepting ourselves with great limitations. It was a wonderful, freeing recognition. It opened me to a rock-hard belief, which has grown only stronger over the years, in a much larger Plan at work than any of our little dealings. The spiritual awakening that began at the Betty Ford Center was, I'm convinced, God's way of preparing me for what was still to come in my life.

Both Fred and Betty believed I had completed all the growth possible for me at the center. "You need to think of this place as the emergency room," said Fred, "and go somewhere else for the real work of healing." He suggested that I go to Florence, Colorado, to Parkside Lodge, an extended treatment center.

The Betty Ford treatment incorporates Alcoholics Anonymous and its famous twelve-step program. Before I could be discharged, I needed to complete the fourth step ("Make a searching and fearless moral inventory of ourselves"). I wrote a list of both my assets and my failures, the hurts I'd caused both others and myself. When the list was complete, I used it when I took my fifth step with a chaplain: "Admit to God, to ourselves, and to another human being the exact nature of our wrongs."

A ceremony is held the evening before people are discharged, and I remember mine well. The people who'd been important in my

treatment formed a circle around me as I took out the fourth-step
inventory I'd written, ripped it up, and burned it—symbolizing the
total letting go of the past. As that list of past mistakes went up in
smoke, we held hands and offered the Serenity Prayer. Even now, a
decade later, it is still a vivid, emotional memory.

The following morning I was given a commemorative coin to take
with me from the Betty Ford Center. I still carry it because it reminds me that I need not bottle up the anger; there is hope for forgiveness. And I do not need to empty a bottle of vodka to find
courage; I can pray. In all the articles I've read about my family,
and my family's wealth, it occurs to me I've never read a sentence
about my most important coin—the one with value far beyond
mere money.

Parkside Lodge was the beginning of a new life for me. In my early
days at Parkside, I reverted to being "Slick." With no Fred Sipe to
challenge me, almost instantly I started playing roles—it was what I
had done longest in my life, and best. If I needed any evidence that
Fred and Betty were right, that I was not yet ready to take on the
world without additional healing, my easy reversion to role-playing
was proof enough. But the lessons of the Betty Ford Center had
been well taught. A counselor at Parkside, Abby, took up where
Fred had left off. And group sessions with people, some of them as
skilled at playing roles as I was, nudged me out of hiding and into
continued discovery.

Before leaving the mountains, I discovered the techniques of trust
in a simultaneously frightening and broadening "Outward Bound" adventure. In the coolness of the upper elevations, we learned the
value of teamwork and togetherness. We learned to forage for survival.
We learned to dare to free-fall back from an elevated platform, believing
that those assembled below would catch us before we crashed
painfully to earth. And I learned to be alone in the woods, and not to
be afraid. I learned to be in touch with my spiritual dimension.

On the porch at Parkside, on April 10, 1985, four days after my thirty-
seventh birthday, I created a simple sketch that opened a new door on
my own soul, encouraging me to risk calling myself an artist.

Finding art was a critical step in the direction of finding myself.
At the same time, I was discovering women. Somewhere I had

picked up the belief that if only I could please a man, he would make my life complete. So I'd gravitated toward men, not women. It wasn't always a healthy gravitation: My passion and possessiveness were fueled by an ocean of neediness. But healthy or not, it had become a life pattern.

When I saw that no other human being could "make me happy"—that there was no perfect man who'd lift me to happiness— I began to open up my relationships with women. I risked telling them the silly things I imagined, the ugly fears that held me back. I remembered the man who had stalked me while I was at Channel 7, who had exposed himself. I remembered ways I'd learned to imitate my mother's worst behavior rather than her best. In the end I made the most stunning discovery of all: I am a woman who is very much like other women. I have models all around me.

And I have art.

A pianist who suffers a great loss might go to the piano to express otherwise inexpressible grief, because it's on the keyboard that she can be most articulate. In the range of notes and chords and accents, she can give herself over to potent, pounding grief.

When my eyes and hands are at work creating a piece of visual art, it is *my* most articulate moment. I may not even know my feelings or beliefs or thoughts until I've seen what I am producing. I begin a work not knowing what to hope for, except an honest expression that will flow from my soul. And then my hands and eyes—and heart—take over; I sketch, I mold, I paint. As the piece nears completion, I finally stand up straight, realizing that my back hurts from the long period of leaning. I get my own first look at what's happened, what's been created. And then, for the first time, I say to myself, "Oh, yes—that's right. That's exactly what I'm feeling, that's just what I believe, that's precisely what I hope." Until that moment, I honestly will not myself have known. It's as if I meet myself, discover myself, in my artwork.

A year after I had fled to Paris and come home again sick, I was a new woman. Something quite wonderful had happened. I had discovered Mary. I was still getting to know her, which I learned is much easier when you are sober. I certainly didn't trust her completely. But I was intrigued by her. Some days, I even liked her. She seemed, in an extraordinary number of ways, normal.

CHAPTER II

"Nesting"

Recovery is a process, not an event. Besides commitment and grace, it requires time and the lessons of experience. This was a hard truth for me to learn.

I'd gone away for treatment and now I'd come home. I was snuggling into my New York City apartment at Seventy-ninth and Madison, living (as they say of people enjoying their first flush of recovery) "on a pink cloud." I saw my old haunts through sober eyes for the first time; they were not the same, because I was not the same. My senses had never been so keen. Being sober was, ironically, like being on a drug. I was high.

When I passed street vendors, I smelled—as if for the first time— the heavy sweetness of their flowers, the sizzling sautéed onions ready to smother their sausages, the smoking wood fire roasting their chestnuts. I heard the steady clip-clop of horses from Central Park punctuating the sound of honking taxis and bellman whistles and distant sirens; had those sounds been there before? Standing at my apartment window at sunset, I watched a kaleidoscope of colors and patterns playing out that I'd never seen before, even from the same window: an orange canopy sky, laced with swirls of pink and red, blanketing the city as it came to life for the evening in a gaudy display of flashing neon, yellow and green and blue and red. Every waking hour, my senses were heightened; I was high.

During a visit to my family in Florida I met a gentleman from France then living in the United States. We began dating, giving me a second reason to spend time in Florida. My parents were by now living much of each year at their home in Palm Beach. I'd earlier found an apartment nearby to use on weekends; now I improved it a bit and settled into life in both New York and Florida.

What I had not reckoned with—not yet—was that recovery was going to be a slow process of rebuilding my life, one piece at a time. Every habit I'd created over the space of decades would need to be re-created to fit a life no longer built around drinking, around avoidance and denial. Each pattern, each relationship, each everyday act—from shopping to entertaining, eating to calling friends—needed to be revised, or replaced, or simply stopped. The Serenity Prayer was important precisely because serenity itself was hard to come by and even harder to hold on to.

In New York, Dr. Valerie Gibbs became my aftercare counselor. Her area of specialization as a psychologist was women with addictions, and she often worked with individuals from families of some financial means. She knew women, and she knew alcoholism, and she knew exactly what it meant to be an adult child of an alcoholic mother. Valerie was always available at a moment's notice, whether this meant a scheduled appointment or a late-night telephone call.

You can't recover until you stop drinking. But once I slid off the pink cloud, the mere fact that I was sober did not in itself make me feel especially useful. I was glad to be clean and sober. But I needed a job now, as I'd needed a job before, and for the same reasons: to earn a living and to feel like a productive person, using whatever gifts I had for some worthwhile purpose. It was one thing to close an unhappy chapter. It was, I now discovered, something else to compose a new life.

I'd run into Ivan Bloch sometime during my first few months back in New York City. We knew each other from Detroit. When I met him again, he was deeply involved in financing and producing a new Broadway show, *Boys of Winter*. Ivan said that if I was interested in getting into "the business," he could get me involved in a wonderful new off-Broadway musical, *Just So*.

Ivan knew that I loved theater. He also knew I had access to cash but lacked the background to be a full-fledged producer. He wanted an investor—a "partner"—and he was willing to trade knowledge (his) for money (mine). We became partners.

Just So was based on Rudyard Kipling's *Just So Stories* for children. The show had great music (by David Zippel and Doug Katsaros) and a first-rate cast and was working toward a holiday opening off-Broadway at the Jack Lawrence Theatre on Forty-eighth Street. I met Liz McCann, the general manager; we got along famously. I loved the script. This was exactly what I'd been waiting for.

With Ivan's promise of partnership, I handed over a large chunk of change and jumped into producing with all the energy I'd stored up since before Paris. There were promotions to be organized, advertisements to be placed, people to be pleased. I went to the theater every day. I reviewed scripts and made suggestions, sometimes taking orders, sometimes mediating conflicts, and sometimes running errands. There was no duty too trivial, no responsibility too heavy: I was committed, I was enthralled, and—Lord knows—I was busy.

Ivan's genius was promotion. He knew how to finesse the box office, how to manage the fickle business end of Broadway. He also knew how cutthroat it could be, because Ivan had cut a few throats of his own. When the time came for us to tackle marketing, I gathered all the needed material and headed for Ivan's office. That was when I realized exactly how much help my partner Ivan would provide: none. He was up to his neck in *Boys of Winter*. He was working on a hit. And he was out of money just now. No time. No money. We'll deal with it later. "We have a wonderful show here," he oozed. "It can't miss."

Opening night for *Just So* was December 3, 1985. Dress rehearsals were, as they can be, uneven; the premiere show was nearly flawless. Without Ivan's genius, our marketing plan was more hopeful than professional. We needed a glowing review from the *New York Times* to start our climb toward the big time. A few days before the opening, all the critics were there. Even with all the busyness backstage, I couldn't help but watch them. It seemed to me they were enjoying themselves.

We all sat up late that night, waiting for the first edition of the *Times* to hit the streets. Someone brought in a copy and began reading. The *Times* had panned us. The bells tolling in the distance were not for the holidays; they were our death knell. We closed the run before Christmas Eve.

The cost of bringing a production to Broadway is staggering; I was a tiny little player in a very big game. Besides, I had none of the cutthroat instincts common in this field. I could endure the loss of my money and the fact that "my show" had fizzled. These stung but were bearable events. What I couldn't bear was telling the cast that they were out of work after all those months of life-investing labor. I'd grown to love them, like family, and I was devastated for them.

My professional redemption was my art. I was filling my apartments in both New York and Florida with everything from miniature sketches to compressor tanks and metal sheets used to make riveted construction. And it was art that brought Brian Campbell more and more deeply into my life.

We'd reconnected shortly after my return to New York, and he was always charming, often funny. We'd talk about common friends and life in the city and eventually ourselves. Brian wasn't feeling well physically. He knew that alcohol and drugs were probably his undoing. I talked about my experience at the Betty Ford Center and Parkside, probably extolling the virtues of sobriety more often than he wanted to hear them. At one point—corny as it now sounds—Brian said, "I think I want what you've got." He stopped drinking and using drugs, started attending AA twice each day, and generally cleaned up his life. I was impressed, and grateful.

But it was not just alcoholism or addictions or even a powerful physical attraction that bonded us; it was art. I needed someone to guide me, to teach me, to help me take the next step. Brian was the perfect mentor. Once he was sober, he began coming to my apartment twice each week to give me lessons. What he knew, what he could do, seemed limitless. He didn't give lectures, he gave examples; he modeled everything. "Try this," he'd say, showing me a technique or an image I'd never seen. Even in his most mindless moments with drugs, Brian never lost his capacity to create; in the days ahead, he never lost his ability to teach me.

Brian—third of six children in a Catholic army officer's family— had been raised mainly near Boston. His days as an altar boy seemed to have left him with more funny stories than religious faith. He'd enlisted in the air force during the heyday of Vietnam, mainly because his draft lottery number was low and unless he did something he was bound for the infantry. After a year of service, he escaped the military through a medical discharge.

After the military, Brian went to Tufts University, graduated with a BFA (bachelor in fine arts), and eventually headed to New York City to find work. Printmaking was his specialty, but he lived off his skills as a designer, of anything—store windows, stage sets, advertising copy. Brian had a world-class eye for composition, for arranging items of furniture or objects on a table. The man could design.

It was Brian the Artist that I admired most. He loved to sketch, using blue pencils and sometimes red. He could sit by a dinner table, casually sketching a plate of grapes, asking about my mother's wardrobe. When he stood up, his sketch was so realistic that you wanted to reach out, take a grape, and pop it in your mouth.

I was ecstatic about what Brian did for my art. After thirty years of a stifling inability to express myself, I had discovered how to do it through art—and now Brian was showing me how to do it more reliably, more effectively; how to reach not only toward my soul but also toward the souls of others. He'd spend an hour showing me how to hold a brush, how to capture a color, how to etch a copper plate or bend an aluminum sheet, and I would work frenetically, staying up two nights in a row in my little studio next to my kitchen, practicing what he'd taught me, waiting for him to come back to give me another lesson, to show me something new, so I could do it all over again.

When he had time, Brian would sometimes visit during his off-hours. We went to Central Park with sketch pads. He showed me how to blend colors, how to play light against shadow, how to translate a detail from a flower to an image of that flower. We went to the beach, where I stood and watched him sketch the most perfect seashells—so perfect that I could imagine the ocean roaring inside them if you held the paper to your ear.

But Brian's lessons went beyond technique to trust. He taught me to believe in my own instincts, to have confidence in my own judgments, to stop waiting for others to tell me if something was good or bad. He'd lead me through a new gallery or an old museum, pointing to paintings being shown. "Do you like that piece?" he'd ask. "I don't know," I'd tell him. "Am I supposed to?"

He wouldn't answer. He just moved a few feet and pointed toward another painting. "Do you like it or not?" Hesitantly at first, I told him, "Well, no, not really . . ."

"Okay, good," he said. "That's okay. That's good."

If Outward Bound at Parkside was intended to teach me to trust others, Brian's guided tours through galleries and museums were intended, at least in part, to teach me to trust myself. He wanted me to have my own sense about art and to trust that sense. It was my judgment, and that was enough for Brian. Eventually it became enough for me.

Brian came into my life as a mentor; he stayed as a wonderful friend. I was still shuttling back and forth between Florida and New York, still dating the Frenchman. One afternoon in early 1986, Brian was working with me at my New York apartment when flowers arrived from Florida, maybe for my birthday. I saw in Brian something I'd not seen before: jealousy. I was impressed. A man I liked actually was jealous of another man who liked me. This was good.

My relationship with Brian was beginning to feel like a healthy pairing of a woman and a man. It wasn't all about my organizing his life, or my living to please him. It was an acquaintance being transformed into a friendship, growing into love. And I liked it, very much.

By the time the summer of 1986 rolled into the city, Brian and I were an item. I'd broken off the relationship in Florida. I was in love. Brian had shown me that I could make art—I could make a difference—not by trying to be what others wanted, but by expressing what was most authentically and essentially me. He was teaching me, whether he intended to or not, that I mattered. No wonder I fell in love with him. No one had ever shown me such love before, or given me a finer gift.

I enjoyed the worldliness of Brian, the funny, mysterious side of him. Perhaps he'd delved too deeply into drugs before I knew him well, scouting for new experiences or better feelings, spurred on by the danger-loving side of his personality. But now he was sober. And he was still funny, still crazy—more than ever, easy to love.

During the summer months I decided that I should sell the New York apartment and move into a larger space. Brian and I were living together more often than not. We found a loft on Broadway and Prince that was begging to be developed. It had what we needed: lots of design potential, and lots of room—five thousand square feet—for storage and studios. Once I made the purchase, we spent most of our time planning the loft together, which was tantamount to planning our lives together.

I had been reluctant to discuss with Brian the fact that my biological clock had become a gonging alarm clock. I was pushing forty—pushing it pretty hard. I wanted children, and I needed to act soon. But by now I also wanted Brian, so I approached the topic gently lest I frighten him off with news he couldn't handle.

To my surprise, Brian was as eager as I was to have a child. What was even more surprising was Brian's conventionality: If he was going to father a child, he wanted the child to have his name. We should probably get married.

Married? Had he said "married"? What a wonderful idea. And have I mentioned how smashingly handsome this man was?

I had already chartered a ninety-eight-foot boat for us to sail in the Caribbean after we'd celebrated winter holidays with my family in Florida. *The Magic Lady* would be perfect for a honeymoon. We'd already invited Valerie and Dominique to join us for the sail, and we decided to leave the plans as they were.

On January 7, 1987, Brian and I were married in a civil service at my parents' home in Palm Beach with a number of their friends as guests. Brian's mother and father and my brother and younger sisters flew down for the wedding. My two "Florida Joys" were there— Joy Anderson with her children and Joy Prouty with her husband, John Irwin. It was a lovely, low-key ceremony. And when it was over we flew to Martinique (on Dad's plane) and boarded *The Magic Lady.*

What was originally slated as a one-week trip was extended, after a few days at sea, to two weeks. Our life on board offered everything needed for a honeymoon. We hopped from island to island, visiting better-known places and my favorite, Bequia. Valerie was a wonderful sailor and spent hours working with the crew. Dominique had been raised on the waters off Corsica and was absolutely at home. At most ports of call, Brian and I went onshore with sketchbooks, like a couple of shipwrecked artists. We'd return late in the day for dinner with Valerie and Dominique.

There was time enough alone so that Brian and I could be newlyweds intent on becoming parents. I had already read every book on pregnancy enhancement. I memorized all the techniques. Now, on

board, all we needed was our supply of thermometers to indicate my peak moments of fertility.

We honeymooned with gleeful abandon—two of the most perfect weeks of my life.

We were home from the Caribbean less than a month when my hunch was confirmed: I was pregnant. It really had been the perfect honeymoon. Max Harrison (for Papaharry) Campbell was born in West Palm Beach's Good Samaritan Hospital at 8:17 A.M. on October 13, 1987.

It had been a fabulous pregnancy. On April 6, my birthday, I heard Max's heartbeat for the first time. On May 30, I felt him kicking for the first time—"like bubbles inside," according to my journal. On June 16, Brian was cupping my tummy with his hands when his unborn child delivered the cleanest kick imaginable. I'd never been happier, or felt better, in my entire life.

Brian and I were spending more and more time in Florida, doing artwork in our apartment. Palm Beach provided a lucrative market for art. Brian and my mother talked about opening a gallery. Although both Brian and I loved New York City, neither of us had been raised in so urban an environment. We felt more confident that we could raise a child in the suburban warmth of Florida. We began to look for a house.

When the sonogram gave unmistakable evidence that I was to have a son, I was frightened. It had never occurred to me that I might have a boy; I was going to have a daughter and, being a woman, tell her everything I'd learned about this feminine, womanly life. "Must be wrong," I told the attending doctor during the sonogram. I feared being unable to answer a boy's questions.

I was rescued from my fears by Joy (Chiles) Anderson. We'd met during my days in the White House when Joy was a secretary in the press office. Like Brian, she'd been raised as an "army brat" (her father was a general). When she decided to marry Dick Anderson, then playing for the Miami Dolphins and later a Florida state senator, she made the commitment to be a full-time mother. She's never wavered.

By the time I was pregnant, Joy's son, Ryan, was already seven and her daughter, Katherine Mary (for me), was six. Joy had faced both a boy's and a girl's questions and answered them all with that sweet, unflappable calmness that I first heard in her voice during noisy, chaotic moments at the White House. Joy was and is the mother who makes all other mothers feel inadequate and amateurish about their mothering. She's also the one who taught me, "Do not, ever, say 'My child has never done that,' without adding the word 'yet.'"

My days were spent more and more in the company of my other "Joy," the incomparable Joy Prouty. My sister Julie had attended an exercise class at Elizabeth Arden's salon on Worth Avenue in Palm Beach sometime in the early 1980s. She came home and announced, "I just met someone just like you." I wish.

Joy Prouty is a former Rockette turned professional fitness instructor (who went on to own fitness centers and become an international fitness consultant). Her first husband, Lloyd, died a lingering death, leaving Joy with three small children to raise alone. If her fate was unenviable, this slight, beautiful woman appears not to have noticed. She is 115 youthful pounds of unbounded energy and happiness, a tap dancer even, always positive and centered, gloriously upbeat and serenely wise. She has the voice of Lauren Bacall and a body without an ounce of fat. If I didn't love her so much, I'd hate her. On days when I was least certain about what was normal, what was real, I would have lunch with Joy for a reality check that—like Joy herself—never failed me.

During my pregnancy, Joy Prouty arranged for someone to walk with me every day to help me stay in shape and feel well. Joy Anderson constantly reassured me that I would be a fine mother. The two Joys in my life are the two key reasons that I remember my pregnancy as a golden time.

Brian and I were both doing art, planning life with and for our child, and becoming increasingly involved in the community. While still in New York we'd become supporters of the Manhattan Center for Living, a day center for people with life-threatening diseases. Anyone facing death in the city could come here to feel life— through a haircut, a meditation, a massage, a meal, or a group therapy session. By 1982, when we were often there, the disease that had found most of the clients had just been given a name: AIDS.

Shortly after our honeymoon I visited Gratitude House in West Palm Beach, a small extended treatment center for alcoholic and addicted women then run by Joan Dunklee. Its clientele bore the scars of incredible poverty, and many of the women came directly from jail, some pregnant, most with desperate histories.

Gratitude House was small and largely unknown. I liked that. This was a place without the aura of fame, without any glitter. And it had needs that I could meet while meeting my need to "give back" as a clean and sober woman. Joan was eager for my help, and I was eager to give it. Through conversation and games and art, I began to show women what had been shown to me: that they were human beings with value, that they had gifts and could make a difference, that they mattered.

For a time I considered building a second career (behind art) out of such service. It never felt like "volunteer time." It was critical work. I needed to do it, and I was needed for it. Betty had always said that alumni of the Betty Ford Center's program needed to become "rocks that we toss into the ponds of their own communities, sending out ripples of service." Here at last was my pond.

Several years later, after Joan had died and I'd left, West Palm Beach was rated as having one of America's highest incidence rates for HIV among women. What earlier had been largely a "gay disease" in New York was a women's disease in Florida. Each week I saw examples of addicted and alcoholic women who had dropped their common sense and given in to unprotected sex, thereby putting themselves at deadly risk for AIDS.

But that was later. During the days I volunteered my time there, as my child grew within me, I would leave Joan Dunklee and Gratitude House astonished and thankful that somehow I'd been spared. I hadn't taken the elevator to the basement. I had a handsome and creative husband with whom to build a family, a wonderful cadre of women with whom to share the journey, and my health. I was sober and clean, working the program. And I was, at last, a mother. My life was good—very, very good. I was nesting, a long way down the road to recovery.

CHAPTER 12

"Motherhood"

Brian got sunburned during our honeymoon. I got pregnant. I felt better, happier, and sexier during my pregnancy than ever before. Brian said, "Seeing you this large isn't tremendously sexy," and he meant it. But what we both wanted, and what we both celebrated, was the arrival of our first son, Max Harrison Campbell.

Phillip had already used the name "Harrison" as the middle name of his son, Chase, but he had no objection to seeing it spread through the family, and Brian liked the sound of the name. Papaharry had died, and giving birth to a child after losing a grandparent made me realize that families really do have "generations." One life had gone and another had come, and I enjoyed connecting them, also by name, in the best of Jewish family traditions.

It is unconventional among Jews to name a child for a relative who is still alive, but I wanted Dad to know of the honor—so Max became Max, and I became a mother.

Because of my medical history, especially the recent bleeding episode and subsequent D and C (dilatation and curettage) procedure that had brought me home from Paris, the doctors wanted Max delivered by cesarean. This had the advantage of allowing me to schedule the event, a feature I deeply appreciated. Once I held Max in my arms, any regrets I might have had for having anything other than a "normal" delivery evaporated. I began to breast-feed and to take on every other maternal task with unbridled joy. Motherhood was all I hoped for, and more.

Less than a week after delivery, my C-section incision became infected. An antibiotic was prescribed, but to take it I needed to give up breast-feeding. This hurt a lot, emotionally and physically. I could hardly sit or walk or—because Max needed attention—sleep. I took on that semiconscious state well-known to new mothers: never quite awake, never dressed with makeup, always trying to get back to bed and never getting to sleep. In the background, as I remember it now, the only two sounds I heard were Max's stirrings and the synthetic "Super Mario Brothers" sound track floating from a television set as Brian played with his Nintendo video game for hour upon hour.

The antibiotic didn't work. I winced when the consulting surgeon said, "I think we'd better open you up again." They said "emergency," which I didn't like, but I insisted that they wait until my anesthesiologist was available, which turned out to be around midnight, so I had late-night surgery. When I woke up, I was booked into Good Samaritan Hospital for at least a week of recovery—and my child was at home with Brian's mother and a private-duty pediatric nurse. I'd gone from the mountain peak to the valley floor. All I had to show for my pregnancy were pictures. When I looked at them, all I could do was cry.

Brian's enthusiasm for sexual intimacy was never the same. At first I blamed it on my pregnancy, on the weight I'd gained but didn't lose; later I blamed it on my illness and, when I came home from the hospital, on the crankiness that afflicts sleepless parents of infants.

Brian had stopped abusing drugs and alcohol, but he hadn't gone through intensive, full-time therapy. After an especially difficult month during the summer of 1988, he headed for the Betty Ford Center. But he stayed only a few days and then used a toothache to justify leaving. After that, any time I raised the possibility of therapy, Brian felt—maybe appropriately—that I wasn't being supportive enough, that I was whining. I'd respond with an "Oh, come on, Bri," I'd tug at his sleeve, give him a little space, and pretty soon he'd be back, smiling, remembering a shared joke.

But Brian's unhappiness, and his capacity to strike out when he felt it, grew more intense throughout the year following Max's arrival. Discussions of money were especially grim, perhaps because he had less to contribute than I did and he felt underpowered. If he brought less to the table, what control could he have over decisions? Whatever the cause, our tense discussions about family finances played into separate discussions he and Mother were having about opening a gallery. Their talks were starting to sound like planning sessions.

Meanwhile, I was pushing to have another child, soon. I usually said, "I want Max to have a brother or sister," which was true. Also true, and not needing to be said, was the reality of April 6, 1988, when I'd turned forty. I couldn't wait much longer.

This time, getting and staying pregnant proved to be a physically and emotionally difficult proposition. I got pregnant after months of trying, then lost the baby before the third month. We started over and again I became pregnant. I carried this baby two months before I lost it. Then I was pregnant again, but for the third time something was wrong. This time I needed surgery. When it was over, the baby was gone.

We started the process of artificial insemination, a clinically "invasive procedure" designed to open the womb to fertility and with the unintended consequence of also opening the body to infections. To raise my estrogen levels, the doctors first prescribed pills and later, to increase potency, taught me to give myself injections, one in each hip, every day. It was all biology and very little intimacy. But I was willing to do anything to have another child.

While I was focusing on children—the one I had and the one I wanted—Brian and Mother grew serious about the idea of a gallery. Mother loved art and since marrying Dad had longed to be a skilled collector. Dad once joked that he'd become part owner of Sotheby's so he could get a share of the profits off his wife's interests. And Mother adored Brian; she loved his taste, his work, and especially his attention.

They decided that Boca Raton's Gallery Center would be the ideal location. They could buy and sell art there, maybe Brian would do some teaching, and I could work in a studio there.

We were a financially lethal combination: Brian, Mother, and I. When Dad would try to offer some helpful counsel on finance or management, we didn't want him intruding in our business. It would be Mother's job to back him out before he taught us something we needed to know. The three of us would do this together, without Dad's help. And we'd do it under the banner we'd chosen together, the Harrison Gallery, named for Papaharry.

•   •   •

By the fall of 1989, Mother and Brian were traveling the world, buy-ing art for our new gallery. I stayed mostly in Florida, enjoying Max, setting up my studio, doing my art, and pursuing a private adoption.

Brian wasn't ecstatic about the idea of adoption, but he was real-istic about the diminishing odds of a successful pregnancy. I was determined. When the attorney with whom we were working found a young woman who wanted a family for her unborn child, I knew this was meant to be. She and I corresponded but never met. I started writing support checks, arranging medical services, and preparing for a second child. We'd have the baby just after the hol-idays of '89. I called the moving company where we'd stored the baby furniture Max used earlier and asked them to deliver the crib.

On October 17, 1989, the week after Max's second birthday, I was finishing our nursery, the little room next to Max's bedroom over-looking the backyard, when a call came: The young woman had changed her mind. She was going to keep the baby.

After months of soaring hopes—the feelings are the same as if you're carrying the child in your own womb—I was crushed. I called the moving company and told them, "Don't bring the crib." I told Brian that I needed to hide for a weekend. We decided to go to Naples, on the southern Gulf Coast of Florida, for a few days, to try to find comfort together, perhaps even enjoy each other again.

Moments later (literally less than an hour after the devastating call), the phone rang again. It was our lawyer. I supposed she needed to tidy up some unhappy details. When she began a little hesitantly, I told her to "just do what we have to do." She paused and said, "Mary, I have another child if you want him. He was born a little early; he's still in the hospital."

The couple who had said they would adopt this infant had backed out at the last minute, saying something about wanting a girl, not a boy. I could hardly believe it. I called Bob Edelman, our pediatrician, and asked if he would agree to take charge of the baby's care. I called Brian to tell him we couldn't leave, after all. I called the movers again: "It's Mary. Bring the crib."

As I was getting ready to head for the hospital the next morning to see my new child for the first time, Bob Edelman called. "Don't come," he said. "There are problems."

The baby had been born five weeks early, a matter of some concern. But there was more. He had a grave illness that none of the doctors had seen firsthand, epidermolysis bullosa. He would need extraordinary medical care throughout his life. Max would never be able to touch or play with his little brother, because on contact his skin would disintegrate as if suffering third-degree burns. His life would be short. He would never see adulthood.

"But who's going to take care of him if we don't?" I asked. Bob kept reassuring me that it was too early to tell, not something we needed to decide right away, and it would all work out. (I learned later that Bob and his wife were planning to take the child.)

I went upstairs and stood in the nursery, unable to believe what was happening. When I walked out, I closed the door as if it would never open again. I had the crib, delivered late the previous day, retrieved by the movers. I was emotionally drained, empty, exhausted.

Brian and Max and I went to Naples, but I was more a mother in mourning than an exciting lover. I was spiritually numb, not knowing what to believe or what to say, even to myself. The marriage couldn't bear much more strain, and I couldn't bear the thought of abandoning this child.

We arrived back home Monday evening. Tuesday morning, Bob Edelman called. He'd spent the weekend with the baby, performing every known test and taking every precaution. "I have good news," he said. "The lab says we've got a simple bacteriological infection here. His mother has checked out and released him for adoption; he's in intensive care, but he should be fine in a few—"

I dropped the phone, grabbed a furry white stuffed bear from the nursery, and ran to the car. Driving to the hospital, I called our lawyer and said, "Do whatever you have to do. I understand the baby is going to be okay. And we want him. I'm on my way to the hospital. Make sure I can get into intensive care. Please?"

I was pulling into the parking lot of St. Mary's Hospital when I remembered to call the movers: "Guess who—I need the crib."

I was spending every day at the hospital. Zachary was so tiny he seemed weightless when I lifted him. He was in intensive care, attached to IV tubes, and needed to be fed every four hours. I never missed a feeding during the two weeks of his stay except during the night when I went home to be with Max.

Meanwhile, Brian and Mother were devoting every day to getting the Harrison Gallery ready for a December 8 opening. When I visited, it was clear that this was their territory, not mine. At first Brian and I would argue; as the opening neared, we fought. They needed my help with some of the administrative functions—making the telephone system work, running the computer. But we reached a negotiated peace around the idea that I should make art and they should run the gallery.

As a gallery owner, Brian's dealings with the artists were either generous or foolish, depending on your view. If they had no time or money to frame their work, the Harrison Gallery would do the framing—and do it first-rate, world-class. If they couldn't afford to ship their goods, we'd pay shipping costs. Money was not the issue. This was about art.

This same philosophy dressed up the gallery itself. It was a stunning place, well ahead of its time. Mother has taste—expensive, refined taste—and Brian wove that taste through his magical design. I remember an artist walking into the gallery once, looking around, drawing a deep breath, and then letting it out slowly in a tone of marvel: "Ohhhh . . ." From his positioning of the art, to his lighting, to his amazing red walls, Brian had inspired a breathtaking sophistication in the place, at a breathtaking cost.

Despite the tensions between us, and despite the split focus of our attention, Brian never gave up being my mentor for my art. It was an island in our relationship, peaceful and calm no matter what other storms were brewing or had just blown by. When he and Mother decided to do a show of artists who had done flowers, he said, "You ought to be in the show."

"I don't do flowers, Bri."

"I'll show you." He started me working on a monotype of flowers. I liked it and kept developing them. Later he encouraged me to add background. Later still, his techniques influenced my handmade paper, which became best recognized, and even commercially successful, when sculpted into brightly colored flowers.

The Harrison Gallery was making local news and consuming lots of money during the winter holidays of 1989. I was celebrating my motherhood, planning the most perfect Christmas I'd ever had. I had stockings and gifts and friends, an extraordinary toddler who "gets into everything," and a two-month-old son who arrived as God's latest miracle in my life. I loved being a mother.

Brian moved out of the house in the spring of 1990. The weeks before he left were hellish. He was alternately angry and listless, short-tempered and sulking. When he wasn't at the gallery, he wasn't happy. Even at the gallery, if I came in, the mood iced over and couldn't be thawed. Brian knew how to sharpen a sentence to a razor's edge and use it to lacerate me, usually in private, sometimes in public.

It may have been lingering memories of George taking his leave of us in Louisville that prompted me to ask, when we'd agreed on the separation, "Can't we arrange it so you don't just walk out?" He agreed. On the appointed day, I would take an aerobics class with Joy Prouty during the morning while he'd be with the children. I'd come home and, together, we'd explain that he was going to be gone for a little while but everything would be okay. We were going to make the time as nontraumatic—as normal—as possible for the children.

Coming home from Joy's class I witnessed a traffic accident. By the time I'd called the police and survived the paperwork, Brian had left home. Max was with a baby-sitter when I got there, crying. I asked him what had happened, and he said, "Daddy left."

"Did he say anything?" I asked. Max nodded.

"What did he say, honey?"

"He said, 'Ask your mother.'"

I hadn't heard that line for forty years.

Our next few conversations were unproductive for both of us. We were neither more nor less distant than we'd been before Brian left. But Brian was depressed, seriously depressed, and he identified it himself. Without prompting from me, he said he needed therapy to relieve the sadness.

Brian and I began having weekly conversations about how we could work things out, how we could make them better. Some conversations produced hope: When the subject was art, we were as bonded as ever. Some conversations produced near-perfect pain: He'd tell me I was fat, I'd cry, he'd storm off.

After one of our more memorable and deeply regrettable conversations, I had lunch with a friend from my White House days. When lunch was over, and we were saying our good-byes, he said, "You're as wonderful as ever. And just as beautiful." The kindness of his words was more deadly than the venom Brian and I had been spitting at each other, because it showed me the stark contrast. I had come to this lunch aware of how sad Brian was; I left knowing my own sadness.

Not long afterward, we (Brian, the boys, and I) were in Michigan visiting Phillip's family. Mother and Brian were leaving in the morning for Chicago on a buying trip for the gallery, and Brian and I were alone for dinner.

"Tell me how unhappy you are," Brian said. In a sentence or two, I said I was terribly unhappy with our relationship. It was a fairly innocent response to a fairly kind question.

"Then I guess we ought to get a divorce," he said calmly.

"Okay."

There was a little pause, and Brian said, "Well, we'd better go tell your mother." And that was it. It had been decided.

Brian's calmness, and mine, lasted through most of our discussions about the divorce. We agreed that I would stay in the house we had purchased in Boca Raton, and that he would get a cash settlement equaling half the house's value. We agreed the children would live with me.

We agreed that he would continue working in the gallery with Mother, who was initially angry about the divorce, angry at seeing her family broken. We agreed that, especially for the children, we should try to stay close, be friends. And of course, we would still do art together.

But the mood didn't hold, and with roiling, roller-coaster emotions, our intentions slipped. Brian was talking about suicide the week the divorce was finalized, and I was growing frightened. He said he wanted more time with the boys, and I wondered if those times should be with supervision. He hadn't been feeling well; maybe the stress of the divorce was making him sick. He had trouble sleeping. I doubted that a baby in diapers was something he wanted to handle all through the night. When I said so, probably unwisely, Brian went into a rage. When he quieted down, it was only to seethe.

"I'm leaving town," he announced abruptly during a call midsummer. "I know you'll take good care of the boys. Have a good life." He wanted five minutes alone with the boys.

I was terrified. I called my attorney who said, "Get protection at the house, and get it now. The last time I heard something like this the man shot his children, his wife, and himself." When the police said there was no action they could take unless Brian did something physically violent, I hired private guards. I moved the children to Mother's house and demanded that Brian's time with the boys be supervised.

Brian responded in full fury. By the time the local papers had a chance to report the court action, both Brian and I had dug up enough dirt from previous lives to smear each other a dozen ways from Sunday. It was a bloody and brutal business. I believed that I was protecting my children. He was convinced that I was trying to destroy him. The judge had a reputation for disliking women, especially if they appeared to have the independence of wealth, and he made scathing judgments from the bench about our mutual incompetence as parents. The whole sorry mess swamped us and then splattered into the public record as a testimony to our shame.

The court ruled in favor of Brian. He could have unsupervised time with the children. I ran from the courtroom, convinced that I had lost not only my marriage but my children. I was humiliated by the proceedings and shattered by the outcome.

The following morning, having scored a victory in court, Brian called me. "How are we going to work this out?" he asked calmly. He wasn't vindictive or even upset. In fact he didn't really want that much time with the children. He had needed to win something, to not have me in charge of his life, to take control. Once he had achieved that, he was satisfied.

From that fall—1990—until he left Florida a year later, Brian became the most regular visitor at the house. He was there for breakfast when the boys came out of bed and spent time playing with them. He'd drop by for lunch, or to spend time with me on an art project, or to take a swim with Max, or to strap on Rollerblades and cruise the neighborhood with me and sometimes Max. He was calm again—not happy, but calm. I could deal with calm.

•   •   •

The divorce was final in August 1990. A month later—September 13, 1990—my father, George Frehling, died.

George had largely faded from my life after the night Mother conquered us all at the Brazilian Court. It might have been two years later when I visited him, still in Florida, and he spent most of our time together trying to involve me in a business deal. He wanted me to invest. This had always been Flohoney's fear— George wanting Phillip or me to give him money—and I could hear her disapproving voice in the distance even as George laid out the reasons I should invest. It was part anger and part common sense that drove my response: "No, George, I can't do that."

Another year or two passed before I visited George and Susan where they were living on a boat in Florida. It was small, quite small for living quarters, but cozily comfortable. He was drinking heavily, and Susan was worried about his heart.

Then his (and Joyce's) daughter, Lisa, had a terrible car accident resulting in a brain stem injury. I didn't hear about the accident for some months. When I did, I immediately headed for the hospital. When I offered to help find specialists in neurology anywhere in the world, George was visibly moved. And when I offered money, if it were needed, he said, "No, no. I don't need any money and neither does she; I'm taking care of everything."

I never knew the actual arrangements, or George's financial contribution to Lisa's care. But I liked the idea, a lot, that one of George's children had needed him, had turned to him in a moment of crisis, and he had been there. George may, belatedly, have learned to behave like a father.

CHAPTER 13

"It's Positive"

It was depressing to be divorced again. Once was a "mistake," but how do you account for twice? Living alone was not so difficult, because I wasn't alone that much. Brian was at the house frequently, and our relationship was usually peaceful. But I hated having failed at marriage again. I was embarrassed in public and shaken in private, doubting my capacity for a healthy, adult, loving relationship.

Brian was fighting occasional colds and infections, but at least he wasn't fighting me. And he continued to be the most insightful art mentor anyone could possibly have: still patient, still affirming. When we worked together, I sometimes marveled that his only interest seemed to be my art, not his, as if mine were more important.

Max became more and more handsome, looking more and more like Brian with every passing day. He had Brian's dark features and some of Brian's moods. Zachary was nearly the perfect opposite: blond, sunshine and smiles. Together they were the center—a very happy center—of my life. I wrote them poems, and I wrote poems about them. I started journals for each of them, recording not only what they did (first step, first tooth, first whatever) but also how I felt about them and about our lives together. I wanted to let them know some of the things that were happening to me. I wanted them to be able to answer questions, when they were adults, that I'd been unable to answer in my own life.

Mother and Brian continued to work together in the gallery, and the red ink accumulated along with the inventory. They were gifted at buying art, which might also have been their keenest interest. Selling art was something else, and less of it was happening. But the gallery had become their business, not mine. And I was investing my time, and finding my satisfaction, in my children and my art.

When Brian and I first broke up, Mother tried to perk me up by buying for me—at a charity auction in New York—a tap-dancing lesson and dinner with Gregory Hines. I'd always idolized him. When *Tap* was first released, I swooned at his dancing. And when *White Nights* came out on videotape, I watched it for days. I could hardly contain myself when she told me what she'd done.

The original plan was for a tap-dancing lesson and dinner in New York, but Hines proposed to come to Florida instead. This was even better, because then I could share the experience with friends in Palm Beach and my children. We finally settled on a date in early 1991 for Joy Prouty's studio in West Palm Beach.

Gregory Hines came, saw, and conquered us all. He charmed every master class participant, leaving me with a spellbinding memory: no music playing, just Gregory speaking gently the sounds of beats and rhythms, bending his knees, gliding effortlessly, encouraging us, softly offering suggestions, tolerating our amateurism with the grace that only a master could possess. After two hours he asked if people wanted to stop. Of course not. He did another thirty minutes, and then patiently posed for pictures with everyone.

Then came the private lesson for Joy and me. My legs had begun to stiffen up; I'd already exceeded my usual limits for stamina. Where I didn't ache, I hurt. "How about a soft-shoe or something?" he offered. He took my hand and led me through familiar steps— familiar to him and most tap dancers, but my mind had turned to mush.

On the way to dinner he spoke of his wife, Pam, and their son, also named Zachary. He was unpretentious, and I was utterly awed. It wasn't his celebrity status that captivated me; I'd lived in a home, and worked both a White House and several television studios, where celebrities were everyday guests. It was being in the presence of brilliance. I was dancing with the artist who had brought that form of dance—tap—to its highest level in our time, perhaps in human history. It was like painting with Michelangelo. Blasting a home run with Hank Aaron. Playing a cello with Yo Yo Ma.

Gregory Hines left Florida to open the New York show that brought tap dance back to life in America: *Jelly's Last Jam.* His picture was everywhere, from the cover of newsweeklies to the feature spread of tabloids. And the euphoria that infused my evening with him has lasted for years; I still tingle at the memory of it. It was as close as a forty-something mother can come to being a teenager again, thrilled by a first kiss that seems as if it will last forever.

I'd read Dr. Brian Weiss's first book, *Many Lives, Many Masters*, sometime after its release in the late 1980s. Joy Anderson and I talked about it. When I learned that Weiss had an active practice in Miami, I called to see if I could meet him. But I never reached him—or maybe our schedules never worked out.

What fascinated me initially was Dr. Weiss's ability to blend two areas of interest: spirituality and psychology. When I read his book, I felt echoes of my own experience, including the sense I had while first at the Betty Ford Center that there was not only a Higher Power but also a Bigger Plan—and that we, as humans, can become active participants in that cosmic plan. My divorce had raised old issues, and I was eager to find a way to ground myself again, spiritually and emotionally, both for myself and for the children.

Brian Weiss broke onto the national scene because of his startling experience with "regression therapy." He was a trained physician and psychiatrist with impeccable credentials and no desire for notoriety. He wanted to heal patients, to relieve their problems and current distresses through this therapeutic innovation. In the process, he had observed that some patients gave very solid evidence of experiencing memories and emotions best explained by previous lives. Given the opportunity—regression therapy—they were able to "go back" (regress) and under hypnosis give vivid descriptions of times and places and events, sometimes with knowledge unavailable to any but actual witnesses.

In April 1991 I got a flyer in the mail announcing a limited-admission workshop Dr. Weiss was going to conduct in Palm Beach. I'd never attended such workshops, and certainly wasn't a "joiner" in the conventional sense. But I'd also never shaken my interest in his work, and I wanted to go.

The workshop with Brian Weiss was all I'd hoped for and more. His gentle voice and quiet demeanor, his acceptance of things that can't be explained with easy answers, his absolute conviction that life has a broad, universal purpose—all drew me toward him. Before I left the

customs & immigration

71791

workshop, I asked for subsequent appointments with him that, over a matter of a few months, not only revived my spirituality but restored it to new heights. I sensed again that extraordinary peace grounded in the knowledge that God has a plan for our lives. Life is about more than the here and now; eternity is a reality, and a comfort.

By early summer I was driving to Miami weekly to spend time with Brian Weiss. We'd become friends. He offered therapeutic insights to the barriers inhibiting my own growth, and we meditated together. He urged me to be more open to messages, to listen as once I had listened in the desert. He was, he told me, convinced that I had a critical role to play in something important, something worldwide. It was, he would say, "all about the Bigger Picture" in which love and courage and art would be blended into God's purpose.

By July of 1991, less than a year after my divorce, I felt that I'd arrived at a new level of spirituality and satisfaction in my life. This was no pink cloud; it was solid stuff. I was grateful not for mysterious or whimsical feelings but for concrete, visible gifts of God: my children, my Joys, my art, my life. I was grounded.

July 3, 1991. I had an appointment with Brian Weiss that was unforgettable. Don Black, the London songwriter and Tony Award–winning collaborator with Andrew Lloyd Webber on *Sunset Boulevard*, had purchased the rights to transform Brian Weiss's *Many Lives, Many Masters* into a musical. They'd already assigned a title: *Forever and Ever, Amen.*

When he told me the good news, Brian welcomed my offer to become involved. I was really interested in theater, of course, and I was happy to become an active advisor. In addition, I knew and trusted Brian's work. I had spoken to Don Black by telephone and explained to Brian Weiss when I arrived at his office that day that everything seemed to be working out "miraculously." Brian just smiled his "of course" smile.

"Don's coming to New York on the tenth; I'll be there on the eleventh, and we'll see what we can work out," I told Brian Weiss.

I was scheduled to go through New York on my way to a vacation cruise off southern France with my parents, Phillip, and a few others. My life was full, the children were busy, and although it sounded like a wonderful trip, I didn't covet the idea of being stuck on board a ship six thousand miles away. I reminded myself this would be considered the vacation of a lifetime by many people, but I was grumpy about it, even irritated. My children weren't coming, and I would have to be cheery and "on" all day long with a group of Mother and Dad's friends.

Brian Campbell had returned from his working trip to Europe not long before, and he wasn't feeling well. He was losing weight. He had strange bumps growing under the skin on his neck. I'd taken a studio at the other end of the Gallery Center, separate from the Harrison Gallery, so I could do artwork in relative peace. We were in that studio one late-June evening when Brian said his doctor had ordered a new batch of tests, everything from HIV/AIDS to viral strep.

"HIV?" I was surprised.

He was unconcerned. "It's crazy." He'd tested negative before, after his drug-using days. I remember thinking to myself that, if he had somehow become HIV-positive, he must have had more energy after our breakup than I had thought possible. At any rate, surely it didn't have anything to do with me.

On July 3, I left Brian Weiss's office and started making calls from the car phone. I arranged an appointment with Don Black in New York. I called home to check on Max and Zachary. The babysitter answered and said, "Brian [Campbell] called." I talked to the boys for a moment, but they were more interested in the swimming pool than their mom. I returned Brian's call while negotiating rush hour traffic coming north out of Miami.

"It's positive," he said. And, again, "It's positive."

It took me a moment to know what he was talking about. Then it registered with the force of a tidal wave. "Oh, my God, Bri—I'm so, so sorry."

"I've already called your mother," he said. I wished he hadn't. She would be crazy with concern not only for Brian, but for me and the children.

I called Mother. She was distraught over Brian. "And don't you need to get a test, too?" she wondered. "And what about the children?"

Sure, when I could arrange it. But first we'd better help Brian.

I had never recovered from my fear of Brian's emotional outbursts, and I couldn't imagine that he would meet this news with much stability. I called Brian Weiss to tell him about my appointment with Don Black and said, almost as an afterthought, "Oh, Brian's HIV-positive."

"We should pay attention to this," said Brian Weiss, who urged me to get tested immediately.

By the time I pulled into Boca Raton, Brian wasn't at the gallery where I'd found him earlier. I called his house. He answered but could barely talk. He was beside himself, nearly hysterical, terrified. I told him I was on my way over.

He was talking about suicide when I arrived. It took a while to calm him. "Okay, okay, okay." I heard myself talking in the tone of voice I'd learned from Brian Weiss: smooth, quiet, easy. "Tell me what the doctor said, exactly. Tell me exactly what he said." Brian didn't know. He was in his own world. He couldn't focus. "I can't forgive myself," he said, pacing the floor and running both hands through his hair, crying. "I can't forgive myself. What about you? What about Max?"

It was at the word "Max" that my world came unhinged. It hadn't occurred to me, for even an instant, that I was seriously at risk. If I weren't, could Max be? And Zachary? He was adopted. He would be okay. Wouldn't he? I sat silently, staring into the uncertain and suddenly anxious future, pondering it all. I resolved to take this crisis, as the twelve-step program proposes, one day at a time, one moment at a time.

"It's July third, Bri—who can I call during the holidays?"

I called Bob Edelman, our pediatrician. He knew a clinic that did anonymous testing; he'd call. Within minutes he'd arranged for a test. A North Palm Beach doctor would get the results. They couldn't do it on the fourth, but they'd take me first thing on Friday, the fifth.

I stayed with Brian for several hours. He didn't want to come home with me, didn't want to see the children. I worried more about his rage than his HIV status. I believed he could kill himself. And he had no one else to turn to. I left him just before the children's bedtime, when he promised me that he wouldn't hurt himself.

July 5, 1991. I went to the clinic for my HIV test. The holiday weekend was in full, sleepy swing. The clinic was slow. They explained that I could use a fake name. I chose "Cher," with no idea why; it was the first thing that came to me.

Bob Edelman and the clinic physician agreed that we shouldn't test Max unless the most improbable results showed up and I was HIV-positive, too. For some reason, I thought I'd have my test results early the next week, Monday or Tuesday. I called both days and was told it would be a while yet.

I saw Brian Weiss on Wednesday, July 10, and his first question was, "Do you have the results yet?" I didn't, and I'd decided to stop calling every day. Just making the call was traumatic, because it meant I had to consider the possibility, no matter how remote.

On Wednesday nights Max would sometimes have an overnight "at Daddy's house." On the tenth, Brian said he really wanted to have Max for the night. I was leaving with the children the next day for New York City, first to work on handmade paper at Exeter Press, and then on the seventeenth flying from New York with Phillip to meet our parents in Europe. The children, meanwhile, would head for Detroit to vacation with Phillip's children, Chase and Amanda.

At two o'clock in the morning my phone rang. It was Brian. "You better come get him. I'm sick and he's scared." I could hear Max sobbing in the background.

Carol, who helped with the children, was staying at the house that night, so I was free to leave Zachary sleeping. I arrived at Brian's in a robe and walked through his garage into his house directly to his bedroom. Max was sitting in the dark on the bed with Brian, caressing his father's hands, still crying.

"I can't make him better, Mommy." Max didn't move, didn't come to me. "I can't make him all better."

Brian had been vomiting over the side of the bed into a trash can. He was so sick he'd crawled across the floor to call me.

I put on my best Joy Anderson "mommy voice" and attempted to reassure everyone—including, I suppose, me—that "it's going to be all right."

"Let's get your things, honey," I said to Max, while checking to see if I could do anything for Brian, who told us to go home. "We'll talk to Daddy later."

Max and I got home about three. Around five, Brian called. He was feeling somewhat better. I put Max on the line so he could hear Brian's voice and be reassured that his daddy was okay.

•   •   •

July 17, 1991. I'd met with Don Black during my first day in New York, the eleventh, and the musical was going to work out brilliantly. We planned to meet again in Europe in a few days. Don was going to be at Andrew Lloyd Webber's home in southern France; I'd be in and out of port; we'd make contact and get together.

The rest of my days were spent at Exeter Press, making paper and then using that paper to make art. Usually I did this work in Boston at Rugg Road Paper, where Brian had first taken me. Exeter Press was more like "my place," not Brian's, and when (some months earlier) I'd scheduled time to spend this week at Exeter, I felt as though I were finally stepping out as an artist—not breaking from Brian, exactly, but emerging.

I'd never had a hard time focusing on my art. It possessed me. My mind wouldn't wander until my body was so tired, so sore from the process of lifting and kneading and bending, that I couldn't keep going. Except this week. I was preoccupied with the test results I didn't have. Until I knew that I was okay, I couldn't know about Max. I was doing Oriental-type work, abstract things I'd never done before, Japanese letters (I don't know Japanese), and very basic colors: red, black, white. Their titles showed my state of mind: "Begin to Heal." "Transformation."

I had called Brian Campbell every day, from Exeter and from the hotel. By Tuesday the sixteenth, his tuberculosis test had come back positive. We assumed we'd been exposed to the TB virus, especially Max. More tests were ordered.

And I'd started calling the clinic again. "This is Cher," I'd say. "I'd like my HIV test results." A woman's voice would always respond, after a momentary check of the files, "I'm sorry, but those results aren't available yet."

I was at La Guardia Airport, preparing to put Max and Zachary onto their late-morning flight to Detroit, when I decided to make one last call to the clinic.

"This is Cher," I said. "I'd like my HIV test results."

"Just a moment, please," said the woman's voice. When she returned, she had a new line: "The doctor would like to speak with you."

I knew. When she said, "The doctor would like to speak with you," I knew. I was HIV-positive. Holding the telephone in one hand, I heard myself climb up onto the road to AIDS. I didn't need to hear what came next.

"I'm sorry, Mary; it's positive." It was the doctor. I knew I was crying because my face was wet. I knew I wasn't saying anything, because I couldn't. Nothing worked. "You've got to come home now, Mary. We don't know your health status. We need to do some more tests right away."

"No, it has to wait," I said. I was too close to shock to make good decisions, and too uncertain of a stranger—doctor or no doctor—to trust his judgments. "I'll get back to you." I hung up.

I was a mess when I reached down to pick up the children for hugs before they boarded their plane with Carol. "Why are you crying?" they both wanted to know.

"Mommy's just going to miss you so much," I said. I nearly choked them with urgent hugs before letting them go.

I'd been dizzy since the telephone call. I was breathing loudly, and my heart was pounding. My mouth was dry. My body was racked, but my mind seemed fairly calm. I remember looking around at the surroundings and realizing that everything was perfectly normal. The telephone call had made no real difference. Passengers were still rushing to catch planes. Announcements were being broadcast by Northwest Airlines staff. The smell of popcorn and hot dogs and tobacco smoke filled the concourse as always.

I wanted to be away, alone, and at the same time I was grateful to be there, to see people, to have some sensation, to know that I was not dead. Not yet. And I knew precisely what I was feeling. It was terror; it was fear at a magnitude and intensity I had never imagined; fear that had a life of its own, a power of its own. It was, almost as I imagine an out-of-body experience, simultaneously paralyzing and freeing. I saw myself in terror. I felt myself feeling shock.

Phillip came off his plane and took one look at me. "What's the matter, Mar?"

"Nothing." I grabbed him and hung on, sobbing.

"Geez, Mar," he said, supposing I was already missing the children. He gave me a long hug, which made me cry harder.

"It'll be okay, kid," he reassured me. "We're only going to be gone for a week."

CHAPTER 14

"Waiting for Someone Like You"

If your father abandons you, your mother might get you another one; you adjust, you cope, you rebound. If people discriminate against you, you may fight back. If you're an alcoholic, you might try recovery. If you're lonely, you could reach out to others. If you're childless, you could adopt. If you have AIDS, you die.

Joy Prouty, whose first husband Lloyd had died a long and difficult death, once told me that although she knew for months that he would die, it was still a powerful shock when he actually did. He had been "dying" for so long that his being "dead" was almost unimaginable. My two weeks of terror, denial, panic, rage, confusion—none of it had made me ready to hear the doctor say, "I'm sorry, Mary; it's positive." It came like a rifle shot out of the dark. When I hung up the phone I was numb, and I knew that I was dying.

I'd been sick, off and on, for weeks; now I understood why. First I'd had a sinus infection and then a general grunge wandered around my body: headaches, colds, sore gums. I'd felt rotten for weeks and now felt even worse. When we spoke by telephone that week, Brian's focus was on his own deteriorating health. He was self-involved. He was scared. So was I: scared for him, scared for me, and beyond scared—unbelievably terrified—for Max.

Members of my parents' generation vividly describe where they were when they heard bells ringing to signal the end of World War II. My generation remembers the November 1963 assassination of President Kennedy; we know where we were, almost five years later, when Dr. Martin Luther King was felled in Memphis. Those just a bit younger describe hearing the news of John Lennon's murder. I learned on July 17, 1991, that I was HIV-positive. No one with AIDS can ever forget the hour and the place at which the news was delivered. Death announcements, especially your own, have a way of grabbing your attention and holding it.

I had no gentle way to explain the news to Phillip. An hour after learning I was HIV-positive—with no rehearsed lines with which to couch the facts or cushion the impact—I told my brother I was dying. "I have AIDS."

He didn't believe me. I told him the whole story, beginning with Brian's test and announcement. Then he believed me. In a matter of minutes, I watched him race through the same set of emotions that earlier befell me: disbelief, horror, rage, confusion. He cried. He hugged me. We both cried. He said he wouldn't let me go, wouldn't let me die. He'd kill Brian. He'd save me. What about the boys? We hugged some more and cried some more.

Eventually, calmer, he asked, "What are we going to do, Mar?"

We called Byron ("Bud") Nease, a gifted Broadway vocal artist and the only close friend we both knew who was HIV-positive. Until very recently, Bud had not disclosed his HIV status because he needed to work, and clients prefer to contract with "healthy people" when they're paying for the job. Like hundreds of thousands of others who are headed for AIDS, he had opted for silence, trusting only a few friends with the knowledge that he was "positive." When I told Bud, he was stunned—but he was also soothing, encouraging, hopeful. He reassured Phillip that it would be okay, that I needed some time and that it would all work out.

After we hung up, going over the conversation we'd just had with Bud, I realized that he'd been grief-stricken. He'd kept saying, "Oh, Mary, Mary . . . I'm sorry, I'm so, so sorry." I was surprised at his distress. I'd not yet learned that being HIV-positive, in some respects, makes the news about others harder to hear: We remember our own first moment of knowledge, and having walked a ways down the road toward AIDS, we know what's coming.

Phillip and I debated for a while whether I should stay home, maybe take the doctor's advice and head back to Florida. But I needed to break the news to Mom and Dad in person, not by phone. Mother already knew Brian was HIV-positive and that I'd been tested; she'd guess, if I didn't show up. It would take only a week. Phillip would be there. The news wouldn't get better with delays. We boarded the flight still talking, still crying.

We landed in Paris where we were overnighting on the way to meet our parents' boat in port. Once at the hotel, I couldn't sleep. I picked up the telephone and busied myself calling Bud and Brian Weiss. I took comfort in hearing their voices, in listening to them talk about ordinary things. I wanted to hear Brian's calm, assuring convictions. I needed to hear Bud speak from his own experience on the road to AIDS, to know that he was ahead of me and that it was okay.

I called Bud repeatedly. With each call, his shock was receding. "Think big, Mary," he said. "Think about the big picture. You need to get beyond yourself. Think about why you have it. . . ." It was a loving and appropriate gesture for him to make, but I couldn't begin to make my brain ask the right questions about the "big picture" and my life's purpose. I was dying. I was wondering who would take care of my children when I was gone.

Bud reminded me that I knew people who could be helpful. He named people in Santa Fe, New Mexico, where I planned a summer vacation. And he added a curious twist at the end of our conversation. He mentioned my family, and my work in TV and the White House, my network of friends. "I've been thinking," he said. "Someone in your position could make a difference in this crisis." I couldn't imagine how.

Sleepless in Paris, I put on my Walkman headphones. Don Black had given me, with apologies for the quality of the tape, a studio cassette of his newest songs as well as a recording of *Aspects of Love*, a Broadway musical. I closed my eyes and played, over and over, "Love Changes Everything."

My mother knew my test results the moment she saw me. I'm not sure if my eyes betrayed the truth, but no words needed to be spoken for her to know. Maybe it's that way with all mothers. For the first time in years I felt very much like a daughter. I was the little girl enfolded in the arms of my mom.

Even beyond the stigma associated with AIDS in America—that this is a dirty disease largely afflicting dirty people who have dirty sex or use dirty needles—there's a feeling, when you are explaining to loved ones that you're infected, that you are intentionally hurting them, that you're the cause of their pain. You feel guilty for their grief. I learned about this when I told Phillip. And I felt it again, instantly, when I saw Mother. In one look at me she had known, and felt the pain of what she knew. She wanted to comfort me, and I wanted to comfort her, and neither of us knew where to find any comfort at all.

I had a special worry about telling Dad: I feared that he would have a heart attack. I didn't know what he knew about HIV or AIDS—he was already past his eightieth birthday, and this was a disease of the young. I didn't know how to break this news gently. And I didn't want to see him in anguish or to feel guilty for telling him the truth.

I'd planned to begin my first sentence with a clear, strong "Dad . . ." But that's not what came out. When he turned toward me, all I could say was, "I'm so sorry . . ." I broke down before I had finished my first sentence.

Sitting next to him on his bed, holding his hand, I went through the story about Brian's being sick and being tested, and his results. Then I explained that I'd been tested. "And I'm HIV-positive, Dad." He did not understand.

"What does that mean?"

"It means I have AIDS, or will get AIDS." A long pause. "It means I'll probably . . . I'll get sick, you know . . . I'll die of AIDS."

His eyes began to glisten. I wanted to hug him, hold him, do something that would keep him from crying, but I couldn't. I reached out to catch a tear rolling from under his glasses, but it made us both cry harder. For a little while, the only noise in the stateroom was the sound of four people crying softly.

We talked for a while. Dad spoke angrily of Brian and tenderly of loving me. Then he stood up. Even past eighty, he's tall; his posture is straight, not stooped. He looked at Mother and Phillip, then back to me.

"Okay," he said in a matter-of-fact tone, "what do we do?" This

was not an expression of helplessness; this was straightforward inquiry. This was Max Fisher talking, the man who took on intractable problems when others had given up. This was my father the businessman, the statesman, the philanthropist. When there's a problem, we face it and we conquer it. Who's got the strategy? What are the goals?

As gently as I knew how, drawing from the shallow well of my knowledge, I explained that really nothing could be done. There are no cures. But Max Fisher was not altogether certain I was right. He may have said something like, "We'll see."

Max Fisher was not going to accept the idea that one of his children had a disease he could do nothing about, or a problem he couldn't fix. Max Fisher had not yet come to grips with AIDS. None of us had.

As I walked my son Max through the corridors of the hospital and down the hallway, through the door marked Infectious Diseases, I was glad he could not yet read. Phillip had agreed to come with us, and I'd given Max as little explanation about what was happening as I could. At age three, he didn't ask the impossible questions. And Phillip, still able to find some humor, helped keep him amused.

I had arranged to have Max tested my first day back in the United States—July 23—in New York City. It was the same day I was introduced to Hank Murray, the man who soon became my "AIDS doctor."

Dr. Henry Murray is professor of medicine at the Cornell University Medical College, and Chief of Infectious Diseases at the New York Hospital. He's very well known within the scientific AIDS community, and I was grateful he had agreed to see me.

When I told him my story, he shook his head sadly. "I'm so sorry," he told me. "I'm so sorry." He wanted to see Max, who was then approaching the age of four, examine his complexion for any warning signs. Max appeared healthy. "I'll test him," he said. "And I want to run a test on you, too, for my record. You never know—false positives happen." Max had his blood drawn while sitting on his uncle Phillip's lap—and Phillip offered me the same arrangement, which I declined.

Dr. Murray (I think of him now only as "Hank") had assured me there would be no more two-week waits for test results. "That's criminal," he'd said when I described the process I'd gone through.

Once the blood had been drawn, I was left with a familiar terror. We used our time to fly home to Florida. Thirty horrendous hours after Max was tested, and I was retested—during which time I couldn't stop my mind from imagining such horrible things as having to leave instructions to put Max's baseball glove in his coffin when he died after me—Hank called with Max's results: He was negative.

"Say it again, please?"

"Max's test is negative. Max is fine, he's okay. Max is negative."

On July 24, for the first time since Brian had told me he was HIV-positive—three weeks to the day since July 3—I was grateful to God beyond all imagination. I wanted to grab Gregory Hines's hand and dance all night! As it was, I had nothing to say to Max himself; he didn't understand what had been happening, so he had nothing to celebrate. But I had something to say to God: "Thank you, thank you, thank you . . ."

Hank must have also tried to tell me that they were confirming the initial positive result from my own test—but all I could hear was the good news about Max.

". . . thank you, thank you, thank you."

Brian and I had lunch, our last for a very long time, the next day in Boca Raton. Phillip joined us. Brian was sick and in a foul mood. I suspect that he'd been as worried as I was about Max; with that fear behind him, he was back to dealing with himself, with AIDS, with us. He was physically drained, and I was emotionally raw. Once the terror of Max's test had receded, I was beginning to feel other emotions, including anger at Brian. Brian didn't want to hear any of it. "You bought your own ticket" was all he'd say, implying that I should have understood he was at risk. We agreed that we weren't very good for each other under these conditions.

Over the next few days, Brian behaved erratically. He would call, angry; then he would call later, conciliatory and crying. He had a cough so severe it bent him over; it was tuberculosis. He was running a high fever and was constantly nauseated. Mother was having emotional moments over Brian's illness and its impact on her life:

She was going to lose one of her closest friends and her business associate. The Harrison Gallery would have to be closed.

As if their crises weren't enough, my anger was beginning to find targets in all directions: I was furious with Brian, with Mother, with me, with God. I was at the edge of exploding. I called Julie Pettit, my counselor at the Betty Ford Center, who came to Florida to help me deal with anger one more time.

On August 7, Hank Murray called to say he had the results of all the tests we'd run, and that my T-cell count was high—just under what is considered "normal." Based on that count, I'd probably been infected two to four years. We imagined, together, that all the invasive procedures surrounding my pregnancies a few years earlier provided an easy opportunity for transmission.

People with AIDS benchmark their disease by their number of T cells (or T-4 and T-8 cells—"helper" cells in our blood that are critical for our bodies to retain an immune system). Each blood test reports our T-cell count. I remembered women at Gratitude House asking one another, "How are your numbers?" Nobody wondered which numbers they had in mind.

Most healthy people have T-cell counts of, give or take several hundred, 1,000. Then comes HIV (the human immunodeficiency virus). When we test positive for HIV, it means the virus is in our blood, working. Without treatment, on average, an HIV-positive person's numbers (his or her T-cell count) will drop about 100 points each year. With effective treatment, it's possible to delay the progression. If we start at 1,000, that gives us eight to ten years between initial infection and symptoms, perhaps death.

When Brian Campbell was tested for AIDS, his T-cell count was only 45. AIDS, the acquired immunodeficiency syndrome, is the name for the later stage of being HIV-positive. A T-cell count under 200 is one definition of having AIDS, as opposed to merely being HIV-positive. At that level, you're likely to be showing symptoms— usually just the inability to fight off infections, especially some forms of cancer. You become vulnerable, susceptible to things like tuberculosis. If you live long enough, AIDS will eventually reduce your numbers to zero. At that point your body has little surviving immune system. In the end, AIDS doesn't kill you; it just takes away all your defenses and invites pneumonia to kill you, or TB to kill you, or some other grim reaper to do the job.

The main point, however, is clear: If you are HIV-positive, you're on the road to AIDS. And you can't get off that road. You finish it when AIDS finishes you.

It was a point I could not evade when I began a week's vacation with the children in Santa Fe at the end of August. On the way out we stopped in Michigan, where I broke the news to Margie, my youngest sister, and her husband, David. They were stunned and loving. I repeated the conversation with Julie and her husband, Peter, but by telephone, because they were out of town. Dad, Mom, and Phillip were all beginning to sort emotion from strategy. They wanted me to know that whatever I needed to do in the coming months, they would support me in every way they could. It was a loving visit.

Before all the crises erupted, back in May, I had planned the trip to Santa Fe on the recommendation of Rob Eichberg, a Santa Fe psychologist, a champion in the fight against AIDS and author of *Coming Out*, a book that galvanized the gay communities in America.

Rob and I had met years earlier, introduced initially by Bud Nease. We'd formed an easy, instant bond. He encouraged me to come to Santa Fe, describing it as the ideal place to blend art and spirituality. "There's a community there you'll appreciate," he said. "And the kids would have a great time."

Rob welcomed me to Santa Fe and introduced me to wonderful people and ideas. He was a veteran in the AIDS community, and I felt like a hapless and helpless rookie. I was at a loss for words when he described what it was like to scratch so many names from his address book. He finally just threw the book away, a revelation that took my breath away.

Bud Nease and Rob had both encouraged me to spend time with Sally Fisher (no relation), a larger-than-life woman who loves to dress in black, wear huge dangling earrings, and speak candidly. She's been involved in theater, in both New York and Los Angeles, for years and founded the AIDS Mastery Workshops to help those who are HIV-positive and those who have AIDS. She's in her fifties, strong, funny, tough, and loving and gentle. She's a member of AA. And she's held the hands of countless people dying of AIDS. She's seen death often and is determined not to let it cheat her or those she loves out of life.

The children and I were staying at Bishop's Lodge in Santa Fe when Sally called to say she would take me out to lunch at the Santa Cafe. It was a perfect place for a leisurely meal and comfortable conversation, she told me. I went downstairs to meet her. Someone driving a red, Jeep-like vehicle—a Mitsubishi Montero— was honking at me and waving. "Hi, Mary! Over here! It's Sally!"

We talked at lunch as if we'd known each other since childhood. When Sally described something silly she'd done, she would lean back from the table, grab it with both hands, and roar. Everyone around us stopped to look, and I sank a little lower in my chair. When we edged into conversations about people she'd lost, she grew quiet and somber.

After discussing mothers, children, alcoholism, homes, and men, she said, "So, I understand you're from a big Republican family. Tell me what's going on in Washington. Have you spoken to [President] Bush?"

"No," I told her, "not yet, but I've talked to others. And Dad has spoken to both the president and Mrs. Bush." I assured her, sincerely, that everyone in the administration was doing all they could do to fight the epidemic. She raised an eyebrow, and I came back even more forcefully: "Everyone says they're not doing enough, but they say they are doing as much as they can . . ." I said everything I thought was the right thing to say, and I said it at some length. Sally let me roll.

When I finished my defense of the Republicans, the administration, and the bureaucracy in general, it was quiet. She was looking at me. With just the hint of a smile, she rolled her eyes toward the heavens and said, "Oh my God, it's going to be a long afternoon!"

It was. I stopped talking and started listening. Sally could no longer remember all those whose bedsides she'd attended at their deaths. She'd taken the measure of the epidemic, not just globally or nationally, but intimately, personally. She'd lost people she loved intensely. She was the battle-toughened veteran, fully aware of the hardships and discrimination surrounding it, gently but firmly offering her wisdom and experience to me, still a somewhat reluctant and nervous recruit in the war being waged over AIDS. She let me know what the war was really like.

When she finished, I was torn. Part of me wanted to march up the hill alongside her. Another part of me wanted to go home and hide under the covers. I'd never before heard someone explain that responsible officials in the government—people I admired, whose children I knew—didn't care if gay men died by the score, or by the thousand. I'd never heard that women were excluded from AIDS research, or that there was no cure anywhere within sight. She was too convincing to be questioned, too calm to be dismissed as a hysterical activist, too loving and appealing to be ignored. But her words were too critical and her message too contentious for me to accept.

As we prepared to leave, she lowered her voice a little and said, almost tentatively, "I can't tell you how sorry I am for all this in your life. But I also need to tell you that we've been waiting for someone like you to come along." She was neither amused nor triumphant. She was telling the truth, as carefully as she could. "You're not a gay man. You're not a Santa Fe liberal. You're in the All-American Republican Power Family, a sweet blond mom with two nice kids. You're just what we've needed. I may cry about all this later, but for now, let me be the first to welcome you to the AIDS community."

I asked her what she thought I should do. "Nothing," she said. No activism? No letter-writing crusade? No nothing? "All you have to do is just tell your story. That's enough. Go one step at a time. But first, tell your story."

"When you speak out, there'll be a backlash," she warned. "Be prepared for a cold-water wash." She described the prejudice and stigma, both bold and subtle. She spoke of the immorality of hatred and the brutalities perpetrated by people who claimed to represent a moral segment of society. "Be careful," she said, in tones more affectionate than I'd expected.

At the hotel that night, I thought of Dad's instruction to each of us to give back to the community that had raised us. The AIDS movement and people like Sally were for me a new community. And it was not at all clear to me that I had much to offer them. When I thought of "the AIDS community," I still thought of a "them," not an "us." Denial was still having its way with me.

"Tell your story," Sally had said. But I couldn't see why I'd do that, or how it could possibly make a difference to anyone.

CHAPTER 15

"Telling My Story"

Next to telling my family, breaking the news to President and Mrs. Ford was going to be the most difficult. They were still summering in their Colorado home near Beaver Creek when I landed in Santa Fe. There'd be no better time to see them.

When I called, Betty thought it would be "just wonderful" if the boys and I could visit for a day. When I hung up, I had a sense of dread. I worried that Betty, when she heard the news, might distance herself from me. I didn't expect it, but I feared it. It was a fear based in my own sense that this was a shameful disease, something more repugnant than alcoholism or breast cancer. What if she recoiled from AIDS, and so from me?

"Aunt Betty" met us with hugs and kisses. For days I'd been rehearsing how I would tell her and the president, and I hadn't been able to work out a good speech. It always came out something like: "I'm great, thanks, and Mother's wonderful, and I love you, too, and, oh, by the way, I have AIDS."

At first, when I thought of how hard our conversations were going to be, I considered going without the boys. But I wanted Betty and the president to see that the children were fine. They're godparents to the boys and have always treated them as their own grandchildren. This morning, when we arrived, the president headed outdoors to play with Max and Zachary, so I asked Betty if we could talk alone for a few minutes. We went upstairs to a study full of pillows and sunlight.

"What's the matter?" she asked.

"I can't do this," I said, and started to cry. She put her arms around me and listened as I poured out the story of Brian's test, my test, and Max's test. "He's okay," I said. By then we were both in tears. We stood up and hugged for a while, then sat down and hugged some more, struggling to recover our composure.

"Well," she finally began, sounding like a grandmother who'd just finished frosting a cake and was ready to serve it. "Well."

She studied me for a moment, straightened her shoulders, and said, "You'll soon be helping women." She needed to find purpose or mission in this, but having said it, she quickly stood up as if to conclude the conversation. "Well, there'll be time enough for that."

I wanted to talk about "helping women."

"Do you think I should go public with this?" I asked. "I'm not a First Lady—I'm not you." I'd thought earlier about her public courage, first about her breast cancer and later her alcoholism. She'd changed so many lives by being honest about her own. I'd seen what my mother's candor about her drinking had done in the lives of others, including my own, giving them courage to take action as she had.

Betty didn't answer immediately. She looked away. "Yes," she finally said, but less certainly than earlier, "maybe it would help. But we need to take time to think this through, to talk it out." I felt her retreating, until she added, "And if you do, when you do, I'll be there for you, every step of the way.

"We'd better go tell Jerry," Betty added.

"Maybe you should do it?" I asked, desperately wanting to avoid this moment. She said she'd stay with me, but I should be the one to tell the president.

Betty and I had talked for an hour. By the time we came downstairs the president was at his office desk, talking on the telephone, his back to us, looking out the window at the boys playing near the pool. It was bright outside. I remembered seeing this same silhouette in the White House when I'd come into the Oval Office, hearing the same voice, smelling the same aroma of pipe smoke.

When he put down the phone, Betty said, "Jerry, would you come over here and sit with us." I sat on a couch with Betty, her hand constantly patting, rubbing, holding mine. We obviously had been crying. With less emotion than I'd feared, I got the whole story out in a few sentences, ending with ". . . so Max is okay, but I'm HIV-positive." He wanted to know what that meant, exactly. I said,

"AIDS." He was silent a long time, just looking at me. He said he was sorry. He shook his head.

"How's your father?" he asked as he stood up to get his pipe.

"He could use a call from you," I said.

When he walked back toward us, I saw that he was visibly angry. His fists were clenched, his face was red, his hands were shaking when he tried to light his pipe. I was worried. The president famous for never losing his temper in public, for being the calm negotiator of thousands of bills in Congress before coming to the White House, was furious. Finally he said it: "I'm angry, very angry." He was angry with Brian, angry with AIDS, angry with his own helplessness. "I'm not angry with you, dear," he said, "but aren't you angry yourself?"

I said something like, "Anger isn't a very good emotion for me with the boys, right now. They probably got enough of it with the divorce."

"Okay," he said, "I'll be angry for you."

The president's anger actually felt good to me. He'd always reserved his wrath for those who went after his family, or someone else he loved. I felt protected. And the degree of his emotion told me how intensely he cared.

In a while, we joined the boys for lunch outside. I'd grown calmer, soothed by the president, who kept touching my hands, giving me smiles, encouraging me. But even at lunch, when he looked away, I could see him clenching his jaw, shaking his head.

Autumn rolled toward winter. Life began settling into a routine. The boys were too young—two and four—to understand anything scientific or medical, and I was just beginning to learn the intricacies of AIDS myself.

Hank Murray, Sally Fisher, Rob Eichberg, and others were teaching me about the epidemic while opening doors for me into the national AIDS community. They introduced me to Dr. June Osborn, the splendid doctor and astonishing woman who was then chairing the National Commission on AIDS, and to Dr. David Rogers, also on the commission, who offered me the wisdom he'd shown during his service at Cornell University and later as president of the Robert Woods Johnson Foundation. Throughout September and October 1991, I listened and learned.

The more I learned, the more I wanted to do something useful, to make a difference. But although everyone was kind, even generous, next to these people I felt incompetent. I was a full-time mother and part-time artist; these were scientists and authors and policy makers.

The American AIDS community was, in 1991, nearly unanimous in its judgment that Republicans in the White House—first President Reagan, then President Bush—had done more to fan the spread of AIDS than to fight it. Research was too little, too late. Compassion was a scarce commodity. The epidemic was years old, and the casualties had passed 100,000, before President Reagan uttered the word "AIDS" in public.

In an accident of history, the initial round of the AIDS epidemic in America had been largely confined to the gay community. Vice President Dan Quayle and others in the conservative wing of the party were seen as particularly antigay and therefore anticompassion. It was a disease tangled in feelings about sex. Some Republicans spoke of "innocent victims of AIDS"—meaning people who'd not contracted the disease through sexual activities—like Ryan White, the Indiana teen who contracted the virus from a blood transfusion, and Kimberly Bergalis, who at the time was near death after apparently contracting the virus from an infected dentist. If Ryan and Kimberly were "innocent victims," what were the rest of us? Guilty culprits and a menace to all decent Americans? If you agreed with some electronic evangelists, the answer was a resounding yes.

My most persistent question to others in the AIDS community during these months was, "What should I do?" More and more frequently they urged me to try working confidentially, behind the scenes, within the Bush administration. But I struggled, perhaps less with the skills required to make the attempt—I knew how to call the White House—than with the person I was, or am, or could be. I was no AIDS activist, no Sally Fisher or June Osborn. I did not see how I could be, at one and the same time, politically loyal to Dad by being "the good Republican daughter" and an effective member of the American AIDS community with my own integrity.

The idea of going fully public—calling a news conference and saying, "Well, for what it's worth, I have AIDS"—simultaneously attracted and repelled me. It was appealing because I could be "me" again, not feeling as if I were carrying this awful secret.

Maybe my example would show people that *anybody* could get this disease, and that women are especially vulnerable. Maybe I could do or say something that would make my children's world better. But I was not a celebrity or famous person. Who would listen to me, anyway? Really, would *I* have listened to me, before?

Besides, I was frightened of media coverage. I didn't want to be the "socialite with AIDS." My last round of public exposure had been coverage of my custody fight with Brian a year earlier. We'd said horrible things to and about each other; seeing such things in print had left scars not yet healed over.

By mid-November Bob Larson—a friend from Detroit who spends his days making international business deals and contributing advice to, among other causes, the National Urban League—encouraged me to get some professional counsel about publicity, if I decided I should go public. He recommended Jonathan Rinehart, now with Powell Tate but then with the firm of Adams Rinehart in New York City. Bob's idea was appealing because by now I was leaning toward going public. But I was uncertain about how to protect my family—especially Dad, who generally favored my going public—and how to create a record my children could someday read without embarrassment.

Jonathan Rinehart, who provided his services without charge, helped all of us—our family, Bob and other friends, me—think through the issues. We were concerned less with facts than with rumors. "Friends" of Brian had already begun calling me with charges that he had been unfaithful, or that he was gay, or that he was still injecting drugs; what if spiteful rumors got more play than simple facts? For years my father had gotten hate mail in conjunction with his work for Israel; what if my speaking out escalated the hatred against him? If I could do something in public that would help others, especially my sons, I was eager to do it; but concern about fallout—the "cold-water wash" earlier predicted by Sally Fisher—was keen.

Just before Thanksgiving we had a meeting at the Adams Rinehart offices. President and Mrs. Ford were in New York, and I met with them privately first. They'd been talking to my parents and reflected the same concerns I'd been hearing from Detroit. They were reluctant to embrace the idea of my speaking out just yet but promised their support for whatever I did. Betty had said to me earlier, "Just remember that whatever you say in public can never be taken back, as if it were private, again." She repeated this in New York.

The Adams Rinehart meeting brought together their public relations experts and my new friends in the AIDS community. After several hours of discussion, there was consensus on one idea: I should go see Mrs. Bush, alone, without public announcement (Betty Ford's advice) to see if such a meeting would lead anywhere.

The media had plenty of AIDS stories already running. Magic Johnson's stunning announcement and upbeat news conference offered an example of how one could make a difference by avoiding the specter of victimhood. Kimberly Bergalis's tragic final appearance at a senate committee hearing provided quite a different image. When Kimberly died on December 8, I took a vow that whatever else I did, I'd do all in my power to avoid being used as a martyr or a victim for partisan political purposes.

Throughout December the whole matter simmered, but nothing happened. People tried to arrange an appointment with Mrs. Bush, but her schedule and mine did not mesh. I asked Dad, in an emotion-laden conversation following an emotion-laden letter I'd sent him, if he would just get me an appointment with President Bush. He declined. Describing my emotions in my personal journal, just before Christmas, I used the word "suicide." Brian Weiss said, "Mary, you are giving away your own power when you let anyone, even your father, have such sway over you, have such impact on your life."

On January 12, 1992, Mother threw a party in Palm Beach for ex–cabinet member and friend Bob Mosbacher and his wife, Georgette. I was still angry with my father for refusing to call the president for me. He was sitting alone in the den when I brought Bob and Georgette into the room with me to tell them my story. Dad said nothing, but Bob expressed first outrage and then kindness. "I'll do anything to help—what can I do?" asked Bob.

"I have a letter I'd like you to take to the president," I told him. Bob agreed and left carrying my message in his pocket.

Dad had listened to it all quietly. When Bob and Georgette were gone, he got up out of his chair slowly, showing all of his age. He walked over to me, put his arms around me, and said, "I'm proud of you, Mary. I love you." And he walked out.

Two days later Earvin "Magic" Johnson was at the White House for a meeting with the president, who was appointing him to the National Commission on AIDS. Magic told me later that President Bush pointed to his coat pocket, where he'd slipped my letter passed along that morning by Bob Mosbacher, and said to Magic, "I've got a letter here from a friend of mine; it's all just shocking."

By the end of January 1992, a meeting with Mrs. Bush had been arranged, but it was too late. Our earlier plan for a behind-the-scenes strategy was crumbling. Telephone calls were coming into the offices of the National Commission on AIDS about "a prominent woman in Florida" with AIDS, and June Osborn called to warn me. Palm Beach reporters had parts of the story and were looking to complete it; all they needed, really, was my name.

I'd talked to Brian Campbell in December. He'd said that if I decided to go public he wouldn't oppose it, but he wanted me to remember that I was going public with my own story, not his. He didn't want me speaking for him. And he added, "Protect the children."

During the first week of February, June Osborn took what became the persuasive position: Before the report leaks inadvertently, choose how and where you want to tell it. She echoed Sally Fisher's earlier advice: "Tell your story." After months of agonizing and changing my mind, I agreed. I began putting out the word—first to my family, where it received mixed reviews, then to friends and other advisors. The issue was no longer where to go public, but how. No heroism was involved: The story was going to break anyway.

Several people suggested releasing the news through, or with, the White House. I never believed this was an option. A senior White House official I trusted had already said to me, "As long as [Chief of Staff John] Sununu is around here, we're not allowed to use the 'A' word."

June and I finally agreed that she would call Joe Stroud, the long-time editor of the *Detroit Free Press*. She'd see if he wanted to tell the story in my hometown. I liked the idea of going public in Detroit. If we could withstand whatever backlash was going to come from people in my hometown, we could take it from any other source.

Joe Stroud and I spoke by telephone. He was eager to do the story and agreed to embargo it until after I'd met privately with Mrs.

Bush. But he wanted a reporter to complete an interview first, at least by telephone, so that if news leaked from the White House he could release the full story. He suggested "a wonderful young writer" on his staff, Frank Bruni, who would do the story "sensitively." Would I talk to Frank, if he called? When he asked the question, I realized we were no longer discussing; we were deciding. If I said "Okay," I was going public.

I swallowed hard and said, very softly, "I think so."

Frank Bruni spoke with me briefly by telephone to schedule another, longer, telephone interview. But before I could set a time for the extended talk, Frank called to say he'd made reservations to fly from Detroit to Florida. Did I mind? I guessed not.

I was growing less confident that I'd made the right decision. I decided to call a friend I'd first met when she was covering the Ford White House, Diane Sawyer. We'd kept in touch over the years, and I respected her as a woman and a journalist. She wasn't in when I called.

Frank Bruni arrived in Florida fourteen hours after our first conversation. He planned to get the story and fly home in one day. One hour became two, then four, and then it was too late for him to catch a plane home that day. Repeatedly during that day he requested permission to bring in a *Free Press* photographer. I refused, then I budged, and finally I yielded. I drew the line at pictures of the children, although I finally permitted a bedtime shot of Max that didn't show his face.

The interview lasted four days. It was both cathartic and frightening, a marathon therapy session whose notes were going to be published. Even though I'd just met him, and he was a reporter, I liked Frank. He was the first "outsider" in whom I'd confided since the awful discoveries of the previous July. When we finished, he wanted to talk to Brian, to my family in Detroit, to friends. He interviewed them all before he wrote his story.

As long as Frank and the photographer, George Waldman, were in Florida with me, the idea of public exposure seemed tolerable. Once they left, I panicked. I called Joy Prouty and told her I'd just made the biggest mistake of my life. I felt as if Frank had gotten me to give myself to him and then taken everything with him. He was in control now. He would determine my future. He would shape my children's lives.

Frank's calls to family members in Detroit for background interviews shook loose an avalanche of other people's anxiety. Some called me to say I was ruining their lives. Some braced for the worst. Dad was amazingly calm, and Mother said, "It'll all work out; I'm proud of you." Most of us just held our breath.

Two days after Frank left, Joe Stroud called to say the story was long, far too long to be suddenly dropped at the last moment into whatever edition was available. He wanted to schedule it for release, not wait for a still-unscheduled White House visit. I said I'd get back to him and called Henry Baskin, my attorney friend in Detroit. "Sounds like it's going to break somewhere," he said. "Might as well be helpful to Joe and go with it."

Frank Bruni had suggested running the story the following Thursday—"a good day to be in the paper"—February 13, 1992. Henry predicted a Detroit media blitz and thought we might control it somewhat by giving local television stations some advance notice. He called his producer friends in newsrooms around Detroit and said, "There'll be a story late Wednesday"—the *Free Press* is a morning paper, printed late in the evening—"you may want to be ready for remotes from Florida on Thursday."

Throughout Wednesday, February 12, I took calls from Frank, who was checking last-minute details. With each call my anxiety mounted. Diane Sawyer, who had returned my earlier call and wound up deciding to put the story on ABC's "Prime Time Live," thought that if the story was breaking in Detroit on Thursday morning, she should do a network feature that night. I said, "Sure." Her "Prime Time Live" crew would arrive at 5:30 the next morning. I called Elizabeth Glaser, and we talked, mother-to-mother, about what it would mean to the children when the world knew their mother had AIDS. She agreed that it wouldn't mean much until they were older, and then it might mean everything. By late afternoon, I was as terrified of going public as I had been of being HIV-positive. Forces were now in motion over which I had not an ounce of control.

Frank knew I was terrified and promised to fax me a copy of the paper as it came off the presses, around eleven o'clock. I put the children to bed at their usual times; they were oblivious to everything going on, and I both rejoiced at and envied their oblivion. Joy

Prouty came to spend the night with me. I told her the story of waiting, years earlier, for the *New York Times*'s review of *Just So* and the shock of having their critic pan us. The memory raised my anxieties another notch.

I was already in tears, caused by nothing but stress, when Henry Baskin called to say, "All the [television] stations are opening their eleven o'clock news with live coverage of papers rolling off the press." Channel 7, my old employer, was running a "tease" for its late news by hinting at the story without my name attached.

At 10:46 P.M. Wednesday, the bell on my home office fax machine signaled an incoming call. The front page of the next morning's *Free Press* was rolling in. As I reached for the paper curling out of the fax, I felt sharp pains in my chest. "I'm having a heart attack," I thought as I unfurled the curling paper to read.

Frank Bruni had done precisely what he'd promised. He'd told my story, and told it better than I could have. It was neither exaggerated nor sensationalized; it was straightforward, gentle, beautifully written. There was more "socialite" than I wanted, but less than I'd feared. Only later, when I saw the photographs and headlines, did I realize that it was the lead front-page story under the heading COMING OUT AGAINST AIDS: WEALTH, POWER AND LOVE DIDN'T BLOCK THE VIRUS. In addition to the long feature, Frank had filed a sidebar featuring an interview with my mother and longtime family friend Kathy Ford, Henry Ford's widow.

"I want to help people get rid of the fear," Frank quoted me as saying. That was true to my experience. He had conveyed the critical message: "It doesn't matter how you got it. It can happen to anyone."

Those two messages were all I had. That was my story, now spread over pages of newsprint in my hometown. In a note of some irony, a headline story that day in the *Palm Beach Post*—without reference to me—read: HETEROSEXUAL AIDS ON THE RISE.

Henry Baskin called again to say, "It's unbelievable up here." In Detroit, many of the reporters breaking the story to television audiences were friends, people with whom I'd worked, people whose work I'd once produced. I was their first AIDS story that wasn't about some distant or anonymous person. For them, this was "our Mary." Their pain showed when they read the news.

I'd always imagined that the story would be big for me, for my life, but not for the media itself. I'd thought this might be a story tucked somewhere in the lifestyle section of the news. Part of what made it worthy of headlines was our collective ignorance at that time. Everyone, including my hometown media, believed this was a "gay disease," "someone else's disease." When AIDS found one of their own, a married woman with kids, they gave it a headline in their papers and lead-story position in their newscasts. At some point in the evening—I truly don't remember exactly when; perhaps when I realized what "big news" it was—I had a distinctly unheroic thought: I wished it were someone else's story.

Joy got no more sleep than I did that night, maybe an hour. We were still talking when the phones stopped ringing sometime after three; we were up by five, making coffee, waiting for Diane Sawyer's crew to show up. While coffee was brewing, I remember going softly first into Max's room, and then into Zack's, just to look at them, to know they were well.

Thursday brought more of the same: telephone calls from press and radio reporters, television crews showing up in the neighborhood to do interviews and shoot footage. The "Prime Time" shoot was first, and there were no surprises; I said on national television what Frank Bruni had reported to his Detroit readers. By the time I put the boys in bed that evening, I was nearing physical collapse. I went to bed too exhausted to feel either elation or depression. I felt nothing.

Friday morning I called Brian Campbell. I'd been thinking of him since reading Frank Bruni's story two days earlier. With his health uncertain and the gallery closed, he had moved to Boston two months earlier. "I've got reporters all over the place here," he complained. "They're camping out in the lobby of my apartment building." He wasn't accusing, but he didn't like it.

"You shouldn't be there alone," I said. "Come down and spend the weekend with us. Be here with us. It's where you belong—with me and the boys." I was surprised when he agreed.

I hung up and realized that the house was still. The children were outside. No phones were ringing. The fax was quiet. No one was at the door demanding an interview.

In the end, friends and advisors had been nearly unanimous, all urging me to tell my story in public. So I'd told it. Now what? I'd gone public and evoked a one-day, mainly regional media blitz. I'd told my story, and now it was over. I was yesterday's news; today, they were concerned about weather in the Midwest, tensions in the Middle East, and whether Kentucky could win another NCAA basketball title. The stir over my story had settled down quickly.

In the quiet, I began to cry uncontrollably. I was tired, and tired of crying, and here I was, crying again. I cried until I could cry no longer.

Seven months earlier I'd heard the diagnosis as if it were an immediate death sentence; indeed, I thought then that I was already near death. It was the "if you have AIDS, you die" conviction. What I began learning this Friday morning—and it did not feel like a significant improvement—added a new twist: If you have AIDS, you live with it. And then you die.

CHAPTER 16

"Sleep with the Angels"

One of the most thoughtful and caring people I've ever known is Stuart E. White, a classmate known as "Stooey" at Kingswood/Cranbrook in the sixties. He went on to become an exemplary public high school teacher in Ann Arbor, Michigan, where he and his wife watched Detroit newscasts on Wednesday night, February 12.

The next morning he wrote me a letter, reminding me that once upon a time we had known another world, before "drug addiction or divorce or children at risk or a disease like AIDS." He remembered a dance scene we'd done together—"a few passes on a darkened stage," he wrote, "[in] a high school production of *Annie Get Your Gun* in a steamy Cranbrook gym on a winter night when George Romney was governor and Vietnam was unknown." He was loving and wise and told me not to pay attention to those "who will be cruel beyond imagination."

Behind Stu's letter came others. Cram (Judy Sherman) offered unconditional love and whatever else I needed. Friends with whom I'd gone to school or worked wrote, faxed, and called by the score; they were sorry, or they were proud of what I'd said, or they would pray for me.

On February 20, a week after the news first broke in Detroit, Diane Sawyer's "Prime Time Live" segment aired nationally, bringing the news to friends from White House days and elsewhere. Hank Murray, my doctor, who'd been reluctant to see me go public, called to congratulate me, and to remind me to get enough sleep.

I'd feared storms of stigma and criticism, perhaps aimed at me, probably aimed at my father or other members of the family. There were a few passing showers, but no terrible gales. The majority of calls came from reporters. Most people who wrote were friendly, some admiring, a few very moving. But in reading the mail, in scanning letters to the editor, in hearing discussions about me on radio or television, I began to understand, really for the first time, why someone had coined the term "public personality." At first I'd wanted to answer each call or letter with a personal note. But then I discovered that these weren't really about me, the Mary Fisher who's a mom, an artist, Joy's and Cram's friend. People were trying to reach Mary Fisher Stereotype, Mary Fisher As We See Her, Mary Fisher Public Personality. I'd never experienced that before.

All this came clear the day I received an offer from a manufacturer to have a special line of condoms produced under my name, a "signature original." I didn't know whether to laugh or be offended. Others had no such problem—my brother Phillip kept calling and asking if I could arrange to have a line named after him.

Equally misguided was the woman caller to a Florida radio station who announced that I'd contracted HIV from Magic Johnson. Her evidence: We had both lived in Michigan. I'd wanted to go public to make a difference in some way. One of the differences, I now discovered, was that I had become fair game: I was a "public personality" in the "public domain."

Brian Campbell stayed in Florida with us for a week. Most of the time was good: good for us to be able to talk, good for the children to see him healthier than he'd been the previous year. We did some art together. By this time, we were both realizing that his illness had contributed in many subtle ways to our divorce. He had been not merely moody, or indifferent, or listless, or uninterested in me; he had been worn down by infections, by the tiredness that refuses sleep, by a virus neither of us knew he had. Nights when I was up caring for the children and he was sitting in a dark room playing Nintendo, I had fumed; in fact, he'd been sick and sleepless, caving in to the silent virus rampaging inside him, trying to fill the hours with some mindless distraction.

After Brian left to go back to Boston, the "going public" chapter of my life felt as if it were over. I needed a future. Brian Weiss, with whom I was meeting weekly, kept pointing me to "the big picture." He was convinced that my purpose would be found outside myself, in world affairs, beyond our interest in things like Don Black's musical based on Weiss's book. I was eager to be, as Mother Teresa once said, "a pencil in the hand of God." But it all seemed so vague, so spiritually ethereal, so out-there-somewhere. I didn't know what to do. I might have been one of God's pencils, but I had no idea what to write. If cosmic insight was being revealed to me in Brian's office, I wasn't getting it; lofty ambitions were buried the moment I walked into my house, where mail needed opening and two boys needed lunch, artwork was half finished and Mother had called. Divine truth got buried under daily obligations and the routine rhythm of life.

But a subtle shift was occurring within me. I was focusing less on dying from AIDS and gradually, imperceptibly, learning to live with the virus. What had been, since the previous July, a sustained and dramatic crisis was slowly evolving into a pervasive concern. I had fewer crying jags and more long, hard thoughts.

At first I grieved that I might have to leave my children before they were grown; now I began focusing not only on my leaving Max and Zachary, but also on the world in which they would be left. I'd gone public with my eye on news accounts of AIDS families whose homes were burned down by concerned neighbors. I felt safe in our home, our neighborhood, but I feared the distant danger—the people not like my friends and neighbors. What would they say, what would they do, to my children?

I felt muddled, confused, aimless, glad to be out of the closet about AIDS but unsure I had anything more to say. I didn't think of myself as "in transition"; I thought I was just getting by. I had no idea that I might be getting ready.

It may have been March—the month after I went public—when I learned that Max had been the only child in his class in a wonderful school who'd not been allowed to have a stuffed animal "visit overnight" at home. I assumed Max had misunderstood, because I was naive. But Max had it right. Someone feared that the fuzzy bear or cuddly kitty or whatever it was would come back to school bearing the AIDS virus.

Although it meant the world to Max, this was not an earthshaking moment; it made no evening news. But it was life-changing in this respect: For the first time my children's lives had been injured by the ignorance and fear that surrounds AIDS. Suddenly I saw us as different—other family names on Max's class roster, and ours; regular rules for the other children, special rules for Max.

No one intended any harm. These were not bad people. They meant only to protect their children, just as I wanted to protect mine. But when Max could not bring home a stuffed toy because people feared his mother's virus, I "got" it: Good people are capable of doing bad things.

I was not raised in the Jewish ghetto of Warsaw; I'd only heard stories of the camps. No one in Papaharry's tradition had been sold at auction or whipped raw along the edge of a cotton field. This was my first experience in the school of stigma, teaching me firsthand that quiet prejudice grows out of common fear, that whispered ignorance leads to blatant discrimination. Now I see that the fire hoses and growling dogs are hauled out only when prejudice has grown into public policy, and someone decides to fight back.

If I'd encountered sex discrimination in both my television and White House experiences, I hadn't understood it clearly enough to fight back effectively. Besides, Mary was a pleaser, not a fighter. But now Mary was a mother. You attack Max or threaten Zachary and, so help me God, I will fight.

I'd never heard of Jim Heynen and he'd never heard of me.

June Osborn had invited me to attend a National Commission on AIDS meeting in Boston early in March. It would be a good place to meet others, including Magic Johnson, who'd just been appointed by President Bush to fill one of the two "White House slots" on the congressionally mandated commission.

The day the commission opened its business, focusing on housing facilities for people with AIDS, I visited Boston's Mission Hill Hospice. I'd never been in a hospice before. The joy of the place caught me off guard; the emphasis on life. But so did the AIDS.

Here was the place Boston families spent their final months, or weeks, or hours with loved ones who had AIDS. In one room I saw snapshots of a handsome, athletic, thirty-five-year-old man on the bedside table next to a semiconscious, emaciated, skeletal, thirty-seven-year-old man. The pictures and the bed had the same person in them.

This was not *my* AIDS. This was not newspaper headlines in Detroit evoking warm letters from old friends, or last week's interview on NBC's "Today Show" after which Katie Couric and I swapped

pictures of our healthy children. This was not show business AIDS, celebrity AIDS. This was dying with AIDS, and dying hard. I took a long, deep breath there, and then a long, hard look down the road to AIDS.

The next morning I was introduced to the other extreme of AIDS: charming, handsome, smiling Magic Johnson. I thanked him for his November news conference that had shown me someone could go public with great dignity. And I told him not to stand up while we talked; as long as he remained seated, and I stood, we were eye to eye. I liked that a lot.

Magic and I talked about doing some events together in Michigan—maybe an "editorial board luncheon" like I used to arrange for President Ford, maybe one huge event with all Detroit school-children. I said I'd make the arrangements, and Magic agreed to participate.

This felt just right. I was back in my element again. I could organize and plan, and get back into my White House Advance Office mode to create an event. All I needed was a "key contact," someone on the ground in Michigan to make it all happen.

A. James ("Jim") Heynen, president of the Greystone Group, Inc., a consulting firm headquartered in Grand Rapids, Michigan, had assumed management of the Michigan AIDS Fund, a philanthropy supported by the Council of Michigan Foundations, a year earlier, the same month I learned I was HIV-positive. Paula Van Ness, then head of the National Community AIDS Partnership, based in Washington, D.C., admired what he had accomplished in less than a year and gave me his name. I made calls, and everyone agreed: Heynen was the person I needed.

So I called him. He wouldn't come to the phone—too busy. Greystone was in the final stage of a major project for the State of Michigan that had become tangled in party politics. He was dealing with media and had no time for me. Could I call later? I asked. He wouldn't have time then either. Could he talk to me for just three minutes? Sorry, not now. He'd call when he had time.

I was learning the difference between calling for the president and calling for myself. I used to say, "This is Mary Fisher from the White House," and everyone I called had time to talk to me. Times had changed. Now I couldn't get through to a consultant in Grand Rapids, Michigan.

Jim finally returned my calls early one morning. Betty Ford had
arrived late the night before to spend a few days. Max was throwing
a cereal box at Zachary when the phone rang; "Aunt Betty" was
wandering about my kitchen hoping for coffee; I'd overslept after
spending half the night writing in my journal. I was standing,
dazed, in my kitchen. I told him, with just a tinge of pleasure,
"Sorry, I can't talk right now." We scheduled a telephone appointment for the weekend, when I'd be in New York City at my parents'
apartment.

When we finally spoke, I immediately knew Jim was unusual. He
asked hard, pointed questions without a hint of intrusion or judgment; he wanted to know me, what I was looking for, what I
wanted, and why. He listened more closely, more carefully, than
anyone I'd ever talked to before. He was both funny and serious,
sometimes at the same time. And it wasn't as if he were the inter-
rogator and I were the subject. He was as open as he wanted me to
be. When I tried to explain about Brian and me and our divorce and
my children and my anger, he said, "Yes, I understand—I'm going
through a divorce myself. I get tired of crying, don't you?"

I'd sent him a copy of the *Detroit Free Press* coverage. He
thought it was nice, but "when you talk about making a difference,
what kind of difference do you have in mind?" I didn't know. I tried
to explain about Brian Weiss, about Betty Ford, about helping people, about maybe having events with Magic, about telling my story.
But it was clear to both of us I didn't know. And Magic Johnson had
no time to visit Michigan.

Jim asked if I'd be interested in becoming a member of the board
for the Michigan AIDS Fund. I said, "Not really, I'm trying to find
my own direction, not just join everything else." He proposed a
swap: "I'll contribute a day or two working with you, wherever you
want, to help you get a clearer focus on what you want to do. I'll
donate my time to you if you'll donate your name to the board." It
was a deal.

On April 1, 1992, Jim came to Florida, and we met for the first
time. He arrived minutes before I got home from a luncheon at the
Breakers Hotel where I'd been scheduled to "make a few remarks."
I'd expected a few dozen people spread around a few tables, but a
thousand women and the mayor of Palm Beach showed up. I stood
up and talked for a few minutes about what I knew: My story.

My children. My line: "If Mary Fisher can get AIDS, so can you."

Over the next two days, Jim and I worked. He asked, I answered. When things got hard and I began to cry, he offered a hug or a tissue. He told a joke and made me laugh. By the first evening, I was confessing my feelings of inadequacy, my fear that if I spoke out I was going to disappoint my children and fail my family, and that if I didn't speak out I'd disappoint myself. He said, "That's understandable. It might be good to let them know." When I talked about my sense that I was no longer a woman, no longer appealing to men, no longer eligible for romance, he said, "That's both what society is telling you, and what you're willing to believe; you're both wrong." I talked late into the night about my fear of losing control, of dying. He told me about his teenage years caring for a father who suffered slow-growing brain lesions; about the morning his father, barely lucid, began calling Jim, then seventeen, "Dad." Jim spoke about God not as a distant concept or an impersonal "it," but as an ever-present source of comfort and help. He used the word "grace" a lot.

Jim kept coming back to my "message"—what was it that I was trying to say, trying to communicate, trying to help others understand? When I told him the story of my comments at the Breakers, he said, "Maybe that's the right strategy for you. Maybe you could speak to communities."

I thought he'd misunderstood. The luncheon at the Breakers was a surprise, not a strategy. If I'd known they expected a speech, I would have been unable to give it. I explained, again, that I was a producer, not a performer, a behind-the-scenes organizer, not an on-camera actress or anchorwoman. Betty Ford is a speaker, but she's a former First Lady. My dad is a speaker, but he's accomplished a lot to speak about. But what had I accomplished that would make me an expert?—even in the field of AIDS, I knew a fraction of what others knew. Mary Fisher, I explained, is a mom, an artist—but not, definitely not, a speaker.

I had an "urgent" message to call Georgette Mosbacher. She was chairing an April 13 dinner gala for AmFAR, the American Foundation for AIDS Research. AmFAR had decided they would like to present me with their Award of Courage. They hoped I'd give a lit-

tle speech at the dinner, in New York City. I'd be introduced by
Elizabeth Taylor. And "of course, there'll be lots of media."

The Award of Courage was obviously a fundraising device, since
I hadn't done anything courageous. But it didn't matter; it was a
good cause, and I'd be happy to help. What concerned me was the
speech. When Mother heard that I was being honored, she bought
two tables so my family and friends would be present. All I could
think of was, "I'm HIV-positive and proud to be here. Thank you
all very much." It would be a reach to stretch that into even ten seconds of eloquence.

I called Jim. He asked questions, and I stumbled over answers.
"It's okay," he'd encourage me. "We can find a way to say that; you
can tell the truth about that in public." He seemed absolutely convinced that if I would be vulnerable and honest, I could be powerful. He was so convinced that he was beginning to persuade me.

The Saturday morning before the AmFAR event, Jim faxed me
an outline of notes and a few paragraphs of copy. I showed what I
had to Brian Weiss, who was elated. "Say it," he said. "Say it just
that way." Sunday I traveled to New York. Monday was the event.

I woke up Monday morning in a panic. I'd tried to memorize the
notes and couldn't remember a thing. Nothing. No opening line, no
ideas, nothing. I called Jim. "It's fine," he said, in that same reassuring voice I'd grown to trust. "Trust the copy; it'll all be fine."

My journal for that Monday is a packed jumble of disconnected
moments, a good if jarring record of what seemed like an out-of-
body experience:

> I'm having a surreal day. . . . Call from the White House, Secre-
> tary Skinner. "President Bush sends his congratulations . . .
> wants to see you soon . . . will set up appointment tomorrow."
> They have a TelePrompTer. This might save me. Getting
> dressed . . . wash my hair . . . flower from Jim arrives . . . Dad's
> late . . . I'm not nervous, I'm hysterical. Okay, we're off . . . 61st
> Street entrance . . . stairway up . . . it's a wall of press, photog-
> raphers . . . I hear them, "She's the honoree" . . . flashbulbs . . .
> "Over here Miss Fisher" . . . I'm all alone, what do I do now?
> keep walking . . . will I take questions from the press? okay . . .
> bank of microphones, never been on this side before . . . the BBC
> reporter wants to know what? "Do I like diamonds?!?!?!"

Dinner was a respite. I sat between Mike Nichols and my friend Kathy Durham. Dad was across the table talking to Diane Sawyer. David Rogers was on one side, Hank Murray on the other, and Mother was urging me to "eat something, dear."

Someone came to get me for a photo with Elizabeth Taylor. By now I was doing whatever I was told, turning obediently in response to directions from photographers, shaking extended hands, smiling. I was thinking about Max, hoping someone had remembered to give him his cold medicine. Now everyone was sitting down again. Georgette Mosbacher was talking about "the Mary Fisher I know."

> Georgette's starting to cry—oh, boy . . . this is it. I'm on. Jim said, "Think bold, be brave, enjoy it." Cameras flashing. Georgette gives me a hug . . . here I go . . . it's noisy out there . . . can't see anyone's faces . . . script rolling over the TelePrompTer . . . it's quiet now . . . what's happening, can't they hear me? Keep going. Can't make eye contact in the lights, can't see Phillip . . . my hands are shaking . . . almost done . . . it's over. It's quiet. No, they're standing up. Where are they all going? Oh, my God, it's a standing ovation. . . .

In the days between the time Jim sent me copy and I stepped up to the podium to speak, I'd changed and rearranged nearly everything he'd written. I had kept one of his early lines ("The numbers are staggering when you take them one at a time, which is precisely how AIDS takes us") and I'd trusted him with this: "My father now knows more about AIDS than I ever wanted him to. He knows, because of me, and he understands that the world is not yet accepting. Where there is stigma, Daddy, you will bear it with me. I wish I could spare you, but I can't."

April 1992 was the turning point. Jim had become a collaborator, a partner, someone I could trust with my soul—and I did. When I talked to him, he knew how to put my thoughts into words that faithfully represented me and spoke powerfully to others. Whether it was a strategic plan aimed at the White House or a thoughtful talk that needed to be given at an AIDS event, I would trust him with my ideas, and he would send me copy that spoke my heart and mind.

The first speech we did entirely together was called "A Letter to My Children." I told him what I hoped for, gave him notes and letters I'd drafted for Max and Zachary, and he wrote the full text as I would deliver it at a luncheon for Mothers' Voices, a national AIDS organization, on May 4. When I first read that speech, composed as if I were writing directly to my children, I told Joy Prouty, "This is more me than me." And the ending of that speech gave us the title for our first book of speeches and photographs two years later—*Sleep with the Angels:*

If I have not told you so before, let me say it to you plainly now. Max and Zack, I not only love you wildly, I need you. I need my family. I need you and everyone else more now than I ever have before. And sometimes when I look too far into the future, I realize how much I will need you then.

But when fear becomes a poison, threatening to rob us of the joy we had rolling on the floor, tickling each other and laughing today, the antidote is us, our family. So long as we have family—you and I—all of us will go on.

Tonight when I tucked each of you into bed, I said to you what you've heard me say every night of your lives. Since the moment you came from my body, Max, and the hour you were placed in my arms, Zachary, I have known that I would, one day, need to give you up.

And so, each night, I rehearse for the day when I must give you over. That is why, as I reach for the day's last kiss and hug, you always hear me say the same four words: "Sleep with the angels. . . ." Love, Mom

The reaction to this speech was electric. We received everything from requests to publish it in national magazines to—more meaningful to me, by far—requests from other AIDS-infected mothers for a copy.

I was beginning to see that I didn't need to stop being a mother, or stop being an artist, to be an effective voice in and for the AIDS community. "Be who you are," Jim urged me, over and over. "That's your power. If you simply tell the truth about your experience, unafraid of what others think, you can make an enormous impact."

I felt that power during and after "A Letter to My Children." All that I'd done was tell the truth, in public. And it had made a difference. I'd found an encouraging ally, and with him, I'd found my own voice and the courage to use it.

Nineteen ninety-two was a political year. By May we could see that the Democratic presidential candidate would be Governor Bill Clinton of Arkansas, and that he would be running against President Bush. Oklahoma senator Don Nickles was organizing the platform hearings for the Republican party when we met in early May. He was cordial, even kind, when we agreed that I would give testimony at the Salt Lake City hearings later in the month. I was surprised when, months later, as he spoke on the senate floor and I listened from the gallery, I heard him comparing HIV-infected immigrants with infected fruit, neither of which, he believed, should be allowed to enter at American borders.

I went to Salt Lake City alone, which was a mistake; I should have had Jim or someone else with me. I felt terribly alone, not just in the pristine city but especially in the platform hearings. I was the only one wearing a red AIDS awareness ribbon; I suspected I was the only one who knew what it meant. I felt as if I'd been invited to speak more as a courtesy to my father's position—he was by then the honorary chair of the finance committee to reelect Bush and Quayle—than as a representative of a million people with AIDS. I felt like a token; I remembered Henry Baskin's warning to me, in writing, at the close of February: "Don't let yourself get used."

It began on an unfortunate note: I was introduced as "an AIDS victim." That was bad. Worse, C-SPAN flashed the words "AIDS Victim" on television screens across America as I spoke. But Jim had written a speech in which I implored the Republican party to "lift our shroud of silence, speak boldly in a voice of compassion, and do justice to the tradition which brought us all here today."

My Salt Lake City speech captured enough media attention to be quoted frequently by both campaigns. When the Democrats announced that Bob Hattoy and Elizabeth Glaser would address their New York City convention in July, during prime-time broadcasting, reporters, especially those who saw AIDS as an increasingly critical political issue, kept asking the Republicans about plans for Houston. Would anyone speak on AIDS? Was Mary Fisher going to be invited?

My first conversations with both Mrs. and President Bush stayed off the record. I thought publicity would only raise defensiveness on the part of the administration. During a July visit, on my way to Amsterdam for the International Conference on AIDS, I'd asked the president to begin speaking out on the issue, to show others that it was safe to talk about AIDS, that there should be no stigma attached to it. He said he'd do his best, and he arranged time with his speechwriters. On July 7, Jim and I spent an hour with the president's (and vice president's) speechwriters. It was largely a courtesy on their part and a waste of time on ours; we were mutually unimpressed.

While I was at the White House, the children were headed for Provincetown, outside Boston, where Brian was now living. I was going to be gone until after I spoke at the Amsterdam conference, and Brian wanted time alone with the boys. It was another difficult time, with Brian becoming violently ill and Max watching his father, among other things, vomiting blood. Jim finally told the children's nanny to take them to a hotel, which she did. When I got back home, I was more traumatized by the children's reports than they had probably been by the events themselves. I was angry at Brian for not sparing them this, and I didn't understand yet that he didn't want me to know the depth of his own illness. He was afraid that if I knew how sick he really was, I wouldn't let him have time alone with the children.

My speech in Amsterdam had been picked up on international wires and was being replayed in New York and Washington, further begging the "will-she-or-won't-she" question about whether I'd be invited to speak at the Republican convention. The day I returned—July 21—Chris Payne, a reporter for the *Houston Chronicle*, ran a story putting the question in public. I hadn't been invited, and he wanted to know if I would be. When that story hit the national wires, others picked it up. The *Washington Post* started calling the Republican convention planners; *USA Today* arranged to do a feature story.

On July 30, 1992, *USA Today* ran a story by national correspondent Patricia Edmonds, along with a large photo of me. *People* magazine was also planning a feature. Which of them called the

White House to ask whether I was speaking, I don't know. Maybe both. But word leaked out to the media that the president hoped I would speak. What the president hoped, the planners implemented. Before I had any official word, reporters were telling me that I'd been invited to address the 1992 Republican National Convention in Houston.

I was happy to get the invitation. I wanted to make an impact on the convention and the party, of course. But more than that, I wanted to deliver a message that would be heard beyond the artificial environment of the Houston Astrodome. I was beginning to believe that I had something important to say to all of America.

I said to Jim, "Do you think we can write something they'd listen to, something they'd hear?"

CHAPTER 17

"Walking a Fine, Tricky Line"

$\mathbb{N}$ational political conventions are impossible events. But like democracy itself, no one has yet devised a better way. At both the 1976 Republican convention in Kansas City and the Detroit convention in 1980, I'd been assigned jobs caring for "VIPs" (very important people). The problem, of course, was that everyone in the arena—thousands of them—believed they qualified as VIPs.

Republicans across America elect mayors and judges, city commissioners and township supervisors, representatives and governors, United States senators and municipal dogcatchers. Most of them think they have something important to contribute to their party's national debate, resulting in thousands of people vying for the opportunity to plug themselves, or their causes, or their candidates, at the national convention.

Jim and I had discussed the value of the convention in Houston not because of politics, but because of the extraordinary venue: Unlike any other setting—and even if no one would listen at the convention—if I could speak in prime time, we could deliver a message to the nation.

We never knew who it was who finally said, "Invite her." Bob Mosbacher was a supporter; so were others with whom I'd worked in the Ford administration—pollsters Bob Teeter and Mary Lukens, for example, who were doing polls for the Bush campaign.

Patty Presock, President Bush's administrative aide, was an old friend who may have played the most critical role in the decision-making process. Some years later she confided that she'd told the convention planners that President Bush wanted me to speak, that it was personally important to him. I didn't know that in August of 1992. All I knew then was that whenever I'd ask for Patty's counsel, personally or professionally, she'd always conclude it with, "Just do the right thing, Mary—don't worry about what others say."

I took the telephone call behind the bar, in the kitchen area, at the Madison Hotel in Washington, D.C. I'd been given advance notice by the White House that the person scheduling convention speakers "wanted to talk to me," so I'd left word at the switchboard where I could be found when I left my room to have late-afternoon tea with friends.

When I got to the telephone, I was surprised to hear a familiar voice: "Mary, it's Red Cavaney." My old boss from the White House Advance Office, "So Sue Me" Red, was vetting potential convention speakers. We hadn't spoken in years, and he was chatty. Before the call ended, I'd grown irritated with what felt like insensitivity. I explained to Red that contrary to what he seemed to believe, I wasn't the only HIV-positive Republican. "The rest," I said, "are just bullied into silence."

The majority of people who appear at the podium of a national convention are given either two minutes (usually an "introduction"), three minutes ("comments"), or five minutes ("remarks"). Anything over five minutes in length is a "speech," and not many speeches are actually given. So length of time at the podium is the first measure of a person's clout; the second is time of day for the appearance, with prime-time evening television coverage offering the most coveted slots.

Once the White House said that I'd speak, and the story ran nationwide, Red Cavaney could no longer threaten to drop me from the list. All we argued about after that was when I'd speak, not whether. I was surprised at how quickly he agreed to an evening: Wednesday, August 19, "Family Night" in the convention program, the night President Bush would be renominated and my brother, Phillip, would celebrate his birthday. I wanted prime TV, between 10:00 and 11:00 P.M., when all the networks would be broadcasting live. No deal. They'd book me right after nine o'clock. "That's prime time to me," said Red. I was going to speak in the same time slot as, among others, Marilyn Quayle and Pat Robertson. "Prime time," he repeated. I said okay. Two telephone calls (and a day or two) later, as the evening's program was being refined, Red announced: "You've got five minutes."

"That's not enough, Red." He rattled off a list of dignitaries who had received two-minute slots and named governors who'd settled for three. He needed to take another call and said he'd get back to me. I called Jim. He thought about it briefly, then said, "I doubt I can do what you want done in three hundred seconds or less." We needed more podium time—more words, more feeling. I called Bob Mosbacher, who said he'd see what he could do. I called my father, who said, "Don't be greedy."

Red called back to confirm that I had five minutes, no more. "I can't do it, Red—Bob Hattoy and Elizabeth Glaser had twenty-five minutes between them." He was unmoved but offered me the services of the lead speechwriter for the convention, Clark Judge. I told Red I needed time, not a speechwriter. Then I played my last card: "I'd rather not speak than make a fool of myself, or not do justice to the issue and deliver an incoherent message. Maybe we shouldn't do it at all." There was a long, distressing silence. "I'll get back to you," he said.

A day or two later Red called. "Look," he said, "I'm going to let you have ten minutes for your speech, but it's going to say five minutes on the published program so I don't get grief from the other speakers. Okay?"

"Okay." I breathed a sigh of relief and rolled on. "But who's going to introduce me?" We took turns ruling out each other's offers and counteroffers. I, still the television producer, finally proposed that I be introduced by a videotape shown on the arena screen. By this time I had plenty of video clips from network programs and a television special that had been done by a Detroit station, WDIV (entitled—and organized around my speech of the same name— "Letter to My Children"). A good video could let people know who I was before I spoke, so my remarks might make sense to them. Red said he'd consider it once we got to Houston, if my speech was short enough to leave time within my ten-minute slot.

As it finally turned out, I wound up producing my own video introduction once we were in Houston, with Phillip's help and a script from Jim. It was twenty-four hours before I spoke that Cavaney gave his final approval.

●   ●   ●

Thursday, August 13, Boca Raton, Florida. Jeffrey Schmalz, the *New York Times* reporter, was interviewing me in my living room while Jim sat upstairs, fielding calls from the White House, lining up other media interviews, and trying to outline the convention speech. We'd talked through the general content of my remarks, and he was trying to turn a tangled conversation into logical ideas.

We'd been told that a draft of my speech was due in Houston the next morning "for retyping on disks for TelePrompTers." We believed that rationale could be translated, "for review of content and appropriate editing," so we'd decided we would send it late, leaving as little time as possible for fights over copy.

I was nervous about Jeffrey's interview. He was a tough political reporter and editor covering the AIDS beat and other issues for the most influential newspaper in America. Rumors about my convention appearance had been flying in and out of print for almost two weeks. Some people in the AIDS community were incensed that someone would speak at a convention of "the enemy." They detested the Bush administration almost as intensely as they had hated the Reagan White House. They had cheered loudest in New York, at the Democratic convention, when Elizabeth Glaser looked into the television camera and laid blame for the death of her child not on the virus but on the president. They didn't know what I was going to say, but it couldn't possibly be helpful; any HIV-positive person appearing on the Houston stage would send the wrong message. Against this backdrop, Jeffrey had flown to Florida to ask what I was going to say.

During the same two weeks, we'd heard consistent reports that convention organizers were wary of me. They feared that I'd been "reasonable" in Salt Lake City, during platform testimony, only to earn a berth in Houston where, in front of God, country, and some fifty million–plus viewers, I could reveal my true colors and upset the Republican applecart in the name of AIDS. ACT UP had already announced plans to picket Houston's Astrodome. Coffins were being shipped to Texas so they could be carried on marchers' shoulders while the president's car drove by. They were anxious to have a look at my speech.

We couldn't show them a speech because we didn't have one. With me tied up in an interview with Jeffrey and someone needing to field other calls, we decided to worry about the speech later that night, when Jim could go back to his hotel room and have some quiet time to think.

Jeffrey's interview was long and, as I'd expected, tough. He had reported on AIDS since before it had a name. It was the *New York Times*, his paper, that broke the story in July 1981, reporting four cases of a strange new "gay cancer" that had been detected in New York. He knew everyone in the AIDS community, had heard all the concerns about my upcoming speech, and was offering me a chance to set the record straight before the convention.

When Jeffrey's story appeared on Sunday, August 16, two days before I was scheduled to speak, it seemed to me a model of insight and balance. I wasn't that happy with how he'd caricatured me: "Ms. Fisher is right out of Republican central casting: The Muffy-Buffy-Jody look writ expensive. And why not? Her Republican credentials are impeccable." But he'd recited the concerns of the skeptics and laid out my responses as I'd given them to him, including my response to his question about whether being HIV-positive had changed my art: "I don't think there's been any change," she said. "But I'm not sure. What does AIDS look like?"

He offered me a piece of advice in the course of his report: "To be effective," he admonished, Mary Fisher "will need to walk a fine, tricky line." How right he was.

But for me the most poignant part of the article was near the close, where Jeffrey injected himself into the story, something he rarely did:

> Always, her conversation comes back to the children, Max and Zachary. She has told them little about her infection, mostly because they are too young. "What anger there is, I work out because of the children," she said. "It's not good for them to be around that."
>
> With that, she seemed to end the chat. But a few minutes later, at the door, she rushed up. "I want a big hug," she said. Then she threw open her arms, squeezing a reporter tight and whispered, "Stay well."

What Jeffrey did not tell his readers—not then, not yet—was that he himself was HIV-positive. Little more than a year later, he lost his fight with AIDS. I remembered our hug when I spoke at his memorial service.

●   ●   ●

Friday, August 14, Boca Raton, Florida. Jim had fielded an endless stream of calls the previous day, and I had talked longer with Jeffrey than I'd planned. Jim's daughter, Emily, who'd been with him in Florida for the week, was yawning widely in the kitchen when they headed for their hotel near midnight, where he'd start writing the speech due in Houston in the morning. We'd discussed the outline but didn't have a single paragraph.

I slept fitfully that night and had just wandered into the kitchen around 7:30 in the morning to start the coffee when Jim walked in, sleepy daughter in tow and with a draft of a speech for my review. I began reading and knew from the opening two paragraphs that the speech was inspired. I read the copy, occasionally looking at Jim. When I'd finished, tears were running down my cheeks. I walked over to him, gave him a wordless hug, and sat down to read it again.

This was it, my message, the one that had been building since last July. It wasn't just my story anymore, the facts of my life; it was a message, a call, a challenge.

I was uncomfortable with the close of the draft, so Jim rewrote the final two paragraphs. We made three other changes—one punctuation mark and two revised sentences—before late afternoon when Jim faxed a copy to Clark Judge, who had by then arrived in Houston.

Clark Judge had nothing but praise for the speech when Jim called him. They spoke briefly, speechwriter-to-speechwriter. He asked Jim how long it would take me to deliver it. "Nine minutes," Jim said. "I know her pace."

We later learned that others had wanted changes, but Clark never demanded them and we never consented to any. In the end, the speech I took to Houston—the speech I gave—was exactly the speech we finished that day, word for word, right down to the commas.

No matter how often I read it over the weekend, it moved me. We had the message now. And no matter how hard I tried to read it faster, it always took thirteen minutes for me to finish.

Monday, August 17, Houston, Texas. The boys and I had flown into Houston Sunday evening. We didn't tell anyone they were there, largely because I had some security concerns. I didn't want media shots of the children. I'd already had one stalker sending me hate mail. He had somehow gotten a note hand delivered to me at my table at the AmFAR event in New York City months earlier, and he'd kept up a fairly steady stream of correspondence, none of it playful. We'd been told that little could be done unless he appeared in person or made some clear physical threat. I half-expected he would show up in Houston.

I spent most of Monday running around Houston with Phillip, who'd arrived over the weekend to be my support system and to help prepare the video introduction. After the man we'd hired to read the video script finished his work in the sound booth, he came over to me and said he didn't want to be paid. "This issue is so important," he said. "God bless you."

Between hours spent on the video, I spent time with Max and Zachary and made return calls to reporters who were being briefed and assigned interview times by Jim. Twice we made the drive from our hotel to the Astrodome, where the convention was being held, to do "local feeds" to Detroit and Florida television stations who had sent crews to cover the convention.

Rumors were rife that speeches were being edited, that the TelePrompTers would carry edited versions, that the convention was being tightly managed. I didn't want my speech diluted by surprise editing, and Jim suggested that the only real safety measure was to memorize the copy. When the children went to bed that night, I finished another round of interviews and then began to commit the speech to memory.

Tuesday, August 18, Houston, Texas. The convention was in high gear and so were the media. We didn't have enough telephone lines into Jim's hotel room to handle all the press calls, and he was working alone. But somehow he sorted out the calls, decided which interviews were most critical, and found time slots for telephone and in-person interviews. While he was organizing, I was interviewing—truly, a reversal of my usual role.

When we visited the Astrodome we ran into Red Cavaney. I asked if he'd make sure the speech I'd brought would be the speech I read on the TelePrompTer. He was reassuring, promising that an additional copy of my text would be on the podium when I got there in the event of some technical glitch in the TelePrompTers.

No speakers were onstage at the moment, and Red offered to take us there so I could see how the podium felt. Even with the auditorium still empty except for a few hundred technicians, it was a humbling setting. The place was monstrous; the permanent seating sections across the arena floor appeared as a blur, they were so distant from the stage. A bank of television cameras—seventy-five of them, maybe a hundred—had been mounted on a platform twenty feet off the floor. They were all aimed where I would be standing.

I walked to the podium and could barely see over it. "There's a step that comes out behind the podium," Red explained. "We have a few officials giving speeches who would be mortified if their voters saw how short they really are." He explained the technology that moved the step: "We have an elderly lady who stands on a ladder below the stage and pushes this thing out when we need it." We all laughed. Later I found out he'd told the truth, although the ladder lady wasn't *that* old.

All convention speakers had been assigned a rehearsal time in one of the trailers parked behind the stage in the Astrodome. The trailer was outfitted with a podium and a TelePrompTer at the same angle as the real stage. There were video cameras, a speech coach brought in specifically for the occasion, and in the very back of the room, seated on a folding chair, a timekeeper (the speech coach's wife, I later learned) who held each speaker's script on her lap while timing the delivery with a stopwatch.

We knew my video introduction was exactly sixty seconds long, so my speech could not exceed nine minutes; in practice, once, I'd gotten it down to twelve.

I stood at the podium at the front of the rehearsal trailer on Tuesday morning and waited for my script to appear on the TelePrompTer. When it appeared, and the video crew signaled "Ready," the speech instructor said, "Start," and the timer clicked on her stopwatch at the rear of the room.

Out of view of everyone in the room except me, since everyone else was looking toward me and I was the only one facing the rear, was Jim. He was standing behind the timekeeper, simultaneously watching her turn pages of copy while the second hand of her stopwatch swept around. He had timed each page of copy to know exactly where I needed to be, minute by minute, to finish the speech in less than 9 minutes. When I slowed down, he gave me a "speed up" sign by rotating his hands; when I was on pace, he gave me the "okay" sign.

One eye on the TelePrompTer, one eye on Jim, I dashed through the speech with all the emotional emphasis I could give while reading every word quickly. With two paragraphs to go, I saw Jim smiling and I knew we'd done it. He wasn't giving me any signs at all. He was just standing there, smiling.

I hadn't quite finished when I noticed the timekeeper turning to Jim, saying something. I heard him say, "Stop your clock," as she dropped the watch, dropped the script, and ran out of the room crying. Jim picked up her watch and brought it to her startled husband. "Eight minutes, fifty-two seconds," he said. The speech coach thanked me, said it was a wonderful speech, asked someone what had happened to his wife, and accompanied us to the door.

Phillip, who'd sat through the rehearsal on a folding chair, closed the trailer door behind us as Jim congratulated me on "a splendid rendition."

"What happened with the timekeeper?" I asked.

"She got involved," said Jim, still smiling.

CHAPTER 18

"Thirteen Minutes of Fame"

I woke early and listened for the boys. It took me a minute to remember where I was, and why. It was Wednesday, August 19, 1992. This was Houston, the Republican National Convention. I was going to speak tonight. My speech manuscript was scattered on the floor next to my bed, where it had landed when I fell asleep trying to memorize it.

I called Jim, whose room was a few floors away. He'd already lined up a long list of interviews I was supposed to do during the day.

I'd appeared on "Larry King Live" and other shows the night before. Most of the interviews were predictable: Would I criticize the president? Did I think his administration was doing enough about AIDS? Larry's interview had been warm, almost too affectionate. "Say hi to your father for me," he said as I left him. He believed he had been interviewing Max's tragically ill daughter, I think; he took it easy on me. And his makeup artist, Antoinette, was fabulous.

We had built in three hours of "off time" for me during the afternoon; it was Jim's idea, and I humored him. Dad and Mom were going to visit and play with the children while I rehearsed—memorized!—the speech. When Jim asked if there was anything else he could do to help me relax, I said, "Sure, you could get Antoinette to do my makeup tonight so I don't have to go over early to the holding room and have someone I don't know do it." Somehow Antoinette appeared.

The midday news from Houston was all about President Bush's fundraising appearance, which had been interrupted by local AIDS activists waving condoms in the air and shouting, "What about AIDS?" Monday night, other activists had been arrested when they clashed with Houston police outside the stadium.

I was working on my script, memorizing, when Dad and Mother arrived at my hotel room that afternoon. Mother hoped I'd attend some receptions with them later in the day and after my speech; I said I'd try but might need to be with the boys.

Dad hadn't seen the speech yet and asked if he could. I gave him a copy. He sat in a chair and read it. Every theme in the speech was something he'd heard from me since February. Perhaps it was more stylized, more elegant, written down, but it was no surprise. When he finished it, he put it down. "That's some speech. Are you going to be able to say all of it?" He wasn't worried about the speech's length; he wondered if I would be able to handle my emotions.

"Of course," I replied. "I have to."

Dad had been one of the previous day's speakers. "Speak slowly," he counseled, "so they can hear every word. There's going to be lots of noise in the Dome, and your words will echo. It's a tough place to give a speech."

Jim had been on the telephone or at the Astrodome nearly all day, working with reporters. Neither he nor I had heard any of the other major speeches of the convention, including onetime candidate Patrick Buchanan's nasty declaration of cultural warfare on Monday night. In fact, we'd seen almost no coverage of the convention itself because we had no time; others later spoke of a "mean-spirited event," but we had no sense of that then.

After three or four recognized reporters asked Jim how heavily my speech had been edited by convention leaders (one said, "So what's left of what she intended to say?"), Jim knew that they'd either heard a rumor or that they knew something we didn't. Jim stuck with the truth as we knew it: The speech had not been edited, not at all. His questioners were skeptical.

Late in the afternoon, less than an hour before we were to leave the hotel for the Astrodome, as I was making dinner arrangements for the boys and trying to get dressed, Jim decided to release to the *Los Angeles Times* the full text of the speech as we'd prepared it. He was no longer confident about the version of the speech that would be waiting on the podium and loaded into the TelePrompTer. This was, as he said later, "a little integrity insurance." He picked the *Times* because its reporter, Bill (William J.) Eaton, was a model of journalistic integrity; because the *Times* had a national readership; and because the *Times* was published in the Pacific time zone. If the speech given to Eaton was not the address I delivered, we'd have time to comment before the *Los Angeles Times* story had to be filed.

I didn't know all this was going on until later. I was trying to keep the children calm, wondering whether to let either of them watch the speech, trying not to worry about what would happen when my speech actually went well beyond the allotted time.

Phillip, Jim, and I rode to the Astrodome together, arriving a little after seven. We went backstage, wearing all the appropriate credentials to pass through every checkpoint. When we arrived at the entrance where speakers were checking in, security, which had been tight everywhere, was in a "clamp-down mode." No one whose name was not on the list could get through; they had my name, but not Phillip's and not Jim's.

"I'm not going in without my brother and Jim," I announced, stepping back and folding my arms across my chest. "I'll just stand out here and wait until it's time for me to speak."

Phillip, whose anxiety had been building noticeably since we'd arrived, saw his opportunity and, after a quick hug and kiss, headed for the auditorium to sit with Mom and Dad in President and Mrs. Bush's box. By the time he was out of sight, a senior security officer had come out with instructions from Red Cavaney to let Jim come in with me.

We were admitted to the "first holding room," where Tanya Tucker, the country-and-western singer scheduled to open the evening with the national anthem, was talking to her children and her dogs.

By now word had spread through the Secret Service detail that I was there, and men I'd worked with during the Ford administration started coming into the room. First came Ron Thomsen to give me a hug and promise me prayers. Then Terry Samway. I was so grateful to see them, and we were all getting tearful together. By the time our reunions were over, a young woman had come to take Jim and me to the final holding room at the base of the stairs leading to the podium.

Mrs. Quayle was already there when we walked in. She nodded. She was having a conversation with Gerald McRaney, the television star of "Major Dad," who was brought in to introduce her. They were enjoying themselves, enormously and loudly. I was not.

Television evangelist and former candidate Pat Robertson had just finished speaking onstage; I was introduced to him and his wife, Dede, as they were escorted past us. He smiled and shook my hand, looking at my large red ribbon.

There were two television sets in the room, tuned to different channels, both broadcasting the convention. But the dominating sound in the room was the continuous, dull roar generated by the thousands of feet moving and shuffling, kicking and stomping the floor overhead. I wondered how anyone could ever hear my message over that din, and I realized why Dad had said I should ignore the noise. The crowd would mill around and chat with one another. "Talk to the television cameras," Jim had said repeatedly during rehearsals, "and everything will be fine."

A man I'd met briefly the day before—he'd given me a strangely emotional hug and said, "I've done work with Elizabeth Glaser"— came down the stairway from the podium into the room and said, "Time to come upstairs, Mary." He put out his arm to take mine. I clung to Jim's hand for just a moment. He said, "Relax, you were called to do this."

I was led halfway up the stairs to a small landing. "You can just wait here, on the carpeted star, until I call you again," the man said, and he climbed the remaining steps out of sight. If it's possible to pace madly in a three-foot by three-foot area, I was pacing. My heart was racing, and I felt dizzy. I needed to go to the bathroom. My mouth was dry. I couldn't remember anything of the speech—not even the opening few words. I thought to myself, "When this is over, I won't have a place to hide; the audience will throw tomatoes and the AIDS community"—some of whose members were at that moment picketing the arena—"will reject me." I felt, because I was, alone.

Then I started to pray, as I'd prayed at the Betty Ford Center years earlier, turning it all over to God, saying, "I'm not in control of this." Amazingly, I was calmed—not just a bit, but thoroughly. I heard the music begin at the opening of the video Phillip and I had made. If only the speech were there, I would be okay.

"Okay, Mary, come on up the steps." I walked up to the voice that had called me. I asked, "Is the step out?" I didn't hear an answer immediately. The stadium had been darkened for the video, but then I heard him say, "Yes." As the video ended, the public address system in the arena roared, "Ladies and gentlemen, Mary

Fisher." I was at the podium when the lights came up. I couldn't see my speech on top of the podium, but the podium was high. I climbed the portable step, put my hand on the side of the podium, and looked down. There was nothing there. No speech. I tried to remember the opening line of the speech, but I couldn't.

When I glanced at the TelePrompTer, my opening paragraph was there, and directly over the screen was President Bush's box, occupied by, among others, My President and Betty Ford. Elizabeth Glaser had told me, during a phone call the day before, that this was the moment—when she first looked over the crowd in New York's Madison Square Garden—that had most given her courage. When she climbed high enough to reach the podium, she'd looked out to find all the delegates wearing red AIDS ribbons. No sea of red ribbons awaited me in Houston. But I could see the president and Betty—and maybe that was a red ribbon on her dress.

The polite applause stopped, I took one deep breath, and I began: "Less than three months ago, at platform hearings in Salt Lake City, I asked the Republican party to lift the shroud of silence which has been draped over the issue of HIV/AIDS. I have come tonight to bring our silence to an end."

I sounded funny. My voice was echoing behind me, delayed by perhaps a second. Jim had said, "Don't listen to the echo; listen to your voice—do it as we've rehearsed it." I'd been looking at the TelePrompTer on the right; I shifted to the left-hand screen. My speech was there, too.

> I bear a message of challenge, not self-congratulation. I want your attention, not your applause. I would never have asked to be HIV-positive. But I believe that in all things there is a good purpose, and so I stand before you, and before the nation, gladly. . . .

The crowd was noisy. I needed to talk to the camera and ignore the people in front of me.

> In the context of an election year, I ask you—here, in this great hall, or listening in the quiet of your home—to recognize that

the AIDS virus is not a political creature. It does not care whether you are Democrat or Republican. It does not ask whether you are black or white, male or female, gay or straight, young or old.

Tonight, I represent an AIDS community whose members have been reluctantly drafted from every segment of American society. Though I am white, and a mother, I am one with a black infant struggling with tubes in a Philadelphia hospital. Though I am female, and contracted this disease in marriage, and enjoy the warm support of my family, I am one with the lonely gay man sheltering a flickering candle from the cold wind of his family's rejection.

Jim was still in the holding room downstairs, standing near one of the Secret Service men who'd given me a hug earlier in the evening. The agent was straining to hear me and his eyes were glistening. The noise of the crowd above was beginning to quiet—"hauntingly quiet," Jim said later—but Mrs. Quayle and Major Dad were carrying on more loudly than ever. As Jim stepped nearer one of the television sets, he heard the agent turn to the wife of the vice president of the United States and say, "Would you *please* be quiet!"

This is not a distant threat; it is a present danger. . . . And we have helped it along—we have killed each other—with our ignorance, our prejudice, and our silence.

We may take refuge in our stereotypes, but we cannot hide there long. Because HIV asks only one thing of those it attacks: Are you human? And this is the right question: Are you human? Because people with HIV have not entered some alien state of being. They are human. They have not earned cruelty and they do not deserve meanness. They don't benefit from being isolated or treated as outcasts. Each of them is exactly what God made: a person. Not evil, deserving of our judgment; not victims, longing for our pity. People. Ready for support and worthy of compassion.

I could hardly believe how calm I was. I looked at the television cameras and wondered if the boys had stayed up to watch in the hotel room. I remembered the speech word for word now, glancing at the TelePrompTer screens for comfort but not for reading. In fact, I was comparing what I knew to what the TelePrompTer said. So far, it was nothing but my speech, exactly as we'd given it to them.

> My call to you, my party, is to take a public stand no less compassionate than that of the president and Mrs. Bush. . . . In the darkest hours, I have seen them reaching not only to me, but also to my parents, armed with that stunning grief and special grace that comes only to parents who have themselves leaned too long over the bedside of a dying child.
>
> . . . [W]e do the president's cause no good if we praise the American family but ignore a virus that destroys it. We must be consistent if we are to be believed. We cannot love justice and ignore prejudice, love our children and fear to teach them. Whatever our role, as parent or policy maker, we must act as eloquently as we speak—else we have no integrity.
>
> My call to the nation is a plea for awareness. If you believe you are safe, you are in danger. . . .

Throughout the convention the press was gathered immediately in front of the podium, in a cordoned-off area that tended to spill into the aisles around it. From the podium, it was hard to distinguish the press from the rest of the crowd. For some reason, I happened to look down into the press area and found myself staring right into the eyes of a grinning Steven Bradley. We'd first met at the International AIDS Conference in Amsterdam, and again here in Houston the day before. He'd come up to reintroduce himself to me and to show off his press credentials as a representative of a gay publication. "I'm a member of Houston ACT UP," he said, laughing. "And—would you believe it?—they gave me press credentials anyway!" I think he was later arrested inside the Astrodome for an altercation with another press person over the integrity of his credentials. But on this night, he was there to support me.

As I spoke, Steven began unbuttoning his shirt. Here I stood, talking to millions of people, and watching this grinning, strapping young man begin to disrobe. When his long-sleeved shirt was fully unbuttoned, Steven pulled it off and leaned back, sticking out his chest at an angle so I could read his T-shirt, looking up at me with a goofy smile as if to say, "Is this cool, or what?" I read the slogan on his T-shirt: "No one here knows I'm HIV-positive." He did not want me to feel all alone.

The crowd had grown eerily quiet by now. I had just finished a part of the speech dealing with my father and his campaign for human dignity and peace. Now that they were hushed, it seemed as if I could talk not just to the cameras, but to them directly. Where was I in my speech? I had to keep speaking. What had I just said? Oh, yes, that my family had supported me, had "helped carry me over the hardest places."

. . . [N]ot all of you have been so blessed. You are HIV-positive but dare not say it. You have lost loved ones, but you dared not whisper the word AIDS. You weep silently; you grieve alone.

I have a message for you: It is not you who should feel shame; it is we. We who tolerate ignorance and practice prejudice, we who have taught you to fear. We must lift our shroud of silence, making it safe for you to reach out for compassion. It is our task to seek safety for our children, not in quiet denial but in effective action.

Someday our children will be grown. My son Max, now four, will take the measure of his mother; my son Zachary, now two, will sort through his memories. I may not be here to hear their judgments, but I know already what I hope they are.

I want my children to know that their mother was not a victim. She was a messenger. I do not want them to think, as I once did, that courage is the absence of fear; I want them to know that courage is the strength to act wisely when most we are afraid. I want them to have the courage to step forward when called by their nation, or their party, and give leadership—no matter what the personal cost. I ask no more of you than I ask of myself, or of my children.

To the millions of you who are grieving, who are frightened, who have suffered the ravages of AIDS firsthand: Have courage and you will find comfort.

To the millions who are strong, I issue this plea: Set aside prejudice and politics to make room for compassion and sound policy.

To my children, I make this pledge: I will not give in, Zachary, because I draw my courage from you. Your silly giggle gives me hope. Your gentle prayers give me strength. And you, my child, give me reason to say to America, "You are at risk." And I will not rest, Max, until I have done all I can to make your world safe. I will seek a place where intimacy is not the prelude to suffering.

I will not hurry to leave you, my children. But when I go, I pray that you will not suffer shame on my account.

To all within the sound of my voice, I appeal: Learn with me the lessons of history and of grace, so my children will not be afraid to say the word AIDS when I am gone. Then their children, and yours, may not need to whisper it at all.

God bless the children, and bless us all. Good night.

It was over. I'd finished. There was a moment of absolute quiet. Then the stadium exploded. They were on their feet, and I was numb. Not calm, numb.

I had visualized every moment except this one: being finished. I stood too long at the podium, my mother told me later. I don't know if that was owing to shock, or to Jim's instructions that I should count to ten before leaving, or simply to the fact that I was enjoying the applause. It was over. I had said what I'd come to say. They were on their feet all over the Astrodome.

A man came out to introduce the next speaker. He took my hand to help me down from the podium and pointed me to the stairway. I walked offstage, alone. As I walked from the podium, I heard a voice on one side of the platform call out, "God bless you!" From the other side reporters were calling my name, asking for quick interviews. I didn't look either way: I needed to concentrate on walking, one step at a time, just getting to the stairway.

I remember crossing from the bright light of the arena into the shadow of the staircase, thinking I was out of sight of the audience, finding a bend in the stairway with a landing with a carpeted star, like the one on the other side where I'd waited to be called onstage. When I reached the landing and turned, I saw Jim at the bottom of the stairs looking up. I ran the last few steps and jumped or fell into his arms. All he said, over and over, softly, was "Wonderful, wonderful, wonderful."

Major Dad and Mrs. Quayle had already gone up the stairs to take the stage behind me. While they spoke, and before I left the first holding room, Bobbie Kilberg, a deputy assistant to the president, came in and said, "Mary, there's a telephone call for you. Please come with me."

I followed her across the hall, where she unlocked a door. A Secret Service agent I didn't know came out of nowhere. "They can't go in there," he said forcefully, nodding toward Jim and me. (The president was making a surprise visit at the arena that night; Bobbie Kilberg was, we later realized, unlocking the room the service had secured for him.)

"Yes, they can," Kilberg said without pausing. "She has a call from the president and he asked that she take it here." The agent backed up, and before Kilberg handed me the telephone, she spoke these words into the mouthpiece: "Mr. Bush . . . President Fisher."

President Bush had watched the speech and was calling to congratulate and thank me. It was a very personal, very touching call. "I wish you could have seen your father's picture on television while you spoke," he said. For a moment, I thought the president was crying. He was ready to say good-bye when I—flush with the excitement of the moment—said, "No, no, wait! Don't hang up! We have a lot to talk about!" He assured me that we would talk soon. Only later did it occur to me that I'd breached every courtesy with the president because I'd been so determined to get in a few words.

By the time Jim and I had worked our way out of the underground labyrinth, Maria Shriver was waiting for me. Other reporters crowded around. A radio technician I'd met the day before, who'd come up to me to say that his brother had died of AIDS and he didn't dare tell anyone, gave me a discreet little hand wave.

I wanted to get to the presidential box where the Fords, my parents, Phillip, and the Mosbachers were all seated. When I arrived, Betty was the first to greet me, and after her, it was tears and hugs all around.

The Mosbachers were giving a party for President and Mrs. Bush after Mrs. Bush concluded her speech that evening. They wanted me to come. But I was fading quickly. My feet hurt. I was hungry. I wanted to see the children, know they were okay, kiss them good-night even if they were asleep.

It was eleven by the time Jim and I arrived back at the hotel. I went to my room; both children were sleeping. Their nanny said that the children watched me speak and cried when I mentioned

their names. I've never known what made them cry; perhaps it was that cameras were showing other people crying, including Dad.

A crowd of my old colleagues from the White House, mainly agents and press people, were in the hotel bar having a drink. When we walked in, they called to us to join them. We did, but we didn't last very long. Jim hadn't slept more than a few hours since he'd arrived in Houston, and I was exhausted.

We of course were the two people who had the least idea what impact the speech might have actually had, if any. It wasn't until the next morning, when we began reading headlines and Jim attempted to field media calls, that we realized how widely the message had been heard.

As we'd expected, the *Los Angeles Times* carried lengthy quotations from the speech itself. AIDS SPEECH SENDS HUSH OVER ASTRODOME, headlined the morning edition of *USA Today*. The *New York Times* said that my "poignant, intimate talk struck the Astrodome audience into silence, and in some cases, tears."

Many of the delegates at first seemed to not hear Ms. Fisher's somber words, and could be seen chatting and wandering about the floor. But as she went on, the room fell gradually to attention. By the middle of her speech almost everyone was staring up at the podium, quiet and with grave expressions.

There were exceptions. A television camera caught Vice President Dan Quayle, standing in his box in the rear of the hall, glad-handing a beaming Arnold Schwarzenegger.

Editorials began on Friday, August 21, offering some perspective on the speech in the context of the convention itself. Joe Stroud's piece in the *Detroit Free Press* was predictably generous ("Bush should heed Mary Fisher's courageous message"). But the *Miami Herald* struck the note that became conventional wisdom: that this had been a largely mean convention with one thirteen-minute exception. GRACE AMID THE GRINCHES was the *Herald*'s title.

Brent Staples of the *New York Times*, now best known for his brilliant memoir, *Parallel Times*, wrote an editorial for the Saturday *Times* under the theme TEACHING MERCY TO REPUBLICANS. He'd sat through the convention that we had largely missed; he had not liked its tone. He used me and my speech to make his journalistic point:

Ms. Fisher took the crusade for decency and compassion into the lion's den. She spoke the message to the people who were most in need of hearing it. For that she has earned our gratitude.

By the time such distant publications as the *London Times* were filing coverage of the speech—they chose to compare it, favorably, to Winston Churchill's speeches, which gave Jim no end of delight— I was headed home with the children. For the first time in months I believed Jim was right: I had a calling.

An Associated Press photographer caught my father wiping his eyes with a handkerchief while I was speaking. The resulting shot was reprinted in newspapers across the country the morning after my speech—often positioned near an AP photograph of me at the podium wearing my rhinestone red AIDS pin (a gift given to me at the AmFAR event where I first spoke).

It is one of my favorite photographs of Dad; it says, graphically, that Dad cares. I've always wondered, and never asked, if he would have preferred not to be pictured in this excruciatingly emotional way.

The morning after the speech something else happened that signaled a change in my relationship with Dad. I'd arrived in Houston, as Larry King so vividly reminded me, as Max Fisher's daughter. As I prepared to leave Houston, Dad told me the following story.

He'd been scheduled to make brief remarks at a leadership breakfast meeting on Thursday morning, August 20, ten hours after I'd spoken from the podium. It was one of "those" breakfasts, he said, meaning one of a thousand he'd attended over the years. Everyone knew everyone, and everyone was powerful. Dad has become a "senior statesman" of the party in these settings and is always invited to make comments.

But on that morning, as he was being brought to the podium, the man introducing him altered the usual script: "Ladies and gentlemen," he said, "it gives me pleasure to present Mary Fisher's father . . ."

"When they said your name," Dad told me, "they gave me a standing ovation."

CHAPTER 19

"A Long Hard Road"

From the beginning of our partnership, Jim and I have tried to measure our effectiveness not by favorable reporting on me as a person but by how much of "the message" gets through. Do the readers or viewers realize, when the story is finished, that they are also at risk? That compassion, not judgment, is the moral response? I can talk to audiences of a few hundred or few thousand; but if we do our job well and the media gets the story right, we can ultimately reach hundreds of thousands or, in an instance as stunning as the convention, millions.

There have been times when, after reading an article that casts me in a heroic light, someone will say to me, "Isn't this wonderful? Look what they said about you, Mary." If Jim's around, he'll explain, without looking up from whatever he's doing, "This isn't a race to celebrity; it's about moral integrity and keeping a generation of Americans alive—it's about the message."

In terms of the message, the convention coverage was spectacular. There were the occasional "AIDS Victim Speaks Out" stories, but not too many. I was more concerned about the implicit message in a fair number of stories that said, in effect, "She could make this speech because, after all, she's an 'innocent victim.' "

From the day I went public, I hammered away at this point. When reporters asked, "How'd you get it?" I was quick to point out that it didn't matter how I got it—it doesn't matter how anyone gets it. We must stop trying to divide the AIDS community into "innocent" and "guilty." Even Jeffrey Schmalz caught my wrath, which he replayed in his preconvention article:

. . . [W]hen asked how her husband got the virus, she bristled, saying: "It makes no difference. It's outrageous you would ask the question. That's how the world gets divided into bad victims and innocent victims."

The American AIDS community in the fall of 1992 was a unified group. What unified it was politics, presidential politics. Governor Bill Clinton had scored an early victory in this territory when he'd promised in May that he would fully fund all the monies appropriated for AIDS research and care (legislation known as the Ryan White Bill).

President Bush and, even more routinely, some of his cabinet members were seen as not merely antigay or anti-AIDS but as indifferent to the plight of those who were now dying at the rate of three or four each hour. I thought the president's image as distant from the epidemic and uncaring stemmed largely from the fact that he had said so little in public that reflected what I'd seen and heard in the Oval Office. From the point of view of the AIDS community, the administration's official policies were—as caricatured by Larry Kramer, founder of ACT UP—built on the moral foundation of the Holocaust. Republicans were allowing AIDS to run rampant so long as it accomplished a political purpose, the "final solution" that would effectively silence the increasingly vocal, bitterly hostile, and overwhelmingly Democratic gay community.

My speech at the convention had evidently delivered to a broad audience the message of compassion and awareness. Friends and family had not been alienated. Brian Campbell called to say that his whole family had watched and finished our conversation with, "I'm proud of you, Mar."

But in the eyes of some, especially some veterans within the American AIDS community, I had become the Republican poster girl for AIDS.

In September I made my first trip home to Detroit since I had gone public in February. In those few months, everything had changed; everywhere I went, I was recognized. I gave a brief after-dinner speech to a group of AIDS caregivers—the occasion for my trip. It turned out to be a very emotional time.

Conversations with administration officials and cabinet members

had begun in earnest before the convention. They accelerated afterward. Both Jim and I were trying, sometimes too hard, to change
both the style and substance of the administration's position on
AIDS. We sent notes and letters. We drafted better paragraphs for
official speeches, position papers, news releases. We offered to meet,
to plan, to organize. At one point, doing an interview for a national
magazine, I showed my frustration when pressed on being a Republican with AIDS: "I'm doing what my father has always done: I'm
going to work within the system until it's clear to me that the system cannot work."

The convention also stirred up a new round of hate mail and
nasty coverage. Right-wing syndicated columnist Cal Thomas, who
helped evangelist Jerry Falwell launch the Moral Majority, wrote a
column suggesting that I had gotten what I deserved. (A couple of
months later, at a White House Christmas party, Falwell backed
away and declined to shake my hand, even though his wife, Macel,
warmly greeted me and told me I had given an important speech at
the convention.) I was beginning to feel lonesome in the Republican
camp when the rest of the AIDS community seemed to be outside
that camp, circling, protesting. I decided to go to Santa Fe to visit
Rob and Sally, and to rest.

On Saturday, October 3, I helped kick off a "Walk for Life"
fundraiser for Santa Fe AIDS organizations. It was great to feel like
part of a community again. On Sunday, October 4, Sally and I got
out of the house and just played: We hiked, we talked, we laughed,
we generally celebrated life. By the time we finally got back to
Sally's house, it was dark. While we'd been gone, my mother had
left a telephone message: "Why don't you tell us when these things
are going to happen?" I was stumped. We replayed the message a
few times to see if we were missing something. We weren't. I was
mystified.

By morning, the mystery had been solved. Magic Johnson had re-
signed from the National Commission on AIDS with a stinging re-
buke of the Bush administration. And while Sally and I had been
trading "girl jokes," the president had announced on Larry King's
television show that he'd named me to take Magic's place.

I could neither refuse the honor nor feel hopeful about accepting
it. Every AIDS leader in the country who had gone on record after
Magic's resignation had underscored his point: Magic had acted to

protect his integrity. If the AIDS community had distrusted me before, what would they think of me if I accepted the appointment?

After long conversations with a number of advisors, I decided that if I could speak in Houston, I could serve on the commission. What I needed was to prove, in public, that my message was both sincere and consistent. Saying "No, thank you" to a presidential appointment wouldn't do it; accepting the appointment and using the commission as an additional forum seemed to be the better option. I accepted the president's appointment.

My stalker, whose hate letters were by now arriving several times per week, used this occasion to write to someone else: the editors of *USA Today*. He let them know that the AIDS community in general, and the gay community in particular, knew I was a spoiled rich witch spending her father's money and living off his power. The nation's newspaper printed the letter and ran my picture next to it. Jim called the editors, and the paper accepted no more letters from that correspondent.

The major event in the life of America's AIDS community that fall was the display of the entire NAMES Project AIDS Memorial Quilt in Washington, D.C., during the first week of October. The display was so huge it was now being measured in acres, rather than just panels, and it blanketed a portion of the Mall in the shadows of the Washington Monument.

I'd invited Mrs. Bush to visit the Quilt with me—unannounced and without fanfare—not as a political statement but as an opportunity for her to experience the Quilt's enormity, its power. Two mornings in a row we were scheduled to go, and both mornings the display needed to be shelved because of rain. We were both disappointed.

The Quilt display had been timed to coincide with a major conference of AIDS leaders and workers from around the country, the annual National Skills Building Conference. It would be an especially charged event this year, because AIDS was being so politicized in the course of the presidential campaign. When I was invited to give a Saturday noon luncheon keynote address, on October 10, to a thousand conference participants and guests, I wondered how I would be received.

Friday, October 9, newspaper headlines were full of the previous day's news conference at which I, standing with the president, had accepted "Magic Johnson's position" on the commission. The next day I needed to appear before, and speak to, those who had been fighting the epidemic from the beginning. It was starting to feel like my political allegiance to the party of Max Fisher could be seen only as disloyalty to my AIDS family.

The speech I delivered that day was direct. There was no defensiveness in it, no apology, and no politics. It was more like an orphan's request to be allowed into the family, or perhaps a mother's soliloquy: "Wrapping the Family in the Quilt."

"I am among the newest members of the HIV/AIDS family which has gathered here this weekend," I began. "Last year at this time, I'd just learned I was HIV-positive. I was huddled alone somewhere, hugging myself and my children, racked with anger and fear, uncertain about my future."

And then I spoke, nervously, to all the leaders of the community at whose door I was knocking:

> This year, I'm here. I've learned to hate the virus, love the family, and be thankful for this reunion and for those of you who have become this family's heroes. I came to Washington, as have many of you, to share the family memorial. . . . The Quilt reminds us all that ours is a family which is never far from grief.
>
> I think of us less as a movement than as a family. Like other families, we are bound by what's in our blood and in our souls, but we are not all the same—even here, in this room. We are black and white and brown; we are gay and straight, young and old, 999 Democrats . . . and me.

I've never had any other speech interrupted by such laughter and applause after just three paragraphs. It let me know that on this day, at this place, I could be accepted. Even if I had been the only HIV-positive Republican in the world, I could still be at home in the AIDS community.

When in November Governor Clinton was elected president, my reign as the Republican AIDS poster girl ended. And the AIDS community was beginning to accept me as one of their own. No less a

presence in that community than the *New York Times* reported that
I was, within the AIDS community, "regarded as bright and committed, not as some dilettante who will move on to the next cause
du jour."

Indeed, the pendulum was rapidly swinging too far in the other
direction. At the convention I had tried to destroy the stereotype of
the poor little rich girl, the "pathetic and innocent victim" of unhappy circumstances. I wanted them to know that I was someone's
daughter and sister, a regular mother with regular children, and
that this was precisely the context of AIDS in America. But in the
months after Houston another image was being built: a larger-than-
life Mary Fisher, a graceful and all-knowing Mary, Mary the Hero.

Some hero worship comes with the territory for any public personality, from ice-skaters to rock stars to crime bosses. In my case,
some of this was encouraged just because I was new on the media
scene; I was the fresh AIDS story, sometimes generating exaggerated reports and sensational nonsense (I received my first Hollywood offer for rights to my life story the day I returned home from
Houston).

Within a few weeks of the convention, I found myself being type-
cast in long and widely read stories reflecting on the convention.
These weren't stories based on interviews with me, but essays written by America's political and literary lights. Norman Mailer, for
example, raised me to new heights in an October 12 essay in *The
New Republic.*

He set the dramatic stage: "The theme for the third day, Wednesday, was Family Values, and it was introduced in the Republican
Gala at noon." He then reported, in several thousand words, stories
of AIDS protestors and President Bush's interrupted speech and
Vice President Dan Quayle's seeming judgmentalism.

The Republicans were making a spectacle of their own insensitivity, he said; they were dying in the broad daylight of Houston. At
which point, he wrote: "Mary Fisher was the Republican answer,
then, to Democrats, and she was effective beyond all measure."

And that was merely the beginning. I was, after all,

a slim, blonde, and undeniably lovely young lady with a delicacy of feature and a poignancy of manner. . . . If a casting director had searched for a fine actress unlikely ever to have

TOWN & COUNTRY

CAN
MARY
FISHER
SAVE
YOUR
LIFE?

DECEMBER
1992 $3.00

To: Mary Fisher

As this year of turmoil draws to and end
we send you our love and our wish that 1993
will be your best year ever~ *Geo Bush*

contact with the virus, he would have selected Mary Fisher if she had been an actress, but she was not. She was in a rare category, a Republican princess. . . . She was not only lovely, but innocent, after all. . . .

Embarrassingly, there was more. Mailer replayed large chunks of my speech, paragraph by paragraph, describing this as Mary Fisher's

> message so old that the coruscated souls of the Republicans, nine-tenths barnacled by now in greed and wealth, cant and bad conscience, fury and fear, began to weep in longing for the old memory of Christ kissing the feet of the poor.
> Republicans were paralyzed before the obscene enigma of AIDS and so, when Mary Fisher spoke like an angel that night, the floor was awash in tears, and conceivably the nation as well.

Even after Mailer and others had finished with me, the drumbeat heralding my "sainthood" continued. *Town & Country* magazine sent word that I'd been selected for their "1992 Generous American Award," which would be presented in the context of a December cover story, cover photograph, and a gala dinner in New York. Jim and I wrestled with whether or not to accept, valuing the opportunity it would provide to reach a largely unreached audience but fearing another round of "socialite victim" coverage. In the end, we opted to go for the story; with it came the dinner in New York.

It was an unbelievable evening, the *Town & Country* affair. Awards were given to a number of people more deserving than I— people who'd spent years, if not a lifetime, devoted to a single cause. Bud (Byron Nease) flew in from Toronto, where he was starring in *Phantom of the Opera*, to sing my favorite songs. When it came time to deliver my brief speech for the evening, I told them they needed to stop worshiping me.

A critical part of my message, perhaps the most critical part— that anyone can get AIDS—was being eroded by kindly but misguided efforts to make me more than I was, more than I am. What had made my speech in Houston effective, what had (finally) disturbed the souls of a few Americans, wasn't that I was a hero but that I was common. And that's it exactly. I was "one of us" instead of "one of them," and I have AIDS. What made me shocking wasn't my distinctiveness, but my ordinariness. I didn't look like America's caricature of AIDS. I am a regular person, a mom; I could be your sister. And that's the point.

Besides, as I told the *Town & Country* audience, I hadn't enlisted in this fight: "I was drafted. . . . I did not march bravely to the head of the line of duty; I was dragged into this arena, kicking and screaming." I'd gone public earlier in 1992 because the story was going to break anyway, and by acting on my own I'd been able to shape the message in the best interests of my family, especially my children.

I'd spoken out not as an act of heroism but as an act of motherhood. And this talk about heroic Mary was dangerous; it threatened to undo the mission.

Since December 1992, whenever I sense "Mary Fisher"—the public personality, the one people think they know—being pushed onto a hero's platform, I send the offending party a copy of the speech given at the *Town & Country* dinner. Its title: "Make Me No Hero."

Arthur Ashe and I were both patients of Dr. Hank Murray. It was Hank who, with his wife Diana, invited Jim and me to have lunch with Arthur in New York City the week before Christmas in 1992. Diana was a trustee of the Metropolitan Museum and had reserved a table in a semiprivate room.

It was a sun-drenched winter day. Arthur was bundled up against the cold in a long coat and beneath it a heavy sweater. I'd just come from giving a speech with Hank at his daughter's school, and I'd brought with me a copy of *Sports Illustrated*, which had that week published Arthur's picture on the cover as their "Sportsman of the Year."

Meeting Arthur was almost mystical. Hank had said that Arthur wanted to meet me, but I was positively elated at the prospect of meeting him. I respected him beyond words: his wisdom, his courage, his civil rights crusades and books, his intellectual integrity, his quiet voice and unyielding manner. When he had stood at the news conference with Jeanne, his wife, and spoken of Camera, their daughter, he had shown the emotion that I knew intimately as well. For whatever divided us, it was more than AIDS that united us. It was parenthood and other mutual concerns, including a desire to give back to those who had given us so much, a commitment to make a difference if we could.

Our conversation was easy. It lasted an hour or more, but it was too short, too little time; he'd just begun, and I could have listened to him forever, describing the things he wanted to accomplish. We discussed doing something special together, a book for children, perhaps, or a speaking engagement. His wife—Jeanne Moutoussamy-Ashe, an extraordinary woman and critically acclaimed photographer— could take pictures of all our children; Arthur and I could provide the text. He told me about Camera's book about her daddy. We described our projects, my Family AIDS Network, his foundation.

Arthur had been in the hospital and was thin, but he ate with a voracious appetite. I watched him eat as I pushed food around my plate. And then I saw him take out, and sort through, his pills. Medication is like talk of one's T-cell numbers, an absolute and undeniable reminder of AIDS. I watched his delicate fingers pick out the right tablet, then a capsule, and I began to feel like a voyeur. Taking his pills in public seemed like such a vulnerable act, an intimacy I imagined I'd never share with strangers. It made me feel even closer to Arthur to know that he felt that comfortable, that safe, with me.

Arthur never left me after that lunch. I carried him with me, and I still do. Whether it was his magical personality, our common bonds, or truly a spiritual union that I cannot understand or explain, Arthur took hold of a part of me and has never let go.

When, after the first of the year, Arthur became too sick to keep his public commitments, Jeanne suggested that he call me to see if I could take his place. I flew to Austin, Texas, the first week in February to fill his commitment to the LBJ High School, the *Austin American-Statesman*, and the local Junior League. Arthur sent down a videotaped message; I sent him a copy of my speeches and all the coverage.

The Saturday after Austin—February 6—Arthur had agreed to be part of a heavyweight panel at the Connecticut Forum, a community event staged in Hartford, which was going to bring together Arthur; Ryan White's mother, Jeannie; Larry Kramer, the founder of ACT UP; Dr. Robert Gallo, a prominent AIDS researcher; Shepherd Smith, a longtime AIDS activist; and assorted others. He asked if I would make that trip, too, and when the forum agreed, I headed for Hartford.

My mind was focused more on Larry Kramer that day than on Arthur Ashe. I was terrified of what Larry would say or do to me. I imagined he would tell me, probably from the podium, that I was not only stupid, but that I was doing the cause more harm than good. I'd read some of his material and it was lethal, and I greatly admired his work as a playwright. Larry Kramer isn't just an angry man with AIDS; he's a revolutionary who, like Thomas Paine before him, knows how to use the arsenal of language. On top of all this, I learned when I arrived that the forum was being taped by public television, which made my terror more complete.

I was talking to Bob Gallo at the site of the forum when I heard someone say, "There's Larry." I thought, "Might as well do it now," and walked over to him, my hand out. "Larry? I'm Mary Fisher." His face softened into a smile, he reached out to take my hand, and he said, "It is really, really an honor to meet you."

"Really?" I said. "I've been terrified of meeting *you.*" We were soon laughing, on our way to becoming friends.

It was a large audience: 2,500 people. The panel itself was predictable. We all said what we'd been saying in other places. Dr. Bob Arnot of CBS News was the moderator and kept the dialogue running up to an intermission break. Just as the other speakers and I were gathering our papers for the break, the head of the forum walked onstage and said, "I have something to announce, and I'm not sure just how to do it."

Arthur had sent a videotaped message to Connecticut, as he had to Texas, and we'd just seen it. I wondered if there were a second tape.

"At 3:17 P.M. today Arthur Ashe passed away. . . ."

I collapsed backward into my chair and began to sob. I wanted to run offstage, out of range of the cameras, but I didn't think I could stand up and walk. It was as if one of my children had been taken from me. I was in shock.

We took an intermission, after which the panelists needed to return to the stage to finish the second half of the program; I was useless. I don't think I said another word. Reporters wanted a comment. Connie Chung asked me to come to the New York City studios the next night so I could close the "CBS Evening News" with a tribute to Arthur.

What happened to me between my holiday lunch with Arthur and his funeral in Richmond, Virginia, and then his memorial service in New York, was quite simple. I had been introduced to the reality of AIDS in a way I'd not known it before. The AIDS I'd seen in the Mission Hill Hospice in Boston a year earlier was, in fact, *my* AIDS. It didn't just infect. It killed.

At Arthur's funeral, New York City's mayor David Dinkens spoke for all of us when he said that, in an age of better advertising and better public relations, better image makers and better spin masters, here we were honored to remember Arthur Ashe "who was, quite simply, a better man."

By the time I returned to Connecticut a month later to speak at the National Institute for Community Health Education conference in Hamden, I had begun to take the real measure of AIDS. "I am deeply grieved to be today's speaker," I told them truthfully. "This was an appointment made by Arthur Ashe, not Mary Fisher, and I wish—more than you imagine—that he had kept the appointment. . . . His was a gentle voice of great wisdom, and I regret beyond words that you cannot hear that voice today."

It was a grim time in the history of the American AIDS community. White House politics were not going as well as those who supported President Clinton had hoped. Many had expected some dramatic new initiative within his first few weeks, but nothing had happened. The White House had remained strangely silent.

The week Arthur died the National Research Council of the National Academy of Sciences released a study under the title "The Social Impact of AIDS in the United States." The report itself was predictable, but someone had condensed the study into a regrettable summary with the result that newspapers, the day Arthur died, told the nation that AIDS was having a significant impact only in "socially marginalized" groups in America. It was, as Dr. David Rogers told the National Research Council in a searing letter, exactly the lie that "every major corporation and every conservative American institution" wanted to hear. Now they could justify the prejudice that says: "Thank God it's them, not us; now we can go back to business as usual and forget about those folks."

Ongoing during all this was a continuing political fight in Washington, D.C., over American policy on immigration by HIV-positive people and the often inhumane discussion about what to do with Haitian refugees with AIDS. Republicans, with whom I was now invariably linked, were making the most grisly speeches.

When I attended Arthur's memorial service at the cavernous Cathedral of St. John the Divine in New York City, Jeanne took me back to the family gathering afterward. It was a place of such comfort, such security, such love, that I could not help but compare it to my own dispersed family. I longed to have people like this gathered around me. For an instant, I resented the few family members who had simply gone on with their lives despite my infection, as if nothing had happened. I did not want them to regard me with pity or sympathetic sentiment, but I missed the closeness, the genuine outpouring of love, that infused this place.

"Who takes care of you?" Jeanne asked me that day. Even in her grief, she was concerned for me.

"Oh," I said, softly, "my children. My mother, Phillip, Joy, Jim."

"Arthur thought what you were doing was wonderful," she said. "I want you to know that I'm here for you. You can't do it alone. It's a long, hard road."

The intensity of both my anger and my grief seemed to grow every day. I had not felt this way before, ever; I never thought I could feel this way. This had very little to do with being either a victim or a hero; it had to do—nothing more, nothing less—with having AIDS.

Jim offered the same counsel he'd given before: Let's find a way to translate your feelings into words, into speeches, to help others know that they're not alone when they endure this same experience. Despite all the work at Betty Ford and Parkside, I still had a hard time recognizing my own anger or grief. But after our long talks together, Jim sent me a draft of a speech in which for the first time I spoke of being a "pilgrim" on the road to AIDS. While it was full of anger and grief, it also reached—as I was beginning to do—for some reason to hope.

"Mary Fisher . . . will replace Arthur Ashe as this year's final speaker of the Salem State College series." The speech was scheduled for April 1, 1993, and it was the last of Arthur's engagements for which a substitute was needed.

Brian Campbell had been sick, very sick, during February and March. He was living not far from Salem State College, where I'd be speaking, and I decided to bring the boys with me to see him. I never said, "This may be their last visit," but I thought it. As it turned out, it was Brian's unspoken assumption, too.

Brian had never before come to hear me speak, although I'd been in or near Boston more than once. He stayed away out of a sense of awkwardness, I think. After all, we were divorced. Given the circumstances, our relationship wasn't terrible, but it wasn't easy. Some people close to me could not forgive him for my infection. But there was also a barrier we'd never taken down: Brian and I had not yet said all we needed to say to each other and were slowly reckoning with that reality.

When Brian said that he wanted to come to the speech and sit with the boys, Jim and I discussed a speech that Brian could hear. I did not want to single him out in such a way that others would know; but I wanted to say things he would know were intended especially and unmistakably for him. Maybe it was a cowardly way to break the ice, to stay safe behind the podium while taking up tough topics, but I didn't know any other way to make it happen.

Brian came. First he needed to quiet Zachary, who thought it important to run up and down the bleachers at the back of the auditorium; then Max needed a drink, and then a bathroom break. I had taken along a baby-sitter to help Brian in case the boys had to be separated. Eventually I saw Brian walking to the back of the auditorium with one of the children in his arms. I wondered if he had enough strength to hold him long.

When I finished my speech, Brian was still standing in the shadows, behind all the seats. Both of the boys had fallen asleep during the final moments. It was as close as we had come to "being family" together—Brian, the boys, and I—in years. So far as I know, no one in the audience knew that much of the speech was for Brian, but I don't think I ever took my eyes off him.

. . . We knew one another in other days, in other moments, before we knew the word "AIDS." And because you've come, we should talk. In fact, I want to say publicly what I've had a hard time saying privately. . . .

We can spend our lives in anger at a tainted needle . . . or an undetected virus in someone we loved. Or we can set aside the anger in favor of forgiveness, and move on.

We can live our lives regretting the moment we were not careful; we can consume our children with our own guilt at leaving them; we can hate ourselves until there's nothing left worth saving. Or we can learn to forgive ourselves as well as others. This is neither pop psychology nor cheap grace; it is merely living out the ancient hope that we will one day learn how to pray, "Forgive us our debts, as we forgive our debtors."

If, in the days of my anger at this virus, you heard only my cries of fear and frustration, diluted by no words of forgiveness and grace, then hear me tonight: The anger has already been eclipsed by commitment. And forgiveness, where it was needed, proved irresistible. If that is a comfort to you, hold it close.

. . . [I]f you need to hear a word of forgiveness, hear it now. The road is hard enough and we will grow weak too soon. We must forgive even ourselves, reach out to take another's hand, and move on. . . . And God give us strength.

I had come to Salem because Arthur was gone, and because Brian was still alive. Before he died, I wanted my children's father to know I'd not given up hope that we could, somehow, say the three sweetest words we knew: "I love you."

CHAPTER 20

"Saying Good-bye to Brian"

Before the April 1 speech at Salem State College, the boys and I had been staying in a Boston hotel for a few days. Brian decided to take a room there, too, so he could be near the children. He wanted to be in a separate room, he said, "to show the boys that we're divorced." Later, he said it had been so that, if he got sick, he wouldn't frighten Max or Zack.

Brian suggested that he and I go to Rugg Road, the studio where he'd first introduced me to handmade paper, and do some work together. He'd started some new work and wanted to show it to me. Brian was on steroids that made him ravenously hungry; he was eating huge volumes of food and looked amazingly healthy.

When we got to Rugg Road, Brian quickly showed me some new pieces he'd started, but he was almost uninterested in his own work. He wanted me to start something, so he could show me a special technique he'd always used but never before taught me. He wanted to help me learn more than he wanted to work on his own pieces.

Brian's sister, Tina Campbell, has always cared for me and the children—before, during, and after Brian and I were divorced. When he was too sick to live alone in Provincetown, near Boston, Tina moved in with him. She'd come to the speech at Salem State College with Brian and the boys as, she'd announced, "the designated driver." Brian's eyesight was failing; he couldn't drive anymore.

When I mentioned to Tina what had happened at Rugg Road, she said, "It's because he doesn't think he has much time left. He wants to give you the gift that he never quite found in his own art. He wants to make a difference, Mary."

After the speech at Salem State, Tina drove Brian back to the hotel with the boys and baby-sitter. "It was a pretty quiet ride," she told me. "He was very touched. I think he was surprised at how powerful you were. And he especially liked the starfish story."

In the speech, I'd said that common people like us can make a difference, and I'd illustrated my point with Loren Eiseley's story about a young man picking up objects off the beach and tossing them into the sea. A second man approached him and saw that the objects were starfish. "Why in the world are you doing that?" he asked.

"If the starfish are still on the beach when the tide goes out and the sun comes up," said the young man, "they'll die."

"That's ridiculous," replied the older man. "There are thousands of miles of beach and millions of starfish. You can't really believe that what you're doing could possibly make a difference."

The young man picked up another starfish and said, as he tossed it far out into the waves, "It makes a difference to this one."

On April 2, the day after Salem State, the boys were scheduled to fly back to Florida and I had a speaking engagement in Cleveland. For whatever reason, Brian and I both knew this would be the last time he would see the children, but we agreed that they wouldn't be helped by a huge, emotional scene.

After getting the boys packed, we all had lunch together—Brian, the boys, and I. The kids were rambunctious, noisy. This was hardly a tender scene accompanied by violin music; it was two boys driving two parents to the edge of distraction. Finally, it was nearly the time Tina had said she'd pick up Brian at the hotel's front door. Brian, the boys, and I left the restaurant and headed to the lobby. Brian and I sat together on a sofa, waiting for Tina, watching the boys, starting to fray at the emotional edges.

Then Max, for reasons still unknown to me, broke into a loud rendition of "God Bless America." Only he didn't exactly sing it; he chanted it, like a cantor or a rabbi, like an old Hebrew prayer. Brian and I both broke up in laughter and Max, embarrassed, threw himself under a nearby chair and wouldn't come back out.

Tina pulled into the hotel drive. It was time to say our good-byes. Brian gave each of the boys a quick hug, said, "I love you," and dashed to Tina's car. I'd told the boys, at Brian's request, that they couldn't follow him outside "because it's too cold." But when I looked out, Brian was facing the lobby glass, looking at his sons with a look I'd never before seen on his face, drawn and sad and grief-stricken. Forgetting my warnings to the children, I ran out to open his car door and give him a last, long hug. "It'll be okay," I whispered, by now in tears myself. "Just go." When I straightened up and turned to go back in, Max was hanging on the hotel door, staring speechless at Brian and me. His face, already hauntingly like his father's, wore the same look I'd just seen in Brian, moments earlier.

I gave twenty speeches and received two honorary doctorates in the seventy-five days that followed our time in Boston. In my travels I saw an AIDS community growing increasingly glum. Hopes had been unrealistically high when President Clinton took office. So many people had believed that President Bush was the problem, and that a new president—*this* new president—would generate a fresh wave of brave new policies and helpful new programs. But after months of apparent inaction, they saw nothing on the horizon to justify their hopes.

The National Commission on AIDS was scheduled to cease existence at the end of June; there was some talk that its mandate would be extended, but in the end it wasn't. By mid-June, word was released from the White House that Christine Gebbie would be named to a vaguely defined position as "AIDS policy coordinator." She served a troubled and brief term.

Meantime, Jeanne Ashe and I became "regulars" on the phone. I never visited New York without spending time with Jeanne and her daughter, Camera, who became Max's first love.

Jeffrey Schmalz and I had become close friends; among other things, he became my most faithful speech reader. When Jim sent me a first draft, I sent a copy to Jeffrey for his reactions. He rarely suggested changes, but he told me over dinner in May that my "voice" had changed since Arthur's death. He thought I was more introspective, sadder, angrier.

"Where do you go with all of it?" I asked. He had been in the middle of this epidemic for more than a decade; he had lost hundreds of friends; he had filed more than a thousand stories on AIDS, grim stories, sometimes brutally depressing, sometimes heartbreaking.

"There's no place to put this, Mary," he said, "except where you're putting it now: in your speeches. Feel the pain, and tell others. What else is there?"

I sold the home I'd shared with Brian in Florida so I could move to the Washington, D.C., area; I was spending more and more time in the capital and thought it would be good for the children to start fresh in a new school. But I'd not yet found a home. We needed to be out of the Boca Raton house by July. Mom and Dad said we were welcome to use the house in Detroit if we needed to, and I started planning a summer near relatives in Detroit.

My Michigan family had stayed steady through all the crises, and I'd gradually learned that we were all going through our own process of dealing with my AIDS, of finding ways to cope. Max's daughter from his first marriage, Jane, and I had never been close; AIDS hadn't changed that. My younger sisters, Julie and Margie, were caring and especially attentive to ways they could stay close to Max and Zack. Phillip was serving as board chair of the Family AIDS Network, the national nonprofit we'd formed to increase community awareness and response to AIDS, and was committed not only to me but to the work we were doing together. Dad was accepting his public role as "Mary Fisher's father" with humor and, I think, some measure of pride. And Mother was proving that, as she had climbed over alcoholism, she'd climb this hill, too. From late-night jokes told on the telephone to critiques of every speech she reviewed, Mother found ways to encourage me. Maybe my own experience as a mother was enabling me to see her differently now. She was strong, fully recovered. If a virus threatened to take away her child, she was going to fight, so help her God.

And all the while, Brian's health was deteriorating. We spoke by phone almost every day. I went back to Provincetown in early May for an art project but mainly to spend time with Brian. I brought with me copies of work I'd been doing that, for the first time, brought human figures into my handmade paper. He smiled and opened his sketch pad for me to see: He'd been sketching exactly the same figures.

Brian's doctors had detected lymphoma in the brain and had given him a choice: He could have chemotherapy, or he could have six more-or-less lucid weeks without the treatment. I wanted to talk to his doctors, and he gave me permission. He told the doctors to treat me as his wife, as if we were still married. But when all the discussions were done, Brian made the decision. He took the six weeks.

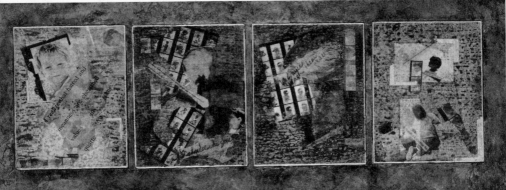

By the end of May, whenever I called, Tina answered. Brian wouldn't let her leave the apartment. He was frightened of being alone. Lumps were forming on his neck literally overnight. His vision was unreliable.

On June 3, Brian's headaches became so intense that he was disoriented. Despite doctors' assurances that if he elected not to have chemotherapy, he'd suffer little pain, he needed time in the hospital and massive doses of morphine to fight off the agony. When the pain subsided, he said to Tina, "Take me home." He was determined not to die in the hospital.

I called and asked Brian if he wanted me to come. No, he didn't. His speech on the telephone was slurred. Tina was wearing down from the constant pressure of being with him, caring for him. When she fell asleep, he wanted her to wake up; when he couldn't find her, he would scream until she came running. I called the local hospice and arranged some help for Tina. Alice Foley, who was the "town nurse" to all of Provincetown, told me she thought Brian had no more than a week to live, maybe less. Manny Souza, who was giving Tina relief when Brian would permit it, agreed. I asked Tina if Brian was doing any artwork at all.

"No," she said. "He doesn't even pick up his pencil." I said I was coming to Provincetown.

"Give me just one day," said Brian on the telephone when I told him I was flying in to see him.

"That's all I'll spare you," I shot back.

"Make it Saturday," he suggested. I didn't dare wait. "Friday," I countered. I was determined to be with him while he was conscious, and he had little choice.

I called Hank Murray, my doctor, for advice. "Be prepared to help him in any way you must," he said. There wasn't anything medical to be done anymore. "Don't be afraid of death," said Hank.

It was hot and sticky when I landed in Boston on Friday, June 18. I was drenched by the time I'd climbed the stairs to Brian's apartment. I was a little afraid of what I'd find. But then again, how many people had I known who'd camped out for weeks on death's doorstep and then miraculously revived to come back to life for months more, even years? This was Brian. With Brian, anything was possible.

Brian had given away most of his furnishings over the past year—most of what had been "ours" at one time. He was in a hospital bed that had been wheeled into the breakfast area. Through the windows that faced the ocean he could see the water and sand dunes where lovers strolled down to the shore and locals would go clamming as the tide eased out.

It was bright outside, but the apartment was dark. Brian had covered all the windows with the heavy paper used for lining shelves. To make sure he didn't see himself as he was, he'd covered every mirror in the place. I studied his face and his features. He looked good to me. I was sure everyone was wrong in thinking that the end was near.

"So," I said as cheerily as I could, "how are you?" He stretched out a hand, and I took it. We hugged each other.

I showed him new pictures of the boys and talked about what we'd do with them later in the summer. We talked about art, my Salem State speech, and the starfish thrower. I hadn't eaten since I'd arrived and Brian insisted that I get food on a plate and, in front of him, eat it. And so the day passed, with Brian giving orders when he was lucid, and complaining about imagined crises when the medications played tricks on his mind.

Brian said he wanted to go to his own bed, which had been set up in the living room. I helped him walk there and, when he lay down, I lay down next to him.

We talked softly and snuggled for a little while. He fell asleep, and I rested next to him, awake, listening to his breathing. I felt for some strange reason that when he woke up next, he would be well again. We would go back to Boston Commons to fly a kite, back to Rugg Road to sculpt wet paper, back to the children to ask if they wanted to Rollerblade. But I also feared that he would die at any moment.

I did not want him to slip away while I slept, so I stayed awake. Sometimes, so softly that I wouldn't wake him, I whispered things I'd not dared to tell him before, about my anger, about my fear of him, about how much I'd missed him.

I could tell when it was morning from the sounds in the apartment. It was Saturday. Tina decided to call Brian's family and friends to come today to say good-bye. Brian got out of bed and we were sitting up, drinking coffee, when his parents arrived.

A priest came, reminding Brian of altar boy stories; he introduced me as "his wife." We had to rifle the kitchen to find olive oil so the priest could perform the ritual of anointing the sick.

I spent some time reading sheets of instructions distributed by the hospice entitled "Preparing for Approaching Death." It was comforting to know what signs I should look for, to know what I should say or not say. I'd spent forty-five years trying to figure out life, but I had absolutely no knowledge about how one approaches death. In five pages, the hospice told me everything I'd need to know.

Then I joined Brian upstairs. He was walking through the bedrooms and into the bathroom, where he packed his toiletries kit as if he were going on a trip. We just stood there for a time, silent. He took some things from a shelf, said they were for the boys, and handed them to me: They were two starfish. We embraced, and we kissed. I wasn't sure he knew where he was, so I said, "Come on, Bri, let's go back to bed."

At 6:30 that evening Brian went to his own, not the hospital, bed. Everyone who was there took turns visiting alone with him for a few minutes; he couldn't talk, but we could tell from his hand motions that he could hear. We could also tell that he did not want a death-watch—no "eyes at the foot of the bed," as he termed it. When the others had left, I climbed back into bed to hold him again.

Candles burned in the living room, dancing light against the papered windows and walls. Music was playing. It was another night of whispers and fears and uncertainty. I guessed it must be near sunrise when Brian woke up, terribly anxious. He was frightened. He couldn't hear the music; I turned it a little louder. I sat next to him, stroking his forehead, until he drifted back to sleep. Tina came in to check on us; Manny dropped by, then Alice Foley. I remember that each of them touched me when they were in the room.

At a quarter after seven Brian's breathing was hard. He was becoming restless again, as he had just before he woke up frightened. This time I heard a voice in the room, talking very softly to Brian. "I love you, Bri." It was my voice; I recognized it. "I'll take care of the boys, don't worry." He relaxed a little. "It's okay, Brian, you can let go now. You can let go. It's enough, Bri. . . . It's enough."

Alice Foley—who is no stranger to death, and no "black box" spiritualist—came into the room moments later. She looked at us on the bed together and said, "Open the window; let his spirit out." I looked at Alice. A family member raised the blind and opened the window in the living room.

And, softly, so softly, he went away.

Everyone said a final good-bye, then left me alone with Brian. I climbed on top of him. It was over for him; not for me. I was still talking, crying, asking him what I was supposed to do now. How could he leave me and the boys again?

After an hour, Manny came in. He put his hands on my shoulders and started to lift me. "Come on, Mary," he said. I helped Manny and Alice change Brian's clothes. They promised me no one would see him put into a body bag.

When we were finished, I started to cry again. "What am I going to do, Manny?"

Manny looked at Brian, and then back at me. "Now that you've seen this, Mary, you can tell them what it's like."

The boys were in Detroit. I didn't want anyone else to tell them Brian had died, and I couldn't do it over the phone. Tina helped me get a plane ticket. I was on board the plane when I checked my calendar to see what I'd missed. It was Sunday, June 20, 1993. Brian had died on Father's Day.

The boys were upstairs in the playroom—the place where we had once had a theater—when I walked in. I sat on the floor with them and said, "Mommy and Daddy both love you very much. And this morning, Daddy went to heaven."

Max looked at me and said nothing. Zachary said, "Okay, Mom," and turned his attention back to the stuffed animal he was trying to dress.

The funeral was scheduled for the following Saturday in Brian's home church. His family had involved me in every way they could, as if Brian and I had never separated. Although Brian had wanted to be cremated, and was, I purchased a coffin so the boys could have a satisfying answer to the question "Where's Daddy?"

Tina explained to me that in some Roman Catholic funeral masses, a member of the family presents something to the officiating priest, something that belonged to the deceased and is somehow symbolic of his life. We decided Max and Zachary would perform this ritual—it would give them something they could do—by having one of them bring some of Brian's brushes and the other present some paints. When the time came, Max wouldn't move; he was going nowhere. Ever willing, Zachary took both the brushes and paints and headed up the aisle to the priest.

But when the priest reached out to take them, Zachary pulled them back. He couldn't give Daddy's things to someone else. He'd thought that, if he brought Daddy's things to the place by "Daddy's box," Brian would open the box and take them from him. He was confused and hurt. Finally he gave the priest the gifts and began to cry.

An American flag was presented to Brian's father at the cemetery in recognition of Brian's military service. When the sky began to turn dark and threatening, I asked Tina to take the boys back to a reception at their aunt's house. I stayed behind at the grave site, alone, to grieve without worrying about what the children would think.

The next day, Sunday, Max and Zachary and I went back to the cemetery and found the grave site. I brought Casablanca lilies; they were Brian's favorite flower, and mine. The children sat nearby. Before we left, they wrote their names in the dirt and drew hearts for their father.

The National Commission on AIDS was going out of existence the next day—Monday, June 28—with a news conference at the National Press Building in Washington, D.C. June Osborn had told me, "Under the circumstances, don't feel that you need to come." She'd also said that if I came, and if I was "up to it," she'd be grateful if I would speak briefly to the media.

Two weeks earlier, when Jim and I had first seen the news conference agenda, we decided that it was important for me to speak. The basic outline of what I would say was finished before Brian died. On Sunday morning I called Jim. For the first time since Brian had died, I was able to get out the words that Manny had said to me. "I need to say something more, something stronger," I said to Jim.

The next morning I was in Washington at the news conference. I'd had too little sleep and hadn't even begun to deal with the emotion of the past ten days.

Jim had sent the speech in large print so I could read the copy under bright television lights. But in front of all the network cameras and assembled journalists, I became teary eyed. I couldn't keep my thoughts straight; I was mixing up copy. I paused. The pages were all stuck together, probably from the tears. Someone handed me a glass of water. I said, "Excuse me," and took a sip. I found the remaining pages, including the new copy Jim had just finished, and sorted them into the right order.

I took a deep breath, looked directly into the bank of television cameras, and started speaking again, talking to the same unseen America that I'd addressed from Houston a summer earlier:

> I spent last week at the bedside of the man with whom I shared two sons and eventually one virus. I've come from Brian's funeral. I spent last Saturday holding our sons at his graveside, writing our names in freshly turned dirt, drying their tears while struggling to see through my own, trying to make sense out of a five-year-old's grief and a three-year-old's questions.
>
> The commission is packing up and going home. And so am I. But I will not go passively, or quietly. When next my children stand at a parent's grave, they may be old enough to ask whether the nation cares. God help the person who needs to answer them.
>
> I am going to ask for leadership today, and again tomorrow, and I'm going to raise my voice each time I ask, until those who have asked for our confidence have earned it—by leading.
>
> Let me be clear: It is not the AIDS community itself which is desperate for leadership, it's the nation at large. Those who imagine that this is someone else's problem, someone else's disease—these are people who need leaders, or they will surely die. The senator who compares HIV-positive immigrants with infected fruit; the preacher who regards the virus as God's good idea—these justify our call for leadership.
>
> Most of all, the nation needs moral leadership. Without it, we will perish; with it, there is hope. Morally, it is no more possible to think of this as a crisis for the infected than it is to think of slavery as an African-American problem, the Holocaust as a Jewish problem, or abuse as a child's problem. When this message finds a leader to deliver it convincingly, we will begin to understand, as a nation, that this is *our* crisis. Perhaps then, for the first time, we will address the epidemic with the moral persuasion needed to wage, and needed to win, a war.
>
> I need to go home and answer hard questions from two children.
>
> But *someone* needs to lead.

AFTERWORD

More than two years have now passed since Brian died. Life has gone on. The boys are growing well in Washington and are busy. Jim and I continue our work together. My mother is still my friend. I still give speeches urging listeners and myself to make our lives count for something—"Since we cannot save our own lives, we would be wise to contribute them for some purpose." In prayers, I still ask God for grace and understanding, I still rage at God about dying. Meanwhile, the toll in the AIDS epidemic mounts, and the national response is still marked mostly by denial and indifference.

Life as a pilgrim on the road to AIDS is bittersweet. I've learned that there is no straight line from hurt to healing. Over and over, pilgrims grow weary, grow frightened, grow sad, grow angry. We never seem to shake off these feelings; they merely rotate to the top of our emotional dials in unpredictable cycles. I've seen far too many other pilgrims fall along the way.

I've begun to think that, at the end of this road, as Elbert Hubbard once put it, "God will not look you over for medals, degrees, or diplomas, but for scars." Somewhere beneath the veneer of ordinary human vanity lurk the unconquerable fears and unmeasured regrets—the scars—that finally shape each pilgrim into something utterly unique, and utterly human. And this is, like it or not, God's purpose with us.

Jeffrey Schmalz died at thirty-nine. Before he died he said it was not death and dying that pained him. It was losing his friends, watching healthy young people lose control of their minds and bodily functions, unable to stop the downward slide toward death without dignity. Paul Monette wrote that he didn't want merely a cure; a cure would come too late. He wanted his friends back. Now, I want Paul back, and Jeffrey.

The losses, more than anything, pushed a change in my art. I'd once prided myself on the beauty of my handmade paper, the colors and textures of the flowers. But my art changed. I never intended the change, I merely did not stop it once it began. The newest collection of work is an assemblage of pieces done along the road to AIDS. It shocks some people, sometimes me. But it is, as art has always been for me, an outlet for my soul. Whether or not it sells, I hope it evokes a response in those who see it. I hope that, at the very least, they walk away from it asking themselves hard questions.

Not long after Brian died I accepted an offer to publish what became my first book, *Sleep with the Angels* (1994), a collection of my speeches illustrated with photographs, mainly of the children, most of which I'd taken. That book led to another like it, *I'll Not Go Quietly* (1995). Then came this memoir.

If my earliest desire in life was to be approved by others, to be a good girl, my ambition today is to prove to myself that an ordinary person, given some moral courage, can make a difference. Part of morality is, I think, obeying common external standards such as the Ten Commandments. But there is also the quiet inner standard of our own conscience, the ability both to distinguish right from wrong and to choose which—right or wrong—we will act on. It's this internal set of standards that I have felt grow more sensitive along the road to AIDS, not because I am uncommonly sensitive, but because any human being who lives with one eye on death sees life more clearly.

What I've learned most during my pilgrimage is that, while no two "AIDS stories" are the same, I am a very, very ordinary woman. Each person's life is unique; AIDS does not change that, so my story is, uniquely, mine. But the hurdles I've encountered in life are common to other women; the joys that make me giggle are the delights of most women blessed as richly as I am: with parents who love me, good friends who cherish me, and children whose lives, I pray, will stretch far into the future. And if I've enjoyed some success in life, if I've accomplished anything that will actually make a lasting difference, it was as an ordinary person, wrestling with ordinary crises, reaching toward God for more courage than I'd have alone, and for a word of extraordinary grace.

I've been tempted to give up on more than one occasion, usually within hours of the death of someone I'd grown to love. As Jeffrey and Paul pointed out, it's the accumulation of deaths that wears us down, like sandpaper rubbed relentlessly into our raw flesh. It isn't

just the pain that ruins us; it's the bone-tired weariness of dealing
with the pain. It's what makes me want to stop, especially to stop
giving speeches in which I'm expected to raise other people's hopes.

It happened again as I was nearing the end of work on this memoir. I needed to say good-bye to Rob Eichberg in Santa Fe. We
hugged our good-byes, and I flew to Chicago, where I was scheduled to give a speech. Before I could get back to Rob, he was dead.

I spoke in Chicago about tiredness, about a weariness that para-
lyzes us. And I ended by remembering Taylor Branch's story in
Parting the Waters, a history of America during the years of the late
Dr. Martin Luther King.

Early in 1956, the Alabama bus boycott was failing. No laws
had been changed; no buses had been integrated. No one was
suffering except those who walked.

Then came a little-known hero from Montgomery's African-
American community, Mother Pollard. For untold decades she
had cared for the sick and raised the orphans, black and white
alike. Now, in her waning years, Mother Pollard joined the
boycott and walked. As the days stretched to weeks, and then
months, she walked. When the winter weather worsened, and
she began to slip and fall, against the advice of King and others, she would pick herself up, time after time, and walk.

A meeting was called to consider ending the boycott and
finding another means of protest. The crowd was divided between speeches and arguments until Mother Pollard rose to
speak.

"I would rather crawl on my knees than ride on a bus," she
told the hushed and now embarrassed crowd. She spoke of
years of humiliation, of self-hatred, of injustice and shame.
She noted that the outcome would have little to do with her
life, but much to do with the lives of her many children. And
then she gave the entire civil rights movement one of its classic
refrains when she concluded, "My feets is tired, but my soul is
rested."

I left the speech as I had come to it, a pilgrim on the road to
AIDS, a mother needing to go home to Max and Zachary, and tired.
But I also left with this hope: that someone will, someday, come

gently to my children, remembering not only their mother, but Mother Pollard.

Perhaps, at the end, someone will bend low and whisper in their ears: Your mother has not gone, Max; she has merely gone ahead. Her body grew tired, Zack, but her soul is well rested.

Until that day, for all who march for justice armed with the courage of compassion, I have this ancient prayer: Grace to you, and peace.

PHOTOGRAPH CAPTIONS

(Captions run clockwise starting from the upper left corner, unless otherwise noted)

PAGE 21: Mary at four months; Phillip Fisher, three, and Mary, five; Brian Campbell, Palm Beach, Florida; First sketch done at Parkside; Mary in the early eighties

PAGE 22: Mary's first watercolors, 1985; Mary and Betty Ford in Beaver Creek, Colorado; *(left to right)* Aunt Ethyl Toor, Brian Campbell, Mary, Caroline Cummings, Max Fisher, Marjorie Fisher, Tony Cummings, Julie (Fisher) Cummings, Florence "Flohoney" Switow, 1987; Brian Campbell and Mary during her pregnancy; Mary in Palm Beach, Florida

PAGE 29: Lizabeth at birth, 1948; Marjorie Switow Frehling and Lizabeth, 1948; Sara "Mama" Klein, Marjorie Frehling, Florence "Flohoney" Switow, and Lizabeth; 2328 Village Drive, Louisville, Kentucky; Grandma Lil Frehling and Lizabeth; Mary, after name change, at one

PAGE 30: Mary in Bluefield, West Virginia; Mary at two; Mary at Humpty Dumpty University, 1953; Mary at one; *(center)* Mary at two

PAGE 43: Mary, 1953, day of Marjorie and Max Fisher's wedding; Joyce and George Frehling (second marriage); Mary at six months; Mary with first-grade class, Brookside School; Molly and William Fisher; Mary with second-grade class, Brookside School; Mary at six (during a 1954 holiday visit with George Frehling); Harry "Papaharry" and Florence "Flohoney" Switow; Max Fisher's parents; Marjorie and Max Fisher

PAGE 44: Marjorie and Max in Tucson; Mary, Julie Fisher, Marjorie Fisher, and Phillip Frehling; Mary at a Halloween party, 1957; Phillip Frehling, Mary, and Octane at home at Parkside; Phillip Frehling, Max Fisher, Mary, and Jane Fisher in Tucson

PAGE 51: *(Left to right)* Phillip Frehling, Max Fisher, Larry Sherman, Jane Fisher Sherman holding David Sherman, Margie Fisher, Marjorie Fisher, Mary, and Julie Fisher; Max Fisher and Mary at Kingswood graduation, 1966; Mary, Max Fisher, and Marjorie Fisher at Mary's Sweet Sixteen party; Richard Burton, Elizabeth Taylor, and Robert "Uncle Bob" Goldstein (on the set of *Cleopatra*); Max Fisher and Governor George Romney

PAGE 52: Mary at Kingswood; Margie Fisher, Julie Fisher, Phillip Fisher, and Mary; *(left to right, back)* Chris Huebner, Molly McGraw, Susie Swan, and (front) Mary; Mary and Johnnie Goodman (at the Sweet Sixteen party); Mary's Kingswood senior-class picture; President Richard Nixon and Max Fisher

PAGE 71: Max Fisher, Marjorie Fisher, Israel Prime Minister Levi Eshkol, and Miriam Eshkol; Mary in Israel with an Israeli general; Marjorie Fisher and Max Fisher at the Channel 56 Auction; Mary and Bozo the Clown at the Channel 56 Auction

PAGE 72: Mary at home in Franklin, early seventies; Mary in a Manufacturers Bank ad for the Detroit Symphony; Bill House and Mary; Israel Prime Minister Golda Meir and Max Fisher

PAGE 89: Mary, Max Fisher, and President Gerald Ford, 1974; Mary and Senator Edward Kennedy; Henry Baskin and Mary

PAGE 90: Mary, Semon "Bunkie" Knudsen, and Soupy Sales at the Channel 56 Auction; Henry Ford II at the Channel 56 Auction; "Kelly & Company" production staff at WXYZ-TV, Channel 7

PAGE 97: *(Background)* Score to the music given to local groups for presidential visits; Mary's White House Commission Book used for identification; Mary's White House Official Passport

PAGE 98: *(Top left and right)* Mary advancing on a windy golf course; Bob Barrett, military aide, aboard *Air Force One*; *(left to right)* Donald Rumsfeld, Max Fisher, President Ford, Henry Kissinger, and Brent Scowcroft; Mary during a quiet advance moment

PAGE 113: *Air Force One* passenger seating card; President Ford, Mary, and Max Fisher on Mackinac Island; President Ford and Mary aboard *Air Force One*

PAGE 114: Mary in the presidential parade at the Cherry Festival, Traverse City, Michigan; Mary saying farewell to President Ford in the White House Oval Office, 1976; Bicentennial First Day Cover, July 4, 1976; Mary standing in for President Ford on the USS *Forrestal*, July 4, 1976

PAGE 123: Newspaper clipping showing Mary and President Ford on the University of Michigan campus, April 1977; Harry "Papaharry" Switow with bride at Mary's wedding to Howard Arnkoff, October 2, 1977; Mary, Phillip Fisher, Margie Fisher, and Marjorie Fisher at the 1979 Switow family reunion in Louisville, Kentucky; President Ford dancing with Mary at the 1977 wedding; Mary and Phillip Fisher

PAGE 124: (*Back left to right*) Phillip Fisher, Marjorie Fisher, Max Fisher, and Margie Fisher; (*front left to right*) Mary, Florence "Flohoney" Switow, and Harry "Papaharry" Switow at the 1979 Switow family reunion; First Lady Betty Ford and Mary at Ford's home in Palm Springs, California, early eighties; Harry "Papaharry" Switow at the 1979 family reunion; Mary with boutique items from Mary Fisher Associates at Bonwit Teller in California; *Women's Wear Daily* clipping showing Henry Ford II and Mary at a charity event

PAGE 141: Vacation shot aboard the *QEII*, 1983; Dominique Fourcade in Corsica, 1984; Mary at Colorado Outward Bound, 1985; Marjorie Fisher, Mary, Julie (Fisher) Cummings, and Margie (Fisher) Aronow; Mary forty feet up at Colorado Outward Bound, 1985; Julie Pettit, Fred Sipe, and Mary at the Betty Ford Center

PAGE 142: Mary and TV producer Geoff Mason at a Betty Ford Center fundraiser; Mary and President Ford in Beaver Creek, Colorado, 1985; News clipping for the opening of Fisher Hall at the Betty Ford Center; Mary and Brian Campbell; Marjorie Fisher and Mary, 1986; Group shot at Marjorie Fisher's sixtieth birthday party in New York City

PAGE 155: Mary and Brian Campbell and one of his paintings; (*left to right*) Max and Marjorie Fisher, Mary, Brian Campbell, Peg and Stuart "Soup" Campbell; Mary and Brian Campbell at their wedding, January 7, 1987, Palm Beach, Florida; One of Mary's metal constructions; Mary and Andre De Shields (star of *Just So*)

PAGE 156: Brian Campbell and Mary during their honeymoon aboard *The Magic Lady*; Mary swinging off *The Magic Lady*; Mary, nine-months pregnant with Max; Max Campbell held by Brian Campbell; Max, one, with Brian Campbell at Disney World; Mary and Betty Ford at the Gratitude House in West Palm Beach, Florida; Brian Campbell, Max Campbell, and Mary (Christmas photo 1987)

PAGE 167: Max Campbell, two, examining Zachary Campbell; Max Campbell at two; One of Mary's handmade paper flower pieces; Zachary Campbell, Max Campbell, and Mary; Max Campbell, Brian Campbell, Zachary Campbell, and Mary (Christmas photo 1989)

PAGE 168: Mary, Max Campbell, Zachary Campbell, and Brian Campbell in New York City's Central Park; Mary at her first "One Woman Show," Boca Raton, Florida; (*back left to right*): David Aronow, Julie (Fisher) Cummings, Peter Cummings, Mary, Brian Campbell; (*front left to right*): Margie (Fisher) Aronow, Andrew Aronow, Max Fisher, Max Campbell, Caroline Cummings, Marjorie Fisher, Tony Cummings, Phillip Fisher, Amanda Fisher, Amy Fisher (then Phillip's wife), and Chase Fisher

PAGE 175: Feet of Mary and Gregory Hines, February 1991; Mary and Zachary Campbell; Marjorie Fisher and Mary in Boca Raton, Florida; Mary at Kennedy Airport, July 17, 1991; Max Campbell and Brian Campbell

PAGE 176: Mary at Exeter Press, New York City; Max Campbell, Mary, Zachary Campbell, and Gregory Hines; Mary and Gregory Hines

PAGE 187: Mary, July 1991; Phillip Fisher, July 1991; Zachary Campbell in Santa Fe, New Mexico, August 1991; Sally Fisher, Robert Eichberg, and Mary

PAGE 188: Max Campbell, Mary, and Zachary Campbell, in Santa Fe, New Mexico, August 1991; Max Campbell in Santa Fe, New Mexico, August 1991; Zachary Campbell in Santa Fe, New Mexico, August 1991

PAGE 199: (*Left to right*) "Aunt Betty" Ford, Max Campbell, Mary, "Uncle Jerry" Ford, and Zachary Campbell, Beaver Creek, Colorado, August 1991; Max and Zachary Campbell, Halloween; Zachary and Max Campbell in the backyard, Boca Raton, Florida

PAGE 200: Zachary Campbell, Mary, and Max Campbell in their Boca Raton home; Mary and President Ford in Beaver Creek, Colorado, August 1991; Max Campbell, Mary, and Zachary Campbell (Christmas photo, 1991)

PAGE 213: Max Campbell, Zachary Campbell, Earvin "Magic" Johnson, and Mary at the National Commission on AIDS meeting in Boston, March 1992; Zachary Campbell, Mary, Kate Anderson, Joy Anderson, Ryan Anderson, Max Campbell, and Tracy Shook, Disney World, 1992; Max Campbell, Mary, and Zachary Campbell, Boston, March 1992; Joy Prouty and Mary, Palm Beach, Florida; Stu White

PAGE 214: Mary and Elizabeth Taylor at the AmFAR Award of Courage dinner, April 1992; Phillip Fisher and Mary, at the AmFAR Award of Courage dinner, April 1992; Betty Ford and Mary in Florida

PAGE 227: Mary on the floor of the Houston Astrodome during the NBC "Today Show" broadcast from the 1992 Republican Convention; Zachary Campbell, Mary, and Max Campbell at the Boston Commons, 1992; Brian, Max, and Zachary Campbell at the Boston Commons, 1992

PAGE 228: (Left to right) Marjorie Fisher, Michael Iskowitz, Dr. June Osborn and daugther, Mary, and Dr. David Rogers in Amsterdam, The Netherlands, 1992; Surgeon General Dr. Antonia Novello, Marjorie Fisher, and Mary at the 1992 International AIDS Conference in Amsterdam, The Netherlands; Judy (Conrad) Sherman, Phillip Fisher, and Mary on the floor of the Houston Astrodome, August 1992

PAGE 245: Zachary, Brian, and Max Campbell, Boston; President and Mrs. Ford congratulate Mary following her Republican National Convention address in Houston, August 19, 1992

PAGE 246: Mary delivering the speech at the 1992 Republican National Convention; Max Fisher during Mary's address at the Convention

PAGE 255: Mary on the cover of the December 1992 Town & Country magazine; A. James Heynen and Joy Prouty, New York City, December 1992; AIDS Memorial Quilt display, Washington, D.C., October 1992; Mary with President Bush in the White House Oval Office, October 1992

PAGE 256: Mary, "Millie," Max Campbell, and Zachary Campbell playing on the floor of the White House Oval Office, October 1992; Mary with Sally Fisher, Washington, D.C., 1993; Max Fisher, President Bush, Mary, Barbara Bush, and Marjorie Fisher at a White House Christmas party, 1992; Carol de Paolo, Jeanne White, Bob Hattoy (in the background), Mary, Elizabeth Glaser, and Miss America 1993 Leanza Cornett, Washington, D.C., January 1993

PAGE 269: A. James Heynen, Joy Prouty, Phillip Fisher, Mary, and Dr. Brian Weiss, Detroit, Michigan, September 1992; An example of Mary's art after Brian's death (part of the "Messages" exhibit banned from the U.S. Senate, September 1995); Max Campbell, Zachary Campbell, and Mary (photo by David Kennerly shot while filming an ABC "Nightline" special, 1993)

PAGE 270: Mary, Zachary and Max Campbell (photo by José Picayo); Max, Brian, and Zachary Campbell during their last visit together, Boston, 1993; Max Campbell, Mary, and Zachary Campbell at Brian Campbell's grave site, June 1993

Index